A

MIRROR

FOR

NARCISSUS

BY
THE SAME AUTHOR

Sailing Across Europe
Seeing Red
The Way of a Transgressor
Transgressor in the Tropics
The Story of a Lake
Behind God's Back
Bomber's Moon
Going Fishing
The Sons of Noah
Last Chance in Africa
Caucasian Journey

Foreword to the American edition. I am leaving this book just as it appeared when published in England on June 11, 1956. The final pages were being printed when Khrushchev did his back-flip on Stalin, and opened his Moscow Pandora's Box, which he will never get closed. So I leave that sentence as I wrote it: "Stalin has already been demoted in the U.S.S.R., and before long will be hated." I also said: "And Lenin is due for a reappraisal. I think the West has been lazy in accepting him at the value the communists place upon him." If we take down Lenin it is like destroying the gods of a sacked city: the communists of the world can no longer have this false prophet as an excuse for their inhumanity. And Lenin can be derated.

I said, furthermore: "I have always cherished the secret hope that if one of the satellites is to let the Russians down—is to double-cross Moscow at some dangerous corner—it will be the Poles. They are the only people who have the nerve for it." Well, Poznan occurred less than three weeks after the British publication of NARCISSUS.

I could, with little trouble, have brought the edition "up to date" in these respects; but I have thought it better to let it go out in America unchanged, with some of its predictions already fulfilled.

Negley Farson

A
MIRROR
FOR
NARCISSUS

by

NEGLEY
FARSON

Doubleday & Company, Inc., Garden City, New York, 1957

For Edith and Mabel Negley

CONTENTS

Contents

A
MIRROR
FOR
NARCISSUS

When I looked out on the beach this morning I saw that the curlew had paired off. There were only a few couples of them probing about sedately among the sitting gulls. The great mass flights of autumn and dead winter are over, when I could look out of my bedroom window on almost any dawn and watch from fifty to a hundred of them come over and whiffle down to the wet sands. In a few days, I know, even these mated curlew will be gone; they will be back among their nests on the uplands, raising their young. I could want no finer sign that spring is here. I love their cry. That lonely haunting call brings back memories of early New Jersey days: surf-casting along the Atlantic when the September sands were empty; duck-shooting down the Delaware and the smell of a salt marsh in raw weather; halcyon days sailing a sneak-box around Barnegat Bay, when all the world that lay ahead of me still seemed so wonderful. In those days, before the clean instinctive vision of youth became plastered over by the muddy self-deceptions we accept in adult life, I knew that that cry, with such a note of reproach in it, came from the very pattern of life: of life as it should be lived, with the full recognition of the essential oneness of us all. And I was right. Destroy me, cried the curlew, and you destroy yourself.

ILLYRIAN
SPRING

In nineteen thirty-five I had to throw up the job I loved. We were broke. Yet never in our lives had we felt so contented. Everything that I stood for, or had not stood for, had worked out to land me where I was. The whole thing was so inevitable that I could not even feel sorry for myself. We spent that spring and summer in the mountains of Slovenia while I wrote *The Way of a Transgressor*.

It was a wonderful place to work. Blue Lake Bohinjsko stretched away from below our bedroom windows. Around us, above the steep pine and beech forests, sparkled the snows of the Julian Alps. There was no settlement around the lake. The two little hotels at its foot, hardly much more than log hunting-chalets, were both owned by a religious order. Ours was the Saint James. Next, half a mile through the beech woods, was the Holy Ghost. For what I should have paid for a double-whiskey in a smart London hotel, the Saint James gave us each bed and board: my wife, self and eight-year-old son. These two little hotels lay at the foot of the late King Alexander's immense game reserve. A wild bit of country for Europe: high, treeless plateaux of snow and grey rock, where the mountain ridges were stirred like cold porridge: large tracts of pine forests which had yet to hear the sound of a woodsman's axe—unpeopled valleys, down which raced some of the finest, most unfished trout-streams in all Europe. The King used to come up here to shoot chamois.

Alexander had been murdered the year before at Marseilles, by Vlada the Chauffeur, a trained killer from Mussolini's terrorist camp at Yanka Pusta. He had been a plain-living man, more soldier than monarch, and now his old hunting companions had faded back into their peasant life. Minka, the royal huntsman's daughter, served our breakfasts. This part of the Balkans, before they lost it at Versailles, had been for centuries under the civilising influence of the Austrians. It had not yet had time to get over it. As a result, when Minka tripped in of a morning, with her happy little "Grüss Gott!", her bare feet pattering across the bare pine-boards of our room, she bore trays laden with Viennese coffee and whipped cream, *croissants* as flaky as those of Paris, a mound of cool butter and a jar of wild honey. I wrote ten pages a day in that delectable spot—before I put my trousers on: that was my formula.

Then after a lazy lunch, during which I read any mail or papers that might have come up by car from Bled, always helped by Josef the waiter who leaned over my shoulder to get me to explain the photographs (the atmosphere of this little place was very *White Horse Inn*), I took my trout rod.

There was plenty of good fishing down by the lake, where the streams flattened out to race through their bouldered beds in the flowered valleys. It would be a poor afternoon if I did not bring back six or seven. Provided we wanted them. They averaged close on half a pound, and they were both wary and lively. It was pleasant, with my work done, to fish up those streams in the fresh airs of spring, investigating every rock or ledge. But the fish were not all of so modest a size; once or twice during that first spring I brought back a spotted beauty that was over two pounds. An old inhabitant. Well, he would never see that blue-green pool again; and taking him out of the wet grass in my bag, with his colours already dimmed, I felt sorry for him. This, as every fisherman knows, is a natural regret. In that part of the world there is a peculiar golden grayling, found, so far as I know, nowhere but in the Balkans. I always came on these in the swiftest water, sometimes in the very pockets of a white rapid. With their small grayling mouths, and the tiny black gnat-like fly I used for them, I always felt, when they made a run for it, that I should suddenly feel my rod straighten up. It was a triumph to land one. And they ran big: some as big as a kilo. The locals much preferred these *esche* to the trout—perhaps because they saw so few of them. But delicately broiled, and served with tartare sauce and a mound of not too crisp slim french-fried potatoes, they took a lot of beating.

Fishing those streams was my Nirvana. A short time after I was in the stream my mind was miles away from it, in another world. In this mood, letting my mind wander freely, I had moments when I was as close to some of the intuitive truths as any Hindu practising yoga. There was the water, as pure as the snows from which it came: the beech and alder in spring bud as the world began to renew it-self: the steady rocks ripping the flow into a dancing white rapid: and up above, where the dark pines stood over a deep pool, a bend, around which lay another infinitely lovely prospect. Here was the grace of life.

My favourite procedure was to take a stream, stick to it, and work it as far up into the mountains as I could use a fly, before the forest and the bush closed over it. Up there, in those utter solitudes, I found pools that had something mystic about them: haunt of the trout that I often thought had better remain undisturbed. Staring into a pool, I felt now and then that I had no right to be there, and that there was something supernatural about the trout being there: they were spectral, possessed, part of the secret of this place. At any rate, they seemed to be part of a thing that I was trying to find out—of some-thing that I was trying to get back to.

When I was working these upper stretches, we always took the frying-pan along in my bag, and about a pound of the hotel's best butter. Delightful days: the trout sizzling in the pan, the tang of woodsmoke, and—the tiredness. I often thought that the last was the best; for lying on the bank in some glade I would think of other fish I had fished, other scenes: catfish in the Chesapeake, and old wharves in the moonlight; small-mouth bass in the spring lakes of New York State, in the days when the chestnuts still rimmed the granite shore-line; golden days on the fierce, flashing rainbow rivers of British Columbia. . . . And I used those fish: they took me back to the very days and scenes I was writing about; even, for fleeting moments, to some of the things I had been sure of at that time. I was no longer so sure. But these Slovenian trout, with the associations of the fly-rod, made me hear the call of the curlew again; and I still knew what it meant. Many a time I have answered it. Fishing up in the Shet-lands or on the Outer Hebrides, and hearing that lonely cry as it came across the moor, I have smiled and said to the bird: "Well, as long as *you're* here, *I'm* all right." The Pattern was still there.

Once a week I took the whole day off, and we climbed. And every two weeks I took four days. With our rolled blankets slung round our shoulders, I became the family pack-mule. I put heavy sweaters, extra pairs of woollen socks, and the coffee-pot and billy in the ruck-sack, with a bulging supply of bread, butter and iron rations; and we tramped wherever the spirit moved us. Our climbing boots had been made for us by an old cobbler in an adjacent valley, who used to make the ski-boots for the officers of the Austrian mountain troops. You could trudge all day in them through snow and slush and yet remain dryshod. I still have mine, with the hobnails under the ball of my foot worn shiny and flat.

In that mountainous corner where Italy, Austria and Yugoslavia meet, there are large fields of eternal snow. Even in midsummer we could climb along the snow-faces for day after day. Once, coming down off a four-day climb from ski-hut to ski-hut, we became lost on the descent—and found we had got ourselves into Italy. That flag, made so detestable by its bombastic fasces, was snapping behind us in a pass. There were no frontier guards with their dogs about, so we carried on. And there, with our legs dangling over the blue depths on the Italian side, we told our young son of a trying summer we had spent in Rome, under the Duce.

I had just been damning Mussolini. For on that climb we had got our boy up to the top of Mt. Triglav—not much of a climb, but I am no mountaineer: and the spikes that the Austrian soldiery had driven into the flaky gneiss during the first World War, with steel cables strung between them for getting supplies up to the observation post on top, had a tendency to come out. I had been warned against them:

"Don't trust them!" chuckled an old ex-Austrian diplomat, who was then at the Saint James. "They will let you down—like England!"

He loved that. This charming old gentleman had begun his career in the Austro-Hungarian diplomatic service when Slatin Pasha was in the Sudan. He asked me, one night when we were admiring some fish I had brought back from the evening rise, where I lived. I replied that up to now, for the last five years, I had been a foreign correspondent in London. "But I don't know where I am going to live now. My so-called future is uncertain." He sighed:

"I can understand the England of John Galsworthy. I cannot understand the England of Aldous Huxley."

"You mean that England is decadent?"

"Precisely. That is why I say: *Don't trust England!* Either England cannot fight, or she will not fight. In either case, her promises as to what she would do as an ally are worthless. Therefore I say: Don't trust England."

"That seems a pretty cold-blooded way of putting it."

"I know. And we Yugoslavs—I am a Yugoslav now, you know—most of our old Empire has been distributed among other nations —inferior people—that was your President Wilson—academic utopian! —we Yugoslavs, as I say, should be the last people on earth to want Mussolini to come out on top in this Abyssinian affair. But what can we do? As you know, I love England—but I can no longer find it possible to admire her. Something has *happened* to England!"

"I think it's Sir John Simon."

He looked worried. "What an unbelievable choice for a Foreign Secretary!"

Part of this (not Sir John Simon) is beside the point: which is that perched up there in the icy snow, sheltering from the high winds in the lee of the old Austrian observation-post on the tip of Mt. Triglav, we could look down through the clouds on the sultry blue Adriatic, across which Mussolini was already raising hell as he prepared to invade Abyssinia. We got occasional glimpses of the beautiful foreshore of Dalmatia nine thousand feet below; and, my mind filled with anger at the things statesmen do, I told my young son (for this was the way he received his most realistic education: being carted around this troubled world with us) how England and France, to get Italy in on their side in the 1914–18 war, had, though it was certainly not theirs to give, promised all this lovely Dalmatian littoral down below us to the Italians—and then, having won the war, diddled the Italians out of it at the Peace Conference. This, I went on, was the secret Treaty of London—by which the Italians had been given the right to invade Abyssinia as far back as 1915. Such double-cross would be an interesting thing for him to keep in mind, I said, if, as I was afraid, he was going to take up the delightful but dis-

illusioning profession of journalism (which he has): a thing to remember when he heard any statesman, of *any* nation, get up on his
hind legs and orate about the boon and the blessing of his own people's morals to an otherwise misguided world. "For," I informed my
solitary contribution (so far as I know) to the continuation of the
human race, "at one time or another—depending upon who was at
the head of it or how desperate the situation was—every nation has
been crooked: so crooked that, if they had been an individual, they
would have been put in prison for it. Collectively, most people have
been murderers. The story of them is what is called History. Now,
you take those statues we put up in all our public places: that man
on a horse, waving a sword. . . ." He yawned.

On another occasion, when we had become hopelessly lost in the
snow-fog after climbing in and out of wet snow-bowls for hour after
hour, and had reached the point of seriously debating where we
might find some shelter for the night, particularly for our son in his
little Austrian leather shorts, the mist suddenly pulled away; we saw
blue sky; and there, on an outcrop of red rock directly over our heads,
stood three chamois staring down at us. They must have heard our
voices in the cloud. But they seemed just as frozen by surprise as
we were. I had never seen a chamois at such close quarters. Then
with a flick of their fat little rumps they vanished. That was all we
needed. We climbed to the red rocks, found their tracks, and although they did lead along one or two stretches that only a chamois
could love, narrow ledges over deep drops, they finally brought us
down to a green grazing alp. We spent that night in a shepherd's
log cabin, sleeping among the cheeses.

We climbed with the spring that year. When, by the lake, the
beeches were a shimmer of green, their buds were tight brown only
a thousand feet up. When the last of a dirty snow-pile finally trickled
away from the shady side of the Saint James, we still came on deep
dry drifts of it in the dark pines up near the timberline. When the
crocuses were pushing their pretty heads up through the glistening
slush in the peasants' highest clearings, the banks of my favourite
trout streams down below were blue with gentians, the big bell-like
kind and the little one of the much brighter hue. Soon we were
counting upon wild strawberries for the best part of our climbing
lunch, and up among the grey rocks we came upon primulas, pink,

mauve and yellow: then it became a breathless climb to reach an edelweiss. About the time of the mayfly came a night when, with much rattle of carts and clunking of cow-bells, the peasants began to move their cattle up to the high alps for the summer grazing. There they lived an arcadian existence, above, and almost out of, the life of worried Europe.

But there was one valley they could not get animals into. No one went there. Its far end was banked by a sea of yellow globe flowers, and its floor was a mosaic of some of the most beautiful and intricate little wild-flowers that I have ever come across. We returned there again and again that summer. On some of the sultry, windless days, when the clouds floated high off the mountains, billowy, motionless, I used to lie on my back among those wild-flowers—and build castles in Spain. At such times I often thought of the old German song *Feldeinsamkeit,* and of the little boy in the painting of that name: also lying on his back among the mountain flowers, unquestionably building castles. I felt that there was little to choose between us: except that I, as it seemed, had come so far from those early dreams that I could no longer imagine what I had wanted. I must try to get back.

It was a fine life. To eat in that high mountain sunshine, lie back against a warm rock, smoke, and look back thoughtfully along the years—this was about as pleasant a period of retrospection as I can remember. The rocks gave me strength. In some strange way I felt that I had come home again—home to myself, at any rate. I don't imagine I thought of Peer Gynt once all that summer, at any rate consciously. But my thoughts must have been very Gyntish. . . . There is that passage when he returns to Norway, and asks Solveig

"Tell me, then—where was my true self,
  Complete and true—the Peer who bore
  The stamp of God upon his brow?"

and she answers him

"In my faith, in my hope, in my love."

I suppose I have always accepted Solveig as the world, and felt, without thinking about it much one way or the other, that if you love this earth you are in its heart all the time. For so I have found it. I have felt more at home in the desert and in the middle of some swamp than I ever have on Fifth Avenue: closer to life. And I have heard more wisdom from a Chesapeake Bay oysterman than from any intellectual or cabinet minister. It may be hackneyed to say that the further up most men get in life the further also they get from real life itself. But it is a fact; and I think that in it might lie the key to much that is wrong with our times. Too many people, too many of the top people, have come too far away from real life—from life as it really could be lived, even at this late day.

In that clean mountain air I could sometimes hardly credit the life I had just given up. For the previous eleven years I had been a foreign newspaper correspondent, and I know of no profession more calculated to kill one's enthusiasm for the human race. I had held down the head office of my paper in Rome, Paris, Moscow, Berlin and London; and I had had all the privileges, and the disillusions, which such fascinating posts carry with them. I had wandered over large parts of the world, writing about peoples and their problems. I had met many of the great men of our time, or those we called great. And I did not like them. Whether politics had made them what they were, or whether it was because of what they were that they had entered politics, I could not know. Nor could I care. I did not like them. Seen at close range, they dwindled to very ordinary proportions: they lied, they cheated, they talked speciously in public and double-crossed one another, and even their own countries, in private. That is politics. Sometimes, when interviewing those I considered the best of the species, I had the uncanny feeling that I was listening to two men. There was the inner, the ethical, man; and there was the outer, the public, figure, always saying what he thought circumstances demanded. In the long run, most of the top foreign correspondents become angry with public men; we dislike having to report so much sham. And some of us go berserk, or take to strong drink: usually both. The word has taken on a new lustre, now that the chips are down and we have to defend it, but there was a long period when a foreign correspondent could not hear the word *democracy* without feeling sick. And when I heard any statesman end his peroration—"and with God's help"—I knew that he was on a bad wicket. They will drag God into it! With the outstanding exception of the Scandinavian, there was not a government in Europe during those wasted years that was not dishonourable, even contemptible. And until the advent of Roosevelt, the American administrations were even more frightening: self-righteous, yet riddled with corruption; ponderously stupid. It is said that the United States had a moral collapse after every war: under the Harding régime we deserved it. (But we have come a long way from those days. So has England. We have been putting the best men we could find in charge of affairs, and most of them have been scared into being honest.) I have never believed in *vox populi*, in the sanctity of numbers: I have seen too many mobs in action. The red river pouring down the broad Nevsky in 1917; the students from Al-Azhar mosque-university rioting in Cairo in 1919; the truck-loads of young Nazi thugs throwing bricks through the plate-glass windows of the big Jewish department stores along the Kurfürstendamm in 1930—I have seen them all. Students will riot for anything. The communists know what they are doing when they appeal to youth—they exploit inexperience.

In the course of my term as President of the Association of American Correspondents in London, largest body of its kind in the world, I was in the chair for many of the most important figures of that day: including Ramsay MacDonald, Stanley Baldwin and Neville Chamberlain. Three duds in a row. Rising to make my speech, necessarily polite, of introduction for these personages, I wondered how England would ever survive them. The answer is that she didn't; England will never be the same again after the rule of these vain, insular, criminally complacent men. In private life Stanley Baldwin was one of the most honourable and kindly men that ever lived, and industrious too: at 10 Downing Street, with the fate of England in his hands, his laziness almost betrayed his country. "Bring me up to date on the Russian situation—but don't make it more than one page." The Strong Hand at the Helm!—but the ship was not brought into harbour.

Reporting their utterances, I always thought of Captain Powell in the opening lines of Conrad's *Chance*:

"If we at sea went about our work as people ashore go about theirs we should never make a living. No one would employ us. And moreover

no ship sailed in the happy-go-lucky manner people ashore conduct their business would ever arrive in port."

Conrad ascribed this universal inefficiency of what he called "the shore gang" to a want of responsibility and to a sense of security:

"They see that no matter what they do this tight little island won't turn turtle on them or spring a leak and go to the bottom with their wives and children."

It is a long time since Conrad wrote *Chance.*

TWO TYPES
OF OUR TIME

I began this book by saying that everything I stood for, or had not stood for, had worked out to land me where I was. The operative words are between the commas. And I can be more specific. This is what I had to think about when, at the age of forty-five, without one red cent, I sat down in the mountains of Slovenia to tell what I had got out of life. It is a story that would make a horse laugh.

It is the account of two men: a tale of materialism and vulgarity: a picture of what could be called, in all sad truth, the ruling class in the good old U.S.A.: God's country—and mine. Writing it brings a strong American taste to my mouth. I rather like it.

While I was still holding my job, but beginning to be dubious about how long I could hold it, Ivy Litvinov, on one of her periodic jaunts outside Soviet Russia, came down to stay with us at a cottage we had taken for the summer on the Sussex coast. When I told her that my reputable and independent old paper had got itself a new owner; that a tough man of the go-getter type, former business manager of the Hearst combine, had bought the *Chicago Daily News;* and that I had an idea he and I were not going to get on very well (he had begun his ownership of the *News* by 'cutting out the dead wood', as he called it; which meant firing without bonus or pension some old faithfuls who had been on the paper over twenty or thirty years), Ivy, who stands in awe of no one, and to whom the arrogant figure of Frank Knox presented the perfect Bolshevik model for a carica-ture of the predatory American capitalist, laughed and said, "Why don't you tell him to go to hell right now?"

I told her life was not quite so simple as all that: I loved the paper. I was not going to get off it until I had to. That same summer, also on his way out of Russia, came Maurice Hindus; and he stayed with us too. When I told him of my forebodings as we lay on the beach one sunny Sunday morning, Maurice ran his fingers through that gollywog head of his, and declared: "Always remember one thing: if you do have to leave the *News*, you have a shot in your locker. Write a book. Your life. But don't you write that book until you absolutely have to!" I never got the chance to act upon Ivy's suggestion. Maurice gave me one of the most useful ideas I've ever had. Also, he wired me from New York when he heard that I had resigned: "Have ten thousand dollars. How much do you need?"

I was forced to resign because Colonel Frank Knox began accusing me of being too pro-British. This was rather ironic, considering that during the five years I had held the London post, those five fateful years between 1930 and 1935, I had been compelled to report a lot of things that had sadly diminished my original, and perhaps too uncritical, admiration of all things British. But, alas and alack-a-day, the unbelievable asininities of the American delegates who came to London for that long fiasco of international conferences, which led directly from the first world war to the second one, were also not something to write home about—or weren't they!—so, what with one thing and the other, I was open to fire from both barrels.

I wrote Knox that Walter Strong, the late owner, had put me in London to report what the British thought, not what the Americans thought the British ought to think; and that there was usually quite a difference. This was not enough for him. After some six months of shadow-boxing, I got a final letter ordering me back to be re-Americanised. It was the letter of a decent man, and almost swerved me. But I had *seen* Colonel Knox. I had met him at Victoria Station when he came up on the boat train with Walter Lipmann, toting a golf bag with about fifty clubs in it and gloatingly satisfied with himself. This was in 1933, when he came over "to hold a watching brief", as he put it, at the World Economic Conference. I had also had the quiet pleasure of seeing him very much in the flesh. He had summoned me to appear before him in his suite at the Savoy Hotel. He was in his B.V.Ds., doing physical jerks: a big, hearty, confident man. He rotated his torso, and, trying not to bend his knees, leaned over in a vain attempt to touch the floor. "One-two-three-four!" he counted. Then he straightened up. "You see I keep myself *fit!*" he said, smiling pinkly. He said it, so he did, with his golf clubs lying on his chair. Then he sat down to "put me right", as he told me, about the World Economic Conference. (At that time he believed that, one fine day, he would become President of the United States himself: and he was going to use the World Economic Conference as a sounding-board. He would cable his news to the ninety-four American papers which, at that time, still took our foreign service, and his voice would be as the voices of ninety-four men.) After about an hour of being "put right", I knew that this man before me knew as much about the life of Europe, its problems and its peoples, as I did of life on the moon. There is a passage in Kierkegaard's *Either/Or* which describes my feelings:

"Of all the ridiculous things, it seems to me the most ridiculous to be a busy man of affairs, prompt to meals, and prompt to work. Hence when I see a fly settle down in a crucial moment on the nose of a business man, or I see him bespatted by a carriage which passes by him in even greater haste, or a drawbridge opens before him, or a tile falls from a roof and strikes him dead, then I laugh heartily. And who could help laughing? What do they accomplish, these hustlers? Are they not like the housewife, when her house was on fire, who in her excitement saved the firetongs? What more do they save from the great fire of life?"

Knox, who hated Roosevelt, but saw his political chance, agreed to serve under F.D.R., and was Secretary of the Navy at the time of Pearl Harbor. What was Colonel Knox doing that morning, when his own Naval Intelligence had already warned him that the big Jap fleet was at sea? Was Colonel Knox keeping fit? "One-two-three-four!" My God.

The bombs rained down on the American fleet.

When *The Way of a Transgressor*, the book I wrote after resigning, became a best-seller in the United States and several other countries, Drew Pearson wrote in his column: "Colonel Knox has fired Negley Farson into prosperity." I shouldn't put it quite like that, but the success of the book did save my skin, and at a time when I had little

hide left. It gave me almost too much freedom for a time, as you
will see: and I shall never get over the home-sickness it gave me—
for the paper, I mean. The eleven years I spent on the *Chicago
Daily News* were among the happiest of my life.

It was two men, really, who had bought the *Chicago Daily News,*
and now for the other of that fabulous pair. This was the man with
the money, and part of his charm was that he would never let you
forget it. I am going to let his name rest in peace. He was such an
unbelievably outrageous vulgarian that I loved him. The first time
I met *him* was also in the Savoy Hotel. It was eleven o'clock in
the morning, and he was lying in bed, tight as an owl, drinking
Courvoisier brandy with Poland Water. He called me Neg as I came
through the door:

"Neg, d'ya know I'm sixty years old . . . yeah—an' I gotta *mill-
yon* dollars for every year!"

Then he sat up. "See these pyjamas?—*real* Jap-an-ese silk! Cost
$150 a pair. Yep!" He kicked off the covers.

"Looka that!" He pulled up his pyjamas. I stared at a couple of
hairy legs, and, tattooed around them, green and scarlet dragons that
crawled, so far as I could see, all the way up to his nether parts.
"Got that done in Japan! Yeah! Japan. When I was jus' a simple sailor
before the mast. Just a poor Gob. Neg—d'ya know I never been to
school?"

"And yet you made sixty million dollars?"

"Tha's the stuff. You got it. *Sixty* years old *and* a mill-yon dollars
for every year! Got it up here." He tapped his grizzled head. (And
he *had* got it there, too. He had invented a printing gadget that was
pouring more money—and cognac—into that fat little belly than he
knew how to handle.) "Lissen," he commanded. "Know wha' you
gonna do . . . ?"

Then, for a few minutes, I watched my job dangling from a thread.
This was when he began to give me some impossible orders. "Neg
—this is not a re-quest; it is a de-*mand.* Get that? Neg—I want you
to have every correspondent of the *News* right here in this room tomorrow morning. Wanna hold a conference."

"Mr. X, we've got a couple of correspondents out in the Far East.
One in China, one in Japan. We have a correspondent in Paris, Rome,
Berlin, Vienna, Moscow—I might get those for you—in a couple of

days—if I can persuade them to leave their posts—you know this will wreck the *Chicago Daily News* service?—but Mr. X, God Himself couldn't——"

"Lissen! I tole you! This is not a re-quest—it is a de-mand. An *order!* Understand?"

I stared at him for a moment, at that bloated little mug; and then I said—"Applesauce."

"Wh-a-a-a-a-t?"

I caught my breath: now I have done it! I thought.

He choked, leaned forward, then grabbed my hand. He stared at me until he could get his eyes into focus, then slowly sank back against the restful pillows. "Neg," he said—"I *like* you. So many tail-kissers on this goddam paper my ass is covered with blisters!"

Well, I had negotiated that corner. He immediately presented me with another. "Get the *Majestic*," he ordered.

"The——"

"*Majestic*, goddam it. Mean to say you ain't never heard of her?"

"Oh. Of course. Where is she?"

"Search me. She sailed from New York yesterday. 'Bout midnight. Wanna speak to her. Wanna talk—telephone—to Miss Devere. She's my Sweetie. Wait till you see her! Neg—you know I lay that baby twice a day. Yuh—an' I'm sixty years old. Ha-ha, well, you just get the *Majestic*, and don't you take all day about it. Hump yourself!"

I tried. After a time the G.P.O. said they could not get the *Majestic* —not until later in the day—she must come out a little further across the Atlantic. "Why?" asked Mr. X. "What's the trouble?" I tried to explain: "It's the curve of the earth——"

"To hell with the curve of the earth! *I* want Miss Devere."

Well—he got her.

After some of the most interesting conversation I have ever heard on the telephone (until the "fat-headed British sonofabitch", the G.P.O. man, cut him off in a huff), Mr. X suddenly had it.

"Say—don't they know their *business?* Get Halifax. Tell Halifax to get New York. Tell New York to put the call out to the *Majestic*. Say, what the hell——"

And sure enough, after about an hour, the call came through. The phone tinkled: "The *Majestic* for Mr. X."

"S-a-a-a-a-y, Sweetie!" I heard him yelling as I made for the door.

"This is *Papa!* Ye-e-e-s! goddam it; Baby, I been a dead man without you——"

So you can see I felt rather sad when a year later, in another posh London hotel—after racing my car through the dawn streets of the West End in answer to a scream from Sweetie over the telephone —I found Papa dead on the bathroom floor. The green dragons were motionless.

The Swiss Manager acted as if Death had no right to come there. The hotel was too rich, too exclusive; only the best people were allowed to register. This was positively shocking: an American millionaire had died in the Marie Antoinette suite, and the lady who had been in bed with him was not his wife. If this got into the newspapers . . . ! The Swiss Manager raised his eel-like eyes and held up his fat hands. This just wasn't fair—to the Babylon.

Death had called for this rich American (a vulgar person, the Manager confided to me) after a midnight supper in the Marie Antoinette suite, in which he had eaten, entirely by himself (I could take the Manager's word for it), two grilled lobsters: and at which he had drunk, all without aid, two bottles of the finest brandy. He had then gone about the hotel's corridors, in striped pyjamas, trying to give £5 tips to everybody, including some startled guests.

"So uncouth!" said the Swiss Manager, "like all these rich Americans." I told the Manager to go easy, I was also an American (though not a rich one), and this man was my friend. And as I looked down at his twisted face, and thought of all the awful things he had done since he had first been an illiterate sailor before the mast, I'll confess that this was the thought that ran through my head: "So, you old roughneck, with all your many millions you even had to die like a tough—always making your best friends afraid of what you were going to do next."

The lady was weeping. I more than half believed her when she said that she loved the man. I happened to know that, only a few days before, she had made him take back to the jeweller's a fantastically expensive diamond necklace he had given her; but in her grief, when she was quite well aware that she had lost everything, she never once mentioned that £25,000 trinket to me. And she told me, I might say, about all there was to be told.

I took my dead friend out by night, down the freight elevator, and his remains were being prepared for shipment back to the United States. Just as it had entered, silently, unseen, Death had left the Hotel Babylon. I moved Sweetie to the floor above the Marie Antoinette suite, to which no one but the Manager—and myself, when I wanted it—had the key. We quickly became friends. I took the law into my own hands, the way I kept control over the dead man's fantastically multitudinous possessions. X had died at the end of a long trip through Europe that he and Sweetie had just finished—a combination of illicit honeymoon and a butter-and-eggs man's Grand Tour. He had bought his own trousseau en route. He had twenty suits, hardly one of them worn, made by Lanvin in Paris; and this was the first time I ever knew that Lanvin made clothes for men. He had a tray of silk pyjamas like those I had first seen him in. The top drawer of one wardrobe trunk was entirely devoted to his personal jewellery—cases of diamond studs, of cuff links; diamond monogrammed cigarette cases, with cigar-cutters to match. He had two tail-coats, just made in Savile Row, and dozens of the most beautiful evening shirts I have ever touched—Sulkas.

"I am sending you back just as you came to Europe," I told Sweetie. "In the most expensive cabin and on the most expensive ship. That's the way *he* would have wanted it. I am thinking about him now—just old Papa X: it would break his heart if he thought that interested parties might get at you. Here are all his things: no inventory has yet been made—so you just take what you like. Take *everything* if you want it."

And I went out of the room and left her to it. What do you think she took? When I came up with the Swiss Manager to the Marie Antoinette suite in the afternoon, and we watched a dumbfounded clerk begin to make a list of X's jewellery before that startling collection was placed in the Babylon's safe, I could not see that she had taken anything. What could it have been? I went up to her room. Still weeping, she pointed to something that lay on her disordered bed. She had taken—

"Exactly what she would take!" cried, a week later, the rich man's attorney, who had raced across the Atlantic to clean up his affairs. "*She* knew what she was doing! A gunman's moll, that's what she was. I've known all about her for years. Just couldn't make poor old Tom see it. He was crazy about her.

"So—she took six boiled shirts, eh? Well, son,—they're going to be worn by her *real* boy friend: something classy from Yurrup! Jee-sus Christ! Six of the best Tuxedo shirts that money can buy in London! And she had poor old Tom hooked for a million, if he hadn't conked out on her. . . ."

So down there in Yugoslavia, as I sat weighing up human values and what I thought of the world in general—wondering what sort of life *I* was headed for—you can see that my thoughts were a bit unorthodox. Often, that corpse I had shipped across the Thames to be put in cold storage until it went back in the *Majestic*—with Sweetie, quite unaware of it, in her *de luxe* cabin up above—kept bobbing up and down like a buoy in the river of my thoughts. Had Mr. X got his money's worth?

Perhaps Sweetie gave it him.

FOR WHAT
IT'S WORTH

Writing *The Transgressor* was literally cashing in on experience. It was making life pay me back. I knew that if that book hit the jackpot I should be free to look for the life that I wanted to live. What was that life? I did not know. I thought writing that book might help me to find out. I can't say that it did. For what would have suited me right down to the ground at one time would have been utterly insufficient after other experiences. Too many wide gaps had appeared inside me.

In writing an autobiography—if you try to make it an honest one, to be honest with yourself at any rate—you put yourself through one of the most painful ordeals that a man can endure. This self-analysis can be even more shattering than being psychoanalysed—and can be, perhaps, as beneficial, or destructive. You go back and meet yourself at many an awkward turn of the road, and are forced to wonder why you did this and did not do *that*: the things you did not do being, of course, the ones you regret most. You need not tell everything—there is no law that requires you to undress in public—but you have met yourself face to face, and that is not always a pleasant encounter. It brings to your thoughts many things you would like to forget—things that can still burn you up; twenty, thirty, forty years later; in that nightmare time, especially if you have a bad hangover, when you lie half-awake, and all your own private little demons come out from the dark caverns of your subconscious to sit on your chest and taunt you. The most terrifying hours of a man's life—if he has had a life.

These sorrows are spiritual. It would be a poor soul who, twenty years later, lay in bed and sweated over some material loss. It is said that if you write these things down you get them out of your system. I don't believe it. What does happen is that you only recall them more vividly: even though, as the term goes, you may think you have "rationalised" them. I don't believe you can write them off or out, nor do I believe that you should allow yourself to be talked out of them. You may be able to buy a dispensation: but you can't buy forgetfulness, even in a bottle, because you will find that there is not another drop in it when you turn it up despairingly in the desperate morning. (And I'd like to have a dollar for every time I've tried.) If they are real tragedies they are real tragedies, and they should be recognised as such. I see no earthly reason why a man should delude himself. Sorrow can make you. A man should live with his mistakes. Life should not be made too sweet; it can't be covered with mayonnaise.

I shall write later of a country I love, land of a wondrous beauty and plenty, where they seem to have everything—including the highest suicide rate in Europe. This is a statistic that has always staggered me. The men are brave, handsome and sporting, the women are delightful. When I asked some of its loveliest inhabitants why their best friends had killed themselves, I knew they were giving me a profound truth when they said: "Life is no trouble." Uninhibited by religion and immune from national catastrophes: neutral to the woes of the world: pairing off in free love whenever they became excited, and coming unstuck just as easily—they seldom allowed desire to get up enough pressure to become passionate love; and, almost free from tragedy, they seldom produced an artist. I have often wished that I had been born in that country. It is hard to be a mere looker-on at such completely consummated self-indulgence. Yet they killed themselves for no reason at all. What is wrong there? This is probably the most highly developed Welfare State in the world, where a person would have to try very hard indeed to be destitute. Is it because by robbing life of nearly all its risks they have also robbed it of its adventures? Made it too dull to go on with? Or that where life has been made so easy even the most ordinary trouble assumes extraordinary, even fatal proportions? It may well be so.

I have always been glad to get back to a sparse, harsher existence again. I have not got the self-discipline to enable me to stand up to a country where "Life is no trouble". I should go to pieces long before its natives (as I have done). I need harsh correctives. And I know that life can be richer because of such experiences: a man should have a certain amount of trouble in his life. It seasons his philosophy. If he hasn't had any troubles then he has taken no chances. I have known just how good life can be, at times, if one would only let oneself live it, and not want too much. But somehow these periods do not last. Not with me. Something always happens. So thinking what sort of life I should go in for if that book gave me the choice, I answered myself with a negative: I knew there was one thing I was not going to do—and this was try for mere happiness. That also doesn't last. It can cloy. I wanted to go on *experiencing*. Perhaps I overrated my own strength, my ability to take punishment. Years later, when I began to get myself into such jams that I thought my steering-gear had gone completely, I went in for a mental overhaul in a Swiss asylum. And there after many months of exploring my dark interior the great Professor gave it up:

"*Keep* your conflicts!" he said. "The best thing for you is not to be normal. A normal man is a mediocre man."

Dreaming high up there in Yugoslavia, where the mountains went on and on until they became part of a dream themselves, I lived in other landscapes—landscapes of the mind. I saw my old cabin again out on that lonely lake in British Columbia. In the background of my mind was always that skyline of pointed firs, and the *Chinook* howling in from the Pacific, and months of grey mist, and the smell of dead salmon, and ducks coming up the river at sunset. For two years I had lived there. Days when I earned my living with both my head and my hands, had to earn it. Days when I was unencumbered by possessions, and need accept nobody's opinions. I had never imagined such freedom. Since then I have often thought that if the worst came to the worst (and I have sometimes hoped it would) I should go back. Not to the same lake, for I do not want an aftermath; but there would always be another lake, somewhere beyond the advance of the thing we call civilisation. Life out in B.C. had had a Homeric quality about it; it was as fresh and as vigorous as the life of the legendary Greeks. "In Argos where the horses graze.

. . ." Out there in the woods, living about as close to the ground as I could get, I found that I had completely lost my fear of life. With a rifle and shotgun, a couple of trout rods and my typewriter, I could have lived there till the end of my days—but I could not let myself.

Life in that unpainted shack floating on its raft of cedar logs, where the trout leapt in the sunsets and the deer often came down to the shore of my bay to drink, was, I knew, about as close to heaven as I was likely to get on this earth. Yet I knew it was not for me. I did not belong there. I was no trapper or timber-cruiser; nothing but bad luck could ever get me to work in a logging camp; the original Siwash had been driven out, and those few who remained, disconsolately spearing salmon before a few rickety old totem-poles down the river, had completely lost the desire to live: the big logging companies were raping their way up the Island, with "To hell with posterity!" as their interpretation of what the hoggish white man felt free to do in that wonderland: and for me to have hung on in that haunted country, writing second-rate stories about a mythical Golden West, in the way empty Rex Beach tried to follow the trail blazed by flaming Jack London—this would have been to accept a make-believe life that, sooner or later, would have made me want to shoot myself.

It was writing about that life in *The Transgressor* that helped me to see its limitations, and a few of my own. It requires more personal worth and self-sufficiency to live a full life in the woods than among the diversions and distractions of a big city. Either you must have something of a super-brain, or just no brains at all; and I must say that most of those I have found living in the wide open spaces belong to the second category. I do not believe most escapist stories. In a life given to quite a lot of wandering about in remote parts, I can count on my fingers, and perhaps one hand would do, the men of whom I could say that they seem to have absolutely fulfilled themselves in solitude. But when you do come on such a character—when you do find one of these men who are completely living up to the majesty of the scene that you usually find them in, what a man! You will meet one or two in this book.

It is all very well to say that a man can find himself in solitude. But then comes the question: What is he going to do with himself afterwards? There's the rub. Toynbee has something to say about that in his 'withdrawal and return', but we ordinary mortals cannot be Mohammeds or Buddhas or Pauls of Tarsus. Though I will say one thing: even the ordinary man, provided he has the will and the wits to take a good long look at himself, cannot fail to benefit from a couple of years' meditation in the desert, if he can get there.

And so I knew, as the seasons passed by in that beautiful life out in British Columbia, that the time was inexorably approaching when I should have to tell myself that I had got all out of life there that it had to give me. And on that day I must go. Go not only because I had exhausted my present habitat, but because I must have something bigger than myself to live for. A cause, if that does not seem too startling. And I did find that cause, just once, in a big American business corporation—in Chicago.

I won't say I wasn't frightened about returning there (I had known the city well). On those last dawns in our houseboat in British Columbia—as I put my rods back in their cases and ran boiling water through my shotgun to proof it against God knew how many years of inaction, my heart was low. I had stood out on our raft many a morning and watched the sun rise and drive the mist off the still lake, watched the reflection of pines slowly appear on the water; and still night after still night we had lain listening to the life in the forest, to the small, tell-tale movements of animals or to the splash of a salmon. Now it was to be the stockyards and the railway tracks.

But when I returned to Chicago it was not with any breathless desire for success; I was going to use it merely as a stepping-stone. And that was just the right sense of values both for me and for the salesmen I soon had under me. American salesmanship at that time was largely a matter of bunk—patter from catalogues. Those were the days of the "Sell 'em *yourself!*" school, and God knows there were plenty of schools for salesmanship. Dale Carnegie's *How to Win Friends and Influence People* must be one of the saddest books ever written. Consider the awful insecurity of soul that it caters to—that biggest, most perpetual best-seller in the U.S.A. after the Bible. I knew, on the other hand, that there was more in American business life than the mere pursuit of money, a lot more; and that if you could give the salesman some real *meaning*, instead of this line of patter that he had to hand out every day (usually to an irate 'prospect' who was telling him to get the hell out of the office), the salesman would bless you. The salesman must believe in what he is saying in order to believe in himself. Put some teeth into what he has to say, some sense of value—and his own life takes on value at once. The purposeless, empty existence that fritters away the lives of so many good people has vanished.

I knew, because I had listened to it only too often, what the average European thinks of the average American's life: that it is one long vulgar pursuit of the Almighty Dollar. And I knew he could not have been more wrong—nor, for the matter of that, could a host of American writers. Dos Passos had not yet written *Manhattan Transfer* and *The Big Money*, levelling his guns on the U.S. capitalists (and whom does he shoot today, anyhow?), but I was in Chicago when *Babbitt* hit that city—and in all the laughter, all the tears of rage, we knew that Sinclair Lewis was close to dead centre on the target. For, burlesque as it was, Lewis loved George Babbitt, and he wrote from inside man: Dos Passos never wrote a line from *inside* big business. He didn't know it. And something of the same lack of inside knowledge characterises the European's mind when he thinks about the American 'way of life', as he is so fond of calling it. The average European hasn't the faintest frog's idea of what an exciting *game* American big business life can be, and you are just wasting your breath trying to get it across to him. Incidentally, he is not worth it. He will often stoop to things that the Americans (I don't speak of crooks) have long given up as bad practice. When it comes to the pursuit of money I have found the complacent Englishman just as fast on his feet as the next man. And behind his mask of self-deprecation (which, in most cases, deceives *him* just as much as it does us) he can, when it comes to a show-down, be twice as ruthless. The English are the most money-conscious people I have ever lived among. The City of London can give New York cards and spades when it comes to putting the financial boots to somebody. They have had centuries of practice, 'developing' all those backward races. But this is not the place to cast aspersions: that comes later. Here, I only wish to say that, except for the Spaniards, I think the Americans are the least materialistic of all the so-called civilised races. They are certainly the most generous.

And so it was that when I became sales manager of my company's big Chicago branch (chiefly because I was the worst salesman in it)

10.4

RANDOLPH BOARD OF EDUCATION

I found my cause. It was working as part of a group. When I got into my car to drive down to the office of a morning, or to pick up a salesman and go out with him to close, or lose, a big order, I knew that the very last thing that either he or I would be thinking about on that crucial day was money. It was the tang of the thing—this was the *finish:* it was like the last mile in the boat race, or taking the last hurdle—with the salesmen of the other big competing companies or their managers waiting in the outer office for us to fail. One or two of those big business deals have given me the biggest thrills I have ever had in my life. How can any writer, even an American, know anything about feelings like that, unless he's had them? It may be that I was lucky enough to work for a company that I really believed in; or the fact that one or two of the top men I worked with were such lovable, even noble characters. (Certainly I had no love for the handful of high-up directors, people we never saw, who speculated in the company's stock and cleaned up millions.) Or it may have been that I was asked to lead the very men I had been working with, and that, after a time, they began to believe that I was some use to them. Whatever it was, the cause was there: the feeling for a thing that was far bigger than yourself, and the losing of yourself in it. Those two years in Chicago were the most *useful* I have ever lived.

I have always believed that a profession can be a cause. A man in love with his profession is free from the trash of life. To him, money really is a necessary evil: all he wants is enough to keep going. (I am not saying what his poor wife and children may feel about all this.) If I were suddenly asked whom I consider the most fulfilled man I have ever met, I should cite a little ex-Russian Jew in New York City. His life is dedicated to research. He is one of the three great biochemists in the world. He gets a salary that a salesman for women's underwear would sneer at. He cannot keep a car, and he gives part of his meagre stipend away, to keep a lame woman assistant who, he says apologetically, is too valuable to lose. I have seen some of the greatest surgeons in New York jump to their feet when that man enters the room. They revere him—as do his adoring, and infuriated, laboratory students, who have to work out their analyses to the seventh decimal point. And who is the man, do you think, that this delicate little Jew cherishes most in his heart? It is a tough

Irish mick: the fighting stevedore who was leading the dock strikers when this Jew, then hardly more than a boy, finally reached New York after he had fled from the pogrom at Odessa in 1905. This great man sat by my bed when I was laid up in his hospital in New York in 1949, and told me his story. Two years later, when I returned and asked him to dinner, I reminded him of his early years: "Are you still thinking of Mr. Shean?" I asked. He laughed joyously. "So . . . you remember? Well . . ." He placed his delicate finger tips together. "Sometimes, you know, I think, I really do, that that big tough Irishman, with his broken knuckles, was one of the biggest and finest men I have ever known." In the story of those two men I saw America.

TOO FREE

This is not a newspaperman's story, though the fact that I have been a foreign correspondent will probably influence every word of it. And I think this is a good thing: no other profession provides one with so many useful yardsticks and the proper attitude of doubt. I am thankful to have had those advantages: just as I was always thankful to have had many years of Europe, witnessed the last three years of the Romanoffs, served a year in Egypt as a British officer, had those two glorious years in the woods of British Columbia, and then survived the maelstrom of big business in Chicago, before I ever became a journalist—and I did not actually become one until, coming out on an Italian tramp steamer from the Black Sea on a windswept winter's day, after my wife and I had finished sailing our yawl *Flame* across Europe (we had left her ashore, iced up, at the Sulina mouth of the Danube), I found a cable at the American Consulate in Constantinople telling me that I had an "assured worthwhile job". The first correspondent's cable I ever sent was from Angora. And it was a beauty. With all the world waiting anxiously to be told whether Turkey, led by the triumphant Mustapha Kemal Pasha, would go to war with England over the Mosul oil, and what the scene was like in that startlingly successful young upstart Republic (because, if Kemal had got very drunk one night, the Turks just *might* have taken on Great Britain), I sent these famous words: BELIEVE IF BRITAIN MAKES REASONABLE OFFER TURKS WILL ACCEPT. The total cable was less than thirty words. My first, it also came within an ace of being my last: only a sense of humour in the *Chicago Daily News* office saved me.

To quote the timeworn truth (the French are credited with it): "Journalism is the finest profession in the world, once you have left it." The cynicism that journalism equips you with is very proper, but can be harmful as well: after years of reporting the conduct of society you will inevitably reach the state, so common in our profession, in which you don't give a damn what happens to anybody, including yourself. It was *after* I left journalism that I cracked up, but it was also because of it, not that I am looking for excuses or even being apologetic about it. I became fed up with the human race, myself in particular.

During my days as a foreign correspondent drink may have made me a nuisance to other people, but it did not trouble *me;* neither inwardly nor outwardly. I think it was love of my job that saved me. What I did after I got my dispatches off was my own affair: always provided, of course, that I did not make an unholy show of myself. Not that this would have been easy in the bottle-party London of the 'twenties, to say nothing of the 'thirties, when lying in high places had become official currency. With such a disgusting exhibition in public life there was little inducement to go in for any priggish personal probity. There are many good reasons why newspaper men take to drink, and we do not need a psychiatrist to help us find them. Chief of them is the disgust we get from reporting the affairs of the poor damned human race. Mark Twain was right when he said that God invented man because He was disappointed in the monkey; but he should have reversed it.

This sounds as if I were giving credit to the correspondents for better morals and foresight than the statesmen's; which is precisely what I am doing. Read the dispatches of any top American newspaper man from Europe during the 1930s. We *hated* most of the statesmen of that time. 1935 was the fatal year. After that, any thoughtful journalist, even though he could hardly believe his own senses, would have to report that the politicians were leading our little world straight to hell. We duly did so, and one or two of us lost our jobs by it. London, with its pageantry, was maddeningly complacent.

Another good reason why so many newspaper men crack up—for drink, as the sad records show, is our occupational disease—is the business of always having to work against the clock. This is a constant strain on the nerves of correspondents working for the big Agencies, which flash the spot news; for to be beaten on a big story by even twenty minutes means that you have been scooped. You might as well never have been on that story at all. Agency men lived in a state of constant nervous tension: they were like hunters prowling through the forest, never knowing what kind of game they are going to jump. And a miss was as good as a mile in that split-second world. With an *interpretative* service, such as the one I worked for, this race against time could be even more trying. We not only had to send the news; we had to send what was *behind* the news—our opinion of what had caused such and such an event, and what it would lead to. Murder, rape, arson and all the minor crimes of the local Sodom were outside our purlieu: we dealt only with the major offences—usually in foreign affairs. But these could be sensational enough: such as when the British gave Hitler the right to build submarines, and so finally took the lining out of France, and made Italy decide to look elsewhere than to Britain for a strong ally.

In our own interpretative service, we were forced to work against one of the most fantastically foolish time-limits ever imposed on foreign correspondents—our infamous 7.30 a.m. deadline in New York. That was the last moment at which we foreign correspondents on the *Chicago Daily News* could get our cables to New York. When old Victor Lawson died the paper came into the hands of a splendid man, Walter Strong. Strong (he insured his life for $1,000,000, and then dropped dead on the golf course) was one of the most lovable, most loyal newspaper chiefs that any body of correspondents could hope to work for: but he was much better as a business man than as a newspaper editor or owner. He made what, from a strictly business viewpoint, was an amazing dicker with the American cable and telegraph companies: this was that if his foreign correspondents got their cables to New York on or before 7.30 a.m.—which was the most idle period—they would be transmitted instantly throughout the United States at an almost ridiculously low rate. And at a ridiculous time too, because our cables reached New York long before the editors had got out of bed—indeed, when most of the Pacific coast ones were just climbing into it. We had ninety-four papers taking our service then. Nearly all of them also took one of the big Agencies, the A.P. or the U.P., and our service was by way of being an additional, highly specialised, analysis of the day's events. We on the C.D.N. were free, theoretically, from having to flash any news; but you can take it from me that we were not very popular if our interpretative cables reached any paper too late to make its editions. The *Chicago Daily News* had, if memory serves me right, eleven editions every day; and in the case of a running story, of the arrest, for instance, of Gandhi, and of how the Indians reacted to it, new cables would hit edition after edition. I filed cables throughout all one day, over two thousand words of them, on the Gandhi story. And all hit that evening's editions, on the same day, in the United States.

In the East, where time begins, our deadline did not matter. I remember how, when Ashmead Bartlett and I drove back to Bombay after seeing the Holy Man being taken off the train at Borivli and escorted to Poona prison, all India was asleep. We watched the peasants lighting their morning fires, watched the flames of sunrise; and in the Bombay Yacht Club, where we were living, we dug out the sleepy Hindu bartender and made him give us a bottle of *Veuve Cliquot*. We poured it into two pint-sized pewter beer mugs filled with ice. We were in no hurry: meridional-time, the curve of the earth, gave us all the ease we needed to let our nerves settle down, and to think over what we had just seen and its importance. "Well, here's to you—you're the one who gets the scoop!" laughed Ashmead, bitterly: that old rogue among foreign correspondents, the hooknosed, arrogant aristocrat who broke the story of the mishandled Gallipoli expedition against Sir Ian Hamilton (who wanted to have him shot for it). "Here I sit—with the same story as you—and I can't beat you!" For so it was: here was where the curve of the earth came in: Ashmead worked for the London *Daily Telegraph*, which was five hours nearer to India than New York is, and the *Daily Telegraph*, a morning newspaper, had already been 'put to bed'. Ashmead could not make his paper before the next day: in the meantime, all the British correspondents in the United States would be cabling my eye-witness story back to their newspapers in London. Ordinarily, I hate champagne: if that were the only drink I should have been sober as a judge all my days: but the *Veuve Cliquot* in the beer mugs, with our scooped and unsuspecting colleagues sleeping in the Club or over at the Taj Mahal Hotel, was what the gods drank on Olympus.

In the East, then, time does not count. In Western Europe it meant everything. You cannot get much sense out of the British Foreign Office before eleven o'clock, if then; and after that—I am speaking of my own case now, though Paris, Berlin, Rome were just about as hard-pressed—there would often be the American Embassy to call on, to get *our* side of the story, or some mission then in London; so there was hardly a day when I was able to reach my typewriter before 12.30. That gave me an hour to write a dispatch of some 800 words or more, which in a few hours was going to be read by the State Department, the diplomats in Washington and the university professors from New York to San Francisco: for those were the people for whom we wrote the 'think pieces', as they were called in our trade. Politics and personalities were our study: political economy was our daily preoccupation. I still have the five scrapbooks of my dispatches sent during those years. They are on the bookshelf by my bed. I have never totted the wordage up, but I should think that for five years I averaged some 300 words a day for six days out of the seven. And nearly every word of those cables was written with nerves taut as a tuned-up violin.

As I have said, I loved that job. It gets into your blood. Such tense riding against time is like taking the jumps at the Grand National. And it can be dangerously exciting if you don't keep a tight grip on yourself. When you are writing like that, with the gun against your head, you have no time to rewrite. Your words are on the air; you can't pull them back; the first words are in the States, usually, before you have finished your cable. You have to know what you are going to say—and especially *how* you will say it—before you type the first word. I usually wrote in short 'takes', with the cable boys waiting in the outer office to snatch my sections of cable as fast as my secretary could vet and hand them over. Many a day, as I ripped the last take from my machine, my hands were shaking; and on such days, even if I was going out to lunch with someone of importance, I rushed straight down to Henekeys' in the Strand and downed four double-whiskeys in a row. That let the nerves down. . . .

But you can't keep on doing that sort of drinking for ever. Sooner or later it will get you. When I lost that deadline I lost myself.

I did not go to the dogs. I went down to Yugoslavia and wrote *The Transgressor*. But when I got back to London in the autumn of 1935 I felt foolishly free. I had been so accustomed to adjusting my daily time-table—and my morals—to that deadline that I felt I had lost a support. I had; or call it a harsh corrective. My life seemed empty, to have no purpose. We had sold the long lease of the two houses I had had knocked into one on Walton Street, scene of many a good party in my newspaper days (the Russian Ambassador, Maisky, with his wit and gay satire, had dined with us there, and so had that fine man Sir Tej Bahadur Sapru when he came over for the Round Table Conference): to say nothing of the quiet pleasure of living among our possessions, the loot of eleven years' wandering. These were stored now.

We were living temporarily in South Kensington. This part of London I knew better than any other; I had known it since the days of my marriage, back in 1920. Known it, loved it, and yet been bored with it. It is too full of pension-minded people. South Kensington is the British Valhalla, stiff with retired officers, military and civil. I doubt whether there is any other district in the world where the density of heroes is so thick. (You can read that both ways.) Men and women who have known the sunsets of India, the snows of the Pamirs and the heart-breaks of lonely out-stations in the Pacific, and who treasure the memory of a warm comradeship when working with 'their people', namely the coloured race they have been administering—what an assembly! Admirable people, splendid leaders; never so dependable as when, in some tight spot, most other people would think the game was up. That is when the Englishman laughs. I have often wondered how people like that, people who have lived such fantastically interesting and even romantic lives, could be content to come home and retire into oblivion.

The answer is, of course, that it is not oblivion. No other country in the world has such a round of official functions for its army of retired officers, or at any rate for those who have distinguished themselves in its service. In America, until quite recently, a man who retired could find no one to talk to. Earn your spurs in Britain, and you wear them for the rest of your life (even in bed, say the French). Had I been an Englishman I should have been content.

But by 1935 the yearly calendar of official functions, with decorations up, meant one thing to the men who had earned those decorations, and something entirely different to us—who had reported what

was happening behind that brilliant scene. We were beginning to
feel that the British were being dazzled by their pageantry. It was
making them blind to the present. True, these glittering functions
were all built round tradition, with its stern obligations; and tradition, one might think, would see Britain through. But, short of war,
tradition can be a very dangerous thing; under cover of it, too many
of the wrong people don the toga. Empire can debauch the mother
country, when it returns too many pewter kings back into its national
composition. And that had happened to England. The Victorian liberals' conception of paternal colonialism had been splendid; its fol-
low-up had not been so good. Strickland Sahib would have found
the stories of Somerset Maugham, *On a Chinese Screen* and his tales
of Malaya, very painful reading. And, accepting Britain's greatness
as their own, there were, even in the 1930s, too many people in England who still talked as if 'the niggers begin at Calais'.

No longer able to take an active part in what was going on, I
found life in London desperately insufficient and exasperating. I was
tired of sitting in the Café Royal, listening to the twitterings of the
sparrow-intellectuals: I was offended by the self-satisfied do-gooders
of that dusty period, the people who rode down Pall Mall on the top
of a taxicab, shouting "ALL AID TO CHINA!": I was fed up with people
like the Webbs, with their paper plans for a test-tube world: (it was
said of Beatrice and Sidney Webb, by an admirer, that "they were
so absorbed with abstract and intellectual affairs that they became
non-human." What a recommendation for people engaged in draw-
ing up plans for the life of man!): and I was tired of the rows of letters after the names of so many public figures, who, I knew from
writing about them, were only stuffed shirts. "Those alphabetical absurdities!" as an American girl called them.

I was too old to be a member of the Bright Young Things, or even
a survivor of the Naughty Twenties. I always had the feeling, as I
looked on at their revels, that I had been born either ten years too
soon or a hundred too late. I belonged to a couple of clubs, but resigned from them both. From one, because I was becoming the club
bore: I will make even a lamp-post stop and listen to me when I'm
drunk. From the other, because the club bored me. Basically, I am
not a club man. One of the weirdest discoveries I made in those
desperate days was that I am a solitary. I was finding English life

"ungracious, unamiable and heavy", as William James, brother of Henry, had found it years before; and that there was "an oppressive ponderosity and superfluity and prominence of the unnecessary" in both the people and their institutions. . . . I began to drink seriously.

It is not pleasant to live with yourself after you have lost your self-respect. The evenings were not so bad, now that drink had given me its fool's paradise. I even began to *like* that chatter in the Café Royal at eleven o'clock at night, when you had to order one of those dummy Welsh rarebits, to comply with the drinking laws. It was the mornings that were so awful—not the remorse so much, or even the hangover, but just the fed-upness. I wanted something to DO—I wanted some interest bigger than the usual round of daily enjoyments, most of them humdrum. I knew that, in my heart, I envied a great deal in British life. It seems absurd to sit here singing their praises; they have a good enough opinion of themselves. And, it must be said, with reason. I envied many Englishmen—though not as individuals: I envied a national tradition which, at one time anyway, held out the prospect of such wonderful lives overseas, in the most interesting and adventurous places . . . "far away, over boundless seas and deserts, to dusky nations living under the stars", as Macaulay has it. I envied the type—though not all the types—that such lives produced: men such as you will see in some of the Service clubs or going into the Royal Geographical—experts on odd places. Some of those lives were fabulous. The old Indian Civil Service was the finest body of men I have ever met, and the African Colonial Service had many wonderful officers. I had seen them at work. The Indian Civil always fought to protect 'their people' from the ununderstanding edicts of Whitehall, and often from those of Delhi; and one of the principal jobs of an African District Commissioner has always been to save the natives in his charge from the rapacity of the white trader and settler. Career and Cause, for these people, were identical: with the result that the one word the British left behind them in India was the best word of all—honour. If we at home had such honest and altruistic men always in public office, we should be lucky.

I can safely say this, for forty years of living outside my own country, and of such things as the left-wing of the British Labour Party and the Cliveden Set, have made me a far better American than I ever thought I could be.

In those days I could still read books, good books, to help me through a hangover. My mind could stand strong meat, even good old British beef. But reading biographies (my favourite pastime), I began to feel nauseated with the British myth of the Great Man. The 'great' Curzon, the 'great' Cromer, the 'great' Milner, the 'great' Joseph Chamberlain—I had seen too much of their achievements, or lack of achievements. Poverty in India, poverty in Egypt, wretchedness in the West Indies—where does all the 'greatness' come in? I am asking this on behalf of the natives, the indigenous people: not of the ruling, occupying, official caste, with all its pomps, pomposities and plumed helmets, and its devotion to the planters, the wares of Birmingham and the Lancashire looms. I am not saying that Curzon can be blamed for the increase in the Indian birth-rate, or Cromer for the fact that the *fellaheen* of the Nile are still the most depressed peasants in the world: I am just saying that these Proconsuls passed by, and left no real record of benefits for the great masses of the people who had been under them. I would not even say this, if the British would only stop holding up for your admiration a figure superb beyond the limitations of ordinary man. That can be irritating. Gladstone, put under a microscope, instead of a magnifying glass, would probably appear as the most blown-up figure of British history. When the Grand Old Man was steaming up and down the country orating against the "Bulgarian atrocities", they were stuffing crippled little children up the flues to clean the chimneys of the stately homes of England.

I worked myself up into a fury about it all. This was serious. I was getting the petty animosities of a sick man. I pulled myself together, took the car across to France, and drove out through Brittany, a country I have always loved, down to the Quiberon peninsula. I had no sooner got the car ashore at Boulogne than I felt that exaltation known by so many English: I had got rid of my nursery governess. I was on the Continent! This in no way implies that I looked forward to orgies of moral laxity: it was just that I had left so many conventions behind me. I reached Quiberon at a time of the year when there were only Frenchmen there with their wives, or other people's wives; and feasting on fried fresh sardines, and writing on the sands, I had a few weeks of perfect bliss. The 'decadent' French struck me as being appallingly athletic: turning somersaults over gigantic push-balls, doing hand-stands on the beach, and battling with their children to build fantastic sand-castles. It was France at play, and very happy. There was not a single tourist to sell anything to. I went over to the Bay, swam naked in the warm shallow water, and dried off on the empty sands as I stared out to where Hawke, flying in from the west in pursuit of the French fleet, in a gale that churned that treacherous sandy-shoaled bay into a maelstrom, rode the top of a wave down on Du Verger and scraped off the *Formidable*'s portlids. I drank my full share of the white wines served with the heavenly shell-fish at Quiberon, and, strange as it seemed to me, held it. I returned to London a new man. For a time. . . .

In the course of my work I had made one or two good friends in the Labour camp. One was George Lansbury. I had started another book (*The Story of a Lake*) at Quiberon; and to get his permission to use some of the material he had given me years before—about the last days of the Labour Government in 10 Downing Street—I went down and sat with Lansbury in his honest little house in Bow Road, with the white plaster bust of Lenin on his bookshelf. It always amused me how that innocent, kindly old man, who would not kill a flea, could have such an admiration for Lenin—who could have blotted out thousands of human beings (and did) with the unconcern with which a biologist would empty his test-tube down the sink. My publisher feared that we might have some trouble over libel, and he wanted Lansbury to agree to substantiate what I had written, if it came to that point. The honest man (in whom much of the *goodness* of the Labour movement was enshrined) said: "Why! Brother"—he always called you Brother—"of course I shall be willing to say that I told you that. I did tell you. It's true." "I *want* to see that printed," he said as I left him. Later, when I came back with more of the book done—I had given short pictures of the Welsh miners during the 1926 strike, standing with their hands in their pockets along the streets of Pontypridd and Tonypandy, afraid to go home for fear their hunger might make them eat their children's food— "Brother!" said Lansbury, with tears in his eyes, "that *has* to be printed."

But when I came back with still more of the book—and he read where I had got my hero all snarled up in a tangle of illicit love—

honest old George just stared at me. "No, no, NO!—I *can't* give my approval to a book like that. It's very hard, Brother, to sort out the wheat from the chaff of this book." I think he was right.

I was drinking again. I began to wait outside the door for the pubs to open in the mornings: walking up and down, so that I should not be observed. I became nervous if a bobby stared too long at me. But I was usually first in—ah, now the day starts. . . . Moreover, which is worse, I began to drink alone. Then I began to embarrass people by talking to them—complete strangers. Life became almost unbearable in my sober moments. I could no longer even sit through a movie, and left theatres after the first act to take a drink, then went right on drinking till closing time. I decided to take a cure.

This was the first and the worst. It seemed a comparatively simple one. I took a room in a nursing-home. I went to bed. A bottle of lovely whiskey was placed before me. I was told to drink all I wanted. Even I, who have some imagination, did not know what was in store for me. A pretty young Irish nurse sat by my bed. "Well, here's how!" I said, and downed half a glass neat. "In just wan minute," she said, "*himself* will be coming along to you." The doctor came. I was given an injection—WOW! I spun like a top. I have never known such retchings. . . . "Aaah!" said the pretty Irish lass, as she held the basin, "what a waste of the grand stuff!"

Between paroxysms I lay prostrate and listened to her story: I wrote it, while I was in there, for the *Daily Express*. It was the story of all too many nurses in England, for the hospitals reeked with petty snobbism, engendering real hatreds. I had heard it all and had seen it all. This one said: "I'm damn' well fed up! When I went into the hospital for my training, I said to myself: 'A nurse is a noble woman—and that's what you're going to be.' Said the others: 'You wait—you wait till you get out—you'll be just as hard-hearted as the rest of us!'"

"The way they *trate* us!" she went on—and now I did persuade her to have a nip of the 'grand stuff'. "I'm not speakin' of only the doctors now, treatin' us like skivvies—the old women are the worst of the whole bloody lot—me own sex, mind you! As soon as they wake up in the mornin' they ring the bell. They don't want anything. They just want to see you jump. The bitches. . . . *Me* kind-hearted? . . .

I could kill the old divvils! Hurry up now—put it down—here he comes. . . ."

That little bit from the bogs of Mayo agreed with me that this cure was "somethin' terrible!" Anyhow, it failed to work. When I got out into the fresh air again, and looked at the city I had once loved (and would love again; but that was to be during the air raids —London under the moon was never so beautiful or so lovable as on those nights), I felt that a change of habitat was imperative. I had had all I could take.

"I have reached a point in my own evolution when I humbly feel that London has nothing left to offer me", said Edmund Blunden in 1953, as he sailed to take up a professorship at Hong Kong. This, as can be imagined, raised a storm. Dr. Johnson was hurled at Edmund Blunden: "Sir, when a man is tired of London he is tired of life, for there is in London all that life can afford."

Anyhow, I sailed for New York.

RETURN OF
THE NATIVE

For me the magic of New York is not in the splendour of its skyline, in the glamour of Fifth Avenue, or in all that dazzle and glitter which affronts your eyes around Broadway and 42nd Street: it lies in the sad companionship of the city slums, in the dreamers of the Ghetto, in life under the Elevated on lower Third Avenue. There, in all that sweating, struggling, stinking humanity, with all its hopes and desperations, you may find an understanding heart. And if there really is a God—a thing which you will come to doubt as you talk with some of the wretched down-and-outers along Skid Row, the lower Bowery—you will know that an understanding heart is the greatest gift that God can give you.

It was an English Jew, Israel Zangwill, who first called New York the great Melting Pot. He wrote a play by that name. He also wrote a play called *The Dreamers of the Ghetto*—the story of the Jews from Eastern Europe, arriving at New York, gateway to the Promised Land, in their millions: the Old Testament folk, who stared at the Statue of Liberty with tears in their eyes as their steamers came up the Bay; who gazed, open-mouthed and appalled, at the towering skyscrapers reaching to the clouds—Babylon, to them—and who then never saw anything of this again in all their shabby lives. They eked out the rest of their existence in the squalor of Hester Street, where they hung their dirty bedclothes on the fire-escapes to air-and-dry them in the mornings, and threw their slops into the steaming streets on top of the rotten refuse and fly-crawling garbage. The weakest among their American-born children rotted, and ended up in the electric chair: the strongest fought their way with a bitter intelligence through the free public schools, driven by their mad urge to escape from the Ghetto: took top honours in the universities and became the great scientists, playwrights, authors, actors, surgeons, musicians, philosophers, philanthropists—and so many of the money-mad maniacs—who have given such fame and ill-fame to that fabled city. Many of these Jews, terrified of what was, and still is, boasted about so loudly as the American way of life, clung apprehensively to their ancient customs: the old orthodox Jewess wore a wig, the old bearded men sought sanctuary in the synagogue and peace in the Talmud. There in the slums of New York you saw life in the raw —life laid wide open, with its steaming intestines exposed to view, and sometimes its beating heart: as plain to see as the insides of any patient who has just been opened up on the operating table. And you didn't know New York at all until you had penetrated that far into its anatomy.

That is the New York I shall always love.

(One of my day-dreams has been that some time or other I would take a room on lower Third Avenue, live there for a year—and just *soak* myself with people: live every day in the presence of so many varied lives, become part of them, and thereby increase my interest in my own life. I want to feel that I am living every day, instead of just being alive. I want to get back to some of that comradeship which the good old grey poet sang about, that 'lover of populous pavements': and perhaps, like him, I shall be allowed to sit up in the wheel-house, and have a good gab with the captain as he steers through the tugs and the steamers and the big ocean liners going about their business in the Bay—that is, if New York still does have ferry-boats; and if the shaghetti in its cheap little Italian restaurants is still spaghetti, and not made half of sawdust; and if I can still get myself a big wire basket of steamed clams, covered by a napkin, raked from the mud flats of Long Island Sound. For—I don't know —so many things have been killed in New York: both men and clams. The city has gone to hell. But I want to hear the voices of old New York again, even if they are only echoes. I often feel that I have been out of my own country long enough: almost forty years now. And perhaps I shall find that companionship? I have seen enough of the world to know that I shall never find its free, generous like in any other country. Yes, I shall go back. And I, too, will lie on Paumanok's grey beach

Recalling now the obscure shapes, the echoes, the sounds and sights
*   after their sorts,*
The white arms out in the breakers tirelessly tossing,
I, with bare feet, a child, the wind wafting my hair. . . .

There is no substitute for your own land.)

I had every reason to be happy when I returned to New York in 1935. I had come back with my shield, instead of on it. It was exciting to step back into the book world, where there was still such good talk and such enthusiasms about the future. (It is far different now, when the written word is fighting for its life.) And my own book had given me the freedom I wanted. I had come over on the *Berengaria* with Sinclair Lewis. He was in his most Puckish mood. We had an English writer on the boat who had done one excellent book, but had been unable to stand success: he was coming over on a lecture tour, as well as to sell us some of his by-products. One of the nicest things about Americans is the way we pay European celebrities to come over and tell us what's wrong with us, and nearly always ask them to come back and tell us more. But this man did not look as if he was going to fill the bill; he was too satisfied with himself. And his sure ideas of what America and the Americans were like, before he had even seen us, were fantastic. Our only consolation was his announcement that, after he had finished this tour, he would go back to England and lecture about the States. Poor U.S.A.—and, for that matter, poor England! This man was constitutionally unable to judge any country. He had a filing-case in his cabin, one of those accordion affairs, neatly tabbed, which seemed just the one idea that Sinclair Lewis had never thought of. "Now this," asked Lewis, putting a finger in one of the tabbed sections; "what's in *there?*" "Why —what it says, of course! From here to here, it is all short stories: this next section is devoted to articles, little—ah—vignettes, you know? And these"—the author strummed some fat divisions—"all this is lecture material." Lewis shook his head in dumb admiration: "I see—you have everything all prepared: how *business*-like!" I thought the man's leg would come off. And, sure enough, when we came slowly up to the staggering skyline of New York he said just the

right thing—"Why! . . . It's Babylon!" There were some ship-re-
porters on board, who had come out with the pilot tug (to interview
Lewis): and the Englishmen turned to see whether they had got
his superb statement. They had: they had heard the same thing from
every first-time arrival. "This city will scare the pants off you," I
growled, as I went below to fetch my Corona. "It's the cruellest city
on God's green earth." I heard no trumpets sounding for him in New
York: I think he went back with his little accordion-case still virgin.
Americans do not mind being told how to live; but, by this time,
we were getting a bit more particular about who did the telling.

I knew Lewis but slightly, the chief reason being that the few
times we had met, usually at parties, we were both in a condition
that precluded friendship. He was one of the noted men whom I
had taken the chair for in London. That particular lunch, at the Savoy, had originally been in honour of Bob Davis, the 'discoverer' of
O. Henry—that old war horse among American editors who was then
wandering around the world writing his column *Bob Davis Recalls*.
Old one-thumbed Bob had bought my own very first short story for
Munsey's; and had sent back the second one by return of post, saying
"This is more pitiful than a schoolgirl's graduation thesis". Fate had
been very kind to me, I thought, in that, when Bob came to London,
I should represent the American newspaper men there to welcome
him. Unfortunately, Red Lewis turned up too, also with the idea
that he would like to make a speech at that lunch: and I asked Bob
Davis whether he minded it being a dual show. Well, I'll draw a veil
over most of this. . . . These two personages, one sitting on either
side of me, started to kid one other during lunch—at least, Lewis
insisted upon making Bob listen to him: recalled adventures they
had had together "in the old newspaper days". This made Davis
nervous; and—fatal mistake—he decided to change the speech he
had originally intended. He saw a chance to be funny: he and Sinclair Lewis would rib each other—for our benefit. One of the stories
Bob told was how he had fired Sinclair Lewis from a paper he was
then editing in San Francisco. "I must say, you certainly were a
dumb bastard," he said, smiling down affectionately at Lewis. "Sure
was, Bob. But just look how I outgrew it!"

As a catalytic agent Lewis was catastrophic. Davis, with one eye
on Lewis and one on us, lost his way in his recollections. He was

pathetic. ("Tell me, Neg; I wasn't really good, was I?"—hoping to God I could convince him he was.) Then Lewis, who was only able to stand because he made a three-point support by resting his weight on his tripod-spread arms, began to speak in German. It took about ten minutes to make him sit down. . . . The denouement came, as in one of O. Henry's stories, in the last line. As I was escorting Bob Davis to the door, he stopped and said to me bitterly: "All that joshing between Lewis and myself about the good old newspaper days—I've never even *spoken* to that goddam man before!"

When I first knew New York it was still O. Henry's New York (he died in 1910): city of *The Four Million*. Bob Davis told me a lot about him—his amazing insistence, for example, on the exact sum when he wanted any money. He always stipulated the precise number of pennies. Bob had constituted himself that openhanded man's banker ("He was the softest touch in New York"), and O. Henry would telephone him: "Bob—I'm up here in the (name of a cheap upper Broadway hotel)—and they've got me. Yeah. Locked me out of my own room. Yes, Bob—they even stole the sheets off my bed this morning, when I was down the hall. Bob—listen—I want $89.47. Get that? Eighty-nine dollars—and forty-seven cents. Come on up: I've got a story for you. Just finishing it." "And do you know what it was?" Davis asked me. "The story he handed me, when I came on him sitting in that bare room, with all his bedclothes gone, was *The Gift of the Magi.*"

Bob Davis was fond of a good story himself, especially if it had a quirk at the end of it, so I don't know whether that one was true or not. But I like to think it was—it was *so* New York. That metropolis really did have magic in the old O. Henry days, when he could write *Springtime à la Carte:*

"The gentleman who announced that the world was an oyster which his sword would open made a larger hit than he deserved. It is not difficult to open an oyster with a sword. But did you ever notice any-one try to open the terrestrial bivalve with a typewriter? Like to wait for half a dozen raw opened that way?"

The New York of O. Henry, as humble and hopeful a person as any of his characters, really was a sort of *Baghdad on Broadway*. Prowling about in its canyons of the night, you felt that you might have an O. Henry adventure yourself—at least you had reason to hope you would—instead of getting 'mugged', as you would today. This was the most heterogenous, diversified cosmopolis on the face of the earth, and the combinations and permutations and possibilities of its populace were beyond imagination. You could live a thousand lives in that city without a previous life ever catching up with you. All you had to do was move a block east or west, for every avenue was its own world.

Baghdad on Broadway! I had known it in the days of the old *Police Gazette*, printed on its pink paper, when broad bottoms were the lure instead of the present Bikini breast-works; when Chuck Conners in his bowler and pearl buttons was the king of Chinatown; when the Bowery was one roar of lights—the saloon doors flip-flapping from dusk to dawn, and bouncers hurling dead-beats into the gutters under the Third Avenue El; when the Tong wars still raged around Chinatown, and Pell and Mott Streets were considered delightfully unsafe after dark; and when a New York sophisticate, after showing some country cousins the opium dens, woke up to find that she had a seagull tattooed on her lily-white arm.

That was the era of Diamond Jim Brady; of Jack's and Shanley's; of Delmonico's, finest eating-place in all the world; of old Oscar Hammerstein. In theatreland, David Belasco was the high priest of realism; and when—more of an actor than any of his casts—he put on *The Darling of the Gods* and we heard the Samurai screaming as he was fiendishly tortured to death in the pit beneath the stage (we could see the flames), we believed every word of the two-page spread in Hearst's *Sunday American,* which revealed that several members of the cast, unnerved by these nightly shocks, had already committed suicide. This was probably the most gorgeous press-stunt ever put over on the *booboisie,* as H. L. Mencken and George Jean Nathan were so gleefully calling us in *The Smart Set.* We were all boobs then, and we loved it. They were still playing the golden harp on the Coney Island boat, and beer was only 5c. a stein. . . . We were wonderfully naïve. And I believe that we were much happier because we were.

At that time, despite all its corruption and crime, New York was an innocent city, chiefly *because* we were so naïve. It has always been run by crooks. But those were the days of Tammany—before gunman rule; and if you knew the East Side, or anything of New York's lower depths, you knew where Tammany's strength lay: it was in 'the boys will always look after you'. Like the Catholic Church, which it worked with in such amicable co-operation, Tammany was very human and understanding of mortal weakness: much more human and understanding than our pitiless, almost empty Calvinist faith. The Catholic priest understands when to put the telescope to his blind eye. From the flophouse, through the crooked cop, the ward heeler, the supine judge, all the way up to City Hall, there was patronage and protection. There was a wealth of helpfulness and warmth in the hearts of those big Irish political bosses who were picking the city's pocket with the full connivance and co-operation of its master crooks: the millionaire Moguls, who had no such tender feelings towards their fellow man and no sense of social responsibility whatsoever—in the days when the *leitmotif* was "Anything goes . . . so long as you can get away with it. . . ."

Now it is the Italians who are at New York's throat: Mafia is behind City Hall. The purifying effect of the Income Tax has robbed the genteel rich of their criminal incentive: it has made the rewards too small. Gunmen don't pay taxes. The great New York fortunes of today are being made by such types as Lucky Luciano, believed to be still running the narcotics ring from wherever in Italy he has been deported to, and by such gentlemen, still at large, as Anastasia, of Murder Incorporated. There was a time when any reform of New York City would have had to begin with its upper world, its leading citizens, so proud, most of them, of their straight Anglo-Saxon or Dutch descent. But such people are harmless now: the Robber Barons, perhaps the greatest plunderers of all time, are as dead as Genghis Khan. New York faces the most vicious, perhaps insoluble problem in all its sordid history—how to do away with intrenched crime in its lower depths: for the Organised Underworld is now the most efficient business organisation in that stronghold of Big Business. And if you study its crime sheet by nationalities, you will see that the peasant emigrants from the Old World brought other things with them from that older culture besides the virtues of simplicity.

I was living at the Brevoort in the winter of 1935–36, the winter of my return. It still held something of the wondrous way of life it had once known. The little French restaurant in its basement was still the favourite lunch-place for writers, critics, and some of the city's most thoughtful drinkers. I had a lovely room, looking out on the backyards and the cats; and I spent many a pleasant afternoon lying on my bed reading, recovering from lunch, and making notes for a new book I had started. This was to be called *Created Equal*. I think that is a good title for a book on the United States: born equal— and how we try to get over it! Greenwich Village, just below, still held the memories of John Reed, and of the writers who had once made life there so exciting. But even the memory was gone of what it must have been like to come out into Washington Square on one of those flaming autumn sunsets, and feel as Frank Norris must have felt when he knew he had batted out the last line of *McTeague*. The triumph was in the cheque-book now: the old exaltations were already dying. It was at the Brevoort that I last saw Louise Bryant, in company with her new husband, Billy Bullitt; and it was there that she told me how, when John Reed was dying of typhus in Moscow, and the Bolshies had put a guard at his door so that no one could come in, "I ran under the guard's arm—and I kissed Jack!" (I had spent my last night in Czarist Russia in 1917 with Louise Bryant and John. They had got married by then, but excused themselves for this concession to bourgeois conventions by saying that it saved passport troubles. I was on my way out to Paris; I had just volunteered, and been accepted, for the French flying corps. And when I put out my hand to say goodbye to Jack, he said to me earnestly "Why don't you stay here? You will soon see something far more important than the Western Front." He was trying to tell me about the coming October Revolution.) And it was at the Brevoort—three years later—that the Sunday editor of the *New York Herald* told me he could not print the full-page obituary he had commissioned from me on the man who wrote *Ten Days that Shook the World*.

"You have made John Reed too lovable," he said. "He was that. And he was, as you have written, a Sentimental Socialist: a man who really did believe that if you turned the earth over—the earth of mankind—no weeds would grow up. That was his weakness as a Bolshevik—John Reed didn't have an ounce of evil in him. But it will be a long, long day before you will ever get any New York paper to print *that!*"

Back at the Brevoort now in 1935–36, I wandered around my old haunts. The Bowery was dead. Its gaudy and bawdy saloons had not been able to survive Prohibition, when drink moved to the speak-easies on the expensive cross-town upper streets. It was dark as the grave, and a grave it half was. There was a boisterously nude burlesque, where some percheron blondes stripped off even their G-strings; but no one in the audience laughed or dared to applaud. This display of so much female flesh, which they were so hungry for but could not buy, frightened the down-and-outers. It was one of the saddest exhibitions of man's humiliation I have met. The Bowery had become a street of doleful silhouettes—the backs of the bums in the Mills Hotels, sitting along the second-floor windows and waiting for 10 o'clock, when the lights are turned out and they are allowed to lie down and escape from this world in sleep. I thought of Hurstwood's last hour in *Sister Carrie*. Of *Maggie*. . . .

Third Avenue was still pretty much the same, though here, it seemed, it was *I* that had changed: I no longer had the vitality, or the credulity, to be a party to its lives. And the slums, I found, had become the most fashionable part of New York; people with the money and taste had moved from Riverside Drive to apartments overlooking the East River. They had found, what the immigrants had always known, the charm of the East Side.

The fact is that unless you have some overflowing fountain of life within yourself, some satisfying interest in the arts, theatre, ballet, music, painting, writing or science—and then New York can give you everything—it can be a dreadfully empty city. The most contented afternoons I have ever spent there have been in the museums. The Metropolitan has one of the most beautiful rooms in the world, the room devoted to the landscapes of the T'ang and Sung dynasties. Brushed in with an ink made from ground-down blocks of pure black, on a silk that was never quite white and has now darkened with age, some twenty scrolls hang there which date back to a time when man and nature were at their most harmonious. In the words of Alan Priest, the curator and guardian of this Chinese splendour, there is a lot of *chi-chi* talked about the mysterious East; but here is something you must pay attention to. The West believes that man is the ultimate purpose of creation, that he was meant to dominate nature: the more forests he fells to turn into tree-stumps, the more prairies he ploughs up to turn into dust-bowls, the more rivers he turns into industrial sewers, the happier he will be. At least he did believe that until yesterday. But the old Chinese gave man only his proper place in the universe. The artists who made these landscapes believed that man in his reaches towards perfection would return as the one spirit that lives in mineral and plant and man. You can sit for hours before these scrolls; and slowly you will see that "the scholar seated under the ancient pine, looking out upon the lofty hills, is not alone: he is part of them and they of him". A good thing to come upon in New York, and be reminded, in this lonely world, of the Oneness of all things.

Apart from living in the world of art and the spirit, I know of only one way in which to beat New York. This is the way followed by two maiden aunts of mine, last members of my family left alive in the United States, and, so far as I know, the sole surviving daughters of a Civil War general. They do not go down to the Bright Lights: they are too old and cannot afford it. They will give themselves the rare treat of a stall at the Metropolitan Opera House, when some singer is on that they want to hear before they die. They will visit their Club for a lecture that may interest them, say on the conservation of American forests. They wait for the movies to come up-town, where they are cheaper. And they live all their lives now within two or three blocks of where they have been living for close on thirty years, in a little apartment on fairly quiet upper Madison Avenue. Here is a world all to itself: everything that New York has to offer, in microcosm.

Here everybody knows them and they know everybody. They saw an Italian grocer start up twenty years ago, and now he has a splendid store where you can get everything from artichokes to almost an elephant. They know his family's affairs: all about the various marriages, Florio's death in France, and the contents of every letter from the Pacific. I am led about and introduced to all the tradesmen, with great pleasure on both sides, whenever I go back to New York. And of all the people I have known in that great roaring city these two maiden ladies seem to have got the most out of it. They feed the neighbourhood's stray cats; they take in any mongrel which, they think, has been left out for the night (and what a row *that* has got them into once or twice!); and they feed all the starlings, sparrows and pigeons that circle down the shafts between the tall buildings, and get their breakfast on the fire-escape landing outside my aunts' breakfast-room window. Once they had a miraculous adventure: a grey squirrel (God knows how he did it) crossed two lanes of roaring traffic from Central Park, and arrived one morning on their window-sill. He was fed with nuts for two days. They are still talking about that squirrel. . . . These two old ladies live in such small things: in their books and in their memory of the old country days, when they would ride through the changing colours of the autumn woods. They have beaten New York because they have made that city *small*.

There is nothing static about New York, as there is in London; and I sometimes think more's the pity. We have no Changing of the Guard or Trooping of the Colour, or any of that royal pageantry: but when we do have a procession—well! The last day I was in New York we had an all-day parade, to celebrate Greek Independence—and there was hardly a Greek in it. I took up my position opposite the Hotel Plaza, across from that gilded statue of Sherman sitting on his horse at the entrance of Central Park, just where the cabbies still line up. (I have a proprietary interest in that statue: my grand-father was one of Sherman's generals when they burnt Georgia "from Atlanta to the sea".) I watched the Irish come past: the Knights of Columbus, with their green bands across their manly chests; the Order of St. Patrick, with their golden harps; the Poles, the Italians—mind you, these were all 100% Americans; and I should not have been at all surprised to see a detachment of Eskimos. *Boom! Boom! Boom! Boom!* Then Boy Scouts, Girl Scouts and a charming force of tiny Negro Sea Scouts (there was a company of mulatto girls down the street I was standing on, dressed in nursing uniforms; they kept breaking into little jazz shuffles, as Negroes do, in spite of themselves; and I felt it would be almost worth getting run over to have one of them attend to me). Then the New York Scottish strutted past, their kilts whipping, their bagpipes skirling: and at last, from behind the statue of General Sherman, came some Greeks!—the *Evzone*, in their little white ballet-dancers' skirts and with red pom-poms on their slippers. New York went wild. People screamed. I related all this in an up-town bar that night, and I said, perhaps a bit too sentimentally, "It's a great town. New York still has a heart."

"You think so?" said a young girl 'solitary' I had seen there before. "You were asking me the other day how I found life here." Then she went on, quietly, *fiercely:* "What do you think it's like to live in a city where cops and crooks are synonymous? A human ant-hill, where the most effective, active, *organised* thing in it is—the Organised Underworld. These terribly clever gangsters who have New York by the throat. A city where the people who are running it work hand in hand with the criminals of its lower depths: where, and this is a fact, you are more afraid of the cops than you are of the burglars —and where you can't even take a walk in its beautiful Central Park after dark. Have you heard of the latest rape case?"

I had. It had shocked even New York. A young man, taking his fiancée for a stroll just after sunset in Central Park, was seized and held down by four hoodlums: then they each raped his sweetheart in turn. And one of these young thugs was the son of a Police Captain.

(But I don't like to leave it like that with the New York Police. With its high incidence of juvenile criminals, its Organised Underworld, and some of the best Judges that money can buy (or gangsters intimidate), New York is probably the most under-policed city on the face of the earth. There are not enough of the City's Finest to handle the city's worst.)

These solitary drinkers are among the most disturbing sights in this frightening city. It is estimated that one family in four in the United States has an alcoholic. Desperate men and women, they never have a word to say to anyone; they sit there all day staring into their glass, and move only to put another dime into the juke-box. The tunes, the last time I took any notice of them, were "My darling! My dar-ling! My d-a-a-a-ar-ling!" and *A Slow Boat to China.* The alcoholics love this sweet, sticky sentimentality; they bathe in the warm forgetfulness it brings them. Then come the sleeping-pills. . . .

I sometimes think that New Yorkers were happier in the days when they worshipped Mammon. Then they knew what to live for. Now, no longer believing that money is the be-all and end-all of life, they are lost. America, as I have found it upon each return after the gaps of long years, is becoming more and more a land of desperate, disenchanted people, good people—all searching for *beliefs*.

And that is just where the hope comes in.

CREATED
EQUAL

While in New York on my 1935-36 visit I received the offer of a big lecture tour, as everyone does who has written a best-seller. Unfortunately, I accepted it. Here is where I return to a very personal *me:* to the crack-up I was then headed for, which put me through some of the worst trials of my life. It was a very rough middle passage. But by making me unfit for the lecture tour it saved me from disappointing many hopeful Americans who had never seen me, and never will. The publicity build-up made me blush with shame: I knew I was never a man like that! I was familiar, of course, with the bunk that can be got away with on the lecture platform—all that profound political philosophising, that wisdom after the event; and yet I know of no better way of giving the general public the feel of what is really going on, and of affecting them, than for a foreign correspondent, a seasoned one, to throw open the talk after he has ended his stipulated lecture and answer questions. It was this rebuttal period that attracted me: there were so many things that I wanted to say. I had not realised, until I agreed to do one, what an immense, highly-organised programme an American lecture tour can be, and how formidable is the preparatory work of fixing the dates to fit in with rail and flying-times and all the rest of it. The whole thing was like a vast jig-saw puzzle where the pieces were a jumble of the map of the United States. These preliminaries took so much time that there could be no question of my doing the actual tour until the following season; and after I had finished my time in the U.S.A. that year I returned to Europe, to bring myself up to date on all four of the special talks that I was going to have in my quiver. As I said, drink saved me, as well as the American people; which is just as well, for I am one of the most unpredictable speakers who ever rose at a table. Addressing a lunch-time audience of the Town Hall Club —some two hundred women and a scattering of grey-beards and professors—I talked for some fifteen minutes and then, with as much still to go, I dried up. For the life of me I could not think of another word. My motor had seized. And while I was standing there, silent as the Sphinx and equally mysterious, the sweat pouring down the back of my neck, two women at the rear of the audience stood up and shouted "Louder! Louder!" Poor dears, they thought they were missing something.

My very first public utterance in the U.S.A. that year had been a fiasco. The day before I left London I had dined with a friend of mine in the Foreign Office. I told him about my conversation with that old ex-Austrian diplomat in Yugoslavia. "Your prestige seems to be pretty low in the Balkans. They really do believe that England is decadent. That's the horrible part of it—they believe it!" "I know," he smiled. "You have left journalism; but for your own information . . ." And he went on to tell me about the stand Britain would eventually make. I had worked with this man for over five years, and had never known him to give me a wrong steer, at any rate knowingly. In New York, the National Broadcasting Company offered me fifteen minutes, on a coast-to-coast hook-up, to say what I thought about "this Ethiopian business". I like broadcasting. And so I let myself go.

For a quarter of an hour I talked dispassionately, precisely, and, it seemed to me, very convincingly. (Had I not been given the inside dope by the British Foreign Office itself?) My friend had told me that I must not quote the source, but was free to make full use of a sentence of his which had struck me particularly: namely, that if the British could not save a man who refused to be saved (Mussolini) then "they will drive the sword into him—up to the hilt". Sounds a bit melodramatic for an Englishman, but that had been the way he put it; and I am quite sure that he believed it at the time. With those words "sword . . . up to the hilt" I ended my impressive talk. "Stuff to give 'em!" asserted Hendrick Van Loon, who was awaiting his turn; the N.B.C. men behind the plate-glass in the control room grinned and gave me thumbs up; I went down some fifty-odd stories to the street, and—"EXTRA! EXTRA!"—the newsboys were running along Fifth Avenue—"EXTRA! EXTRA! DIVIDE ETHIOPIA! ENGLAND AND FRANCE AGREE TO——" I bought a paper and read: the Hoare-Laval Proposal.

"Ha-ha!" laughed one of my publishers as I came in next morning, the one who thought I was always a bit sappy about the British. "Good old England let you down, *didn't* she?"

Defeat for me had begun right at the start, that year in the United States. As soon as I had set about collecting material for *Created Equal* I knew that I did not want to write the book. It seemed that no American I talked with could be himself: they were all in violent reaction to "that man" Roosevelt. The utopians, and we do have a few among us, seemed to expect impossibly much, though it was touching to see how he affected young Americans who wanted some selfless cause; but every man with a dollar regarded F.D.R. as a personal enemy. After the first scare Big Business had recovered its nerve, and now had its nose back in the trough. Out in Chicago I found that I had only to mention the name Roosevelt to give the whole table rabies. This was disconcerting, for they were all very decent people, poisoned though they were by hate. Also, with every business man boasting that he was "going to pull the tail-feathers out of that God-damned bird!"—the Blue Eagle was the symbol of Roosevelt's National Industrial Recovery Act—situations were changing so rapidly that anything I might write would be out of date before it reached the printer. So I decided to let the book ride until the country settled down, and do magazine and newspaper articles —mostly for the British press, as no British correspondent thought it worth his while, at that time, to go west of Washington. Some of the material—about the sharecroppers of the cotton states, our form of peasant peonage, and the chain gangs, for instance—was lurid.

Thus, freed from the moral obligations that a book imposes upon you, I went on the loose; and as New York life was a bit loose itself at the moment, scene of some of the wildest parties you could imagine, my blinds did not attract much attention. On one of them, which was a classic, I apparently kidnapped the editor of what was then regarded as America's *avant-garde* monthly. We were gone a night and a day, like the owl and the pussycat, and then another night. He was a charming young man, of the New England type, and I think it was our both having gone to Andover that started the thing. On the morning of the third day I thought I had better put him in touch with current events again, so I called up his wife. "I've got Roger here. I just called up to let you know everything is all right." There was no answer for a time, then she asked: "Where is he?" "He's right here. I've got him in bed with me—he's all right; I've got him pressed against the wall, he can't fall out. Want to speak to him?" "No—no—*never!*" He shied like a horse whenever we met after that. Drink and dismay—they nearly did for me. I steered clear of all the literary cocktail parties, except one given by the *New Yorker* (not for me), at which I met some of the most disturbing lovelies I have ever encountered—all Dorothy Parkers in embryo— and got nowhere with them. I might have been Rip Van Winkle. Then I bought a beautiful black Ford V-8, and headed South. . . .

I had seen the snows of the Himalayas and the golden shrines of Kiev: now I wanted some good old Chesapeake Bay mud. And I knew the patch of mud that I wanted to see most. It was the flats across from Blackwalnut Point at the foot of Tilghman's Island, where they used to have the pond-nets up and where you put about to enter the Choptank River and beat up to Oxford, Maryland. That little town, so like a Currier & Ives print when I first saw it, has stayed with me ever since I first beached my gunning-skiff there in almost forgotten summers, and lived a Huck Finn existence down the Bay. Another day-dream of mine has been that when I retire, if I ever get enough money for that and want to pull off the road, I shall buy a place somewhere on the Eastern Shore of Maryland. Eastern Shore is always printed with a capital E and a capital S; for before the day of the motorcar it was something far more than a geographical term. A low farming country, deeply indented by rivers and estuaries; a land of magnolia, crab-grass, coons and possums, where the waters teemed with duck, oysters, crabs, geese and terrapin and the land was rich with melons, sweet corn, tomatoes and lima beans—it was a way of life. You saw sails going across dry country, or so it seemed, miles inland: this was two hundred and fifty miles of heaven on earth—and the finest expanse of sailing water in all America.

When I first knew little Oxford there was not a building in it, except the church steeple, that projected above its magnificent trees. And the slanting masts of the oyster bugeyes on the far side of its point topped the weather-beaten roofs of the little white homes along its green foreshore. Out in the tranquil pool of its broad harbour there was always a skiff or two, with a couple of Izaak Waltons abroad, waiting for a catfish to bite. Oxford was an American Oblomovka, where it was always summer and the peaceful days would never end. I borrowed my brother's boat in Baltimore and sailed across to it. And it was not there.

"It's just not there any more!" I said to him. "The bugeyes are all gone. It's just motorboats now. The waterfront's a glare of plate-glass windows and Coca-Cola signs. Filling stations. And that little white oyster-shell road that you and I used to know—cut our bare feet on—well, it's all cement now. Oxford has gone."

"What did you expect?" he said. "Nothing is 'here' any longer in these United States. You have some surprises coming to you."

How I mourned the end of the oyster bugeyes! These fine craft, with their clipper bows and tall raking masts, were probably the most beautiful commercial schooners ever put into the water. They were built only on the Chesapeake, and were used for dredging on the shallow beds in all kinds of weather, and for racing with full holds to the Baltimore market. (Now the oysters are brought up to Baltimore in motor-trucks.) These beautiful bugeyes were the ultimate development of the American dug-out canoe—plus that skill, that peculiar American skill, which had turned out the original Baltimore clippers: fastest sailing ships in the world. The clipper ship *Lightning* logged the quickest day's run ever made under sail: 436 knots, from noon to noon, on March 1st 1855, when running from New York to Liverpool—which means that the *Lightning* was making an *average* of 18.75 knots per hour. Think of what speed she must have made at times! And think what it must have been like to have been aboard her, slashing through the seas. . . . The bugeyes, built only on the Chesapeake, were part of the romance of that bay. And pride went with them.

I was taken out on a bugeye long before I could walk, for my father was part-owner of one. He was a waterman to his last breath. The Delaware River, on which he was born, was "the valley of his being". To putter about in a boat: to smell the water, to feel the

wind, to see buff marshes in the autumn with the wild geese string-
ing over them—he wanted nothing else. And to row home in the sunsets. . . . Tired and dirty . . . with a couple of ducks lying on the
floor boards. This blood-love for the river and for the two bays was
the best part of my heritage, of the things he handed on to me. He
was a much better yachtsman than business man. He left me nothing else.

The Chesapeake Bay bugeyes were part not only of my, but of
the American, heritage. With their passing, and that of the fine lives
that were lived in them—Maryland oyster-laws made it obligatory
for them to be sailed by their owners—went some more of the skills
that had once given so much happiness to American life—of the
skills and the craftsmanship and the prides, with their daily satisfactions, whose loss now makes us feel so empty. No wonder I always
go on a drunk in Baltimore.

Although I knew that I was going to find plenty of things I did not
like on this trip of rediscovering my own country, I did not set out
to look for the bad things. I was looking for the opposite, for things
that would make me happy. As far as the land itself was concerned,
about the only places I found encouraging were those that the go-
getters had as yet been unable to tamper with. When I came to a
swamp I took off my hat to it; as I always do when driving through
the United States. And sometimes, eating my lunch by the road,
I would sit there and listen to the swamp; to the call from its centre,
as I heard the red-wing blackbird sing. I had lots of conversations
along the road. In Baltimore, I looked up F. Scott Fitzgerald, to see
what *he* was thinking about God's Country.

I don't remember much of that evening—except that he was writing, *standing up,* at an old-fashioned accountant's desk. "Why do
you do that?" I asked him. "Because," he said with that attractive
smile, "if I sit down, I do *that*." He nodded at a half-finished bottle
of gin on the floor by a sofa. "Let's sit down," he said. "I've got another bottle."

He was writing *The Crack-Up* then. It was obvious that he did not
himself know what he was thinking about life in the United States.
Its features were blurred in the outline of his own life, which was
no longer distinct. The only specific thing I recall was that he was

interested in a young Irishman in Baltimore, a taxi-driver, who had
just written a book about that life: this could be a whale of a book,
said Fitzgerald, if . . . we talked on and on. We finished that gin.
And then, suddenly: "My God!" he cried, jumping to his feet. "I've
got to go! I've got to go!" It was long after midnight. He was living
in a flat at the very top of an apartment house. We went down. At
the door was a big black car waiting for him. The driver got out
and helped Fitzgerald in. The Packard purred off. I think only the
driver knew where.

In Washington I was invited to one of those exclusive White House
receptions at which Eleanor Roosevelt took the line and shook a
thousand hands. The President, in his chair, smiled artlessly, not
missing one trick: beside him, with politician written all over his
tough Texas mug, stood little Nance Garner, whom F.D.R. had to
accept as his running mate, Vice-President, in order to clinch the
big South-West vote: he looked, as someone so neatly put it, "about
as out of place as a mouse in a mince-pie". From the waist up Frank-
lin Roosevelt was as fine a figure of man as ever sat in the White
House, and I thought of what he must have been like in his yachting
days, and of the fun that all the Roosevelts must have had: most of
all Teddy, with his ranch in the Kootenies and the books he took
with him (and let the country know it) when he went to pot lions
in darkest Africa. A patrician like that knew automatically how to
handle the Irish when he was Police Commissioner of New York
City. These men, these lucky men, and their like, who knew how
to get the most fun out of life in the United States, were far closer
to the American working man, and the American working man knew
it, than any of these great big bouncing know-it-all self-made Americans who are always so afraid of their own immediate past.

I used to give people fits by merely asking "But what has Roosevelt
done—to you, I mean?" Knox, my old boss, was at that moment declaring: "It is my sober and solemn judgement that four more years
of such government may destroy our system of free enterprise and
our system of constitutional government . . . no life insurance policy
is safe; no savings account secure." I asked the steel workers in the
saloons of Gary (which was about the only place where I could
meet them on an equal footing) what they thought about all this;

to which they grinned and replied "Mister, we'll tell you—Roosevelt will just have to drop dead not to get in."

Well, there it was. 1936 was a presidential election year, and with every big newspaper in the United States frantically against F.D.R., and trying to scare the populace into believing he endangered everything they stood for or possessed; with big business bringing every gun to bear on the organs it controlled and which, it thought, controlled public opinion—press, radio advertising, even jobs—Roosevelt was returned to office with the most overwhelming electoral landslide in the whole history of the United States.

I looked around the White House, wondering in which room it had been (could it have been in this?) that at a Ball after the American Civil War Sherman, who was waltzing with my grandmother, suddenly lifted her off the floor, held her up, and said: "My God, Mrs. Negley—what a small waist you have!" A family legend? Well, it could easily have happened, for my grandfather had been a divisional commander; he and Sherman had been friends; they had ridden stirrup to stirrup in the Army of the West.

The next day I saw John L. Lewis. He had just founded the C.I.O., the Congress of Industrial Organisations. When I told him that I had come from Gary; that I had been there with the American Federation of Labour Leaders in 1934, when they were trying to organise unions inside United States Steel; and that one of their delegates had said to me hopelessly: "The most terrible thing we have to face here is that there is no *class-consciousness* among the workers in the United States. These big shots working in the rolling mills just won't have anything to do with the Polaks and poor Bohunks out on the slag pile—the real snobbishness in U.S. industry is not at the top—between employer and worker—*it's between workers!*"—when I told John L. Lewis that, he simply soared up and hit the ceiling.

"When *I* call a strike," he roared, pounding the table, "all Steel will come out! It won't be just those poor Polaks out on the slag pile— it will be from slag pile to drawing-board: *I'm* going to call out the white-collar guys! And it won't be in just one town, or in one plant, either: I'll bring out all Steel! All Steel!"

And so he did. John L. Lewis, Welsh immigrant, made the United States Steel Corporation recognise trade unions for the first time in its vicious history; he did the same with rubber and autos. And I knew where his strength came from: it came from the 400,000 soft-coal miners of Pennsylvania and West Virginia, where the towns, with their Company Store and the sewers running down the stinking streets, were human cesspools that a Welsh miner would not have lived in for a day. I had seen them in all their dirty misery.

I haven't got the space to go into the diminishing career of John L. Lewis after he had reached those peaks; but as employers supply better working conditions, agree to more generous collective bargaining with their workers, and stick to the results of it more honestly, the power of the rabble-rousing leader—which is about what John L. Lewis has now dwindled to—will correspondingly diminish. A new, intelligent, almost intellectual type of labour leader will begin to appear—such as Walter Reuther of the Automobile Workers of America. The brains of Labour and of Management will make agreements *outside* Government—outside the corruption and the stupidity of politics. And that is the way American industry will go. The day Walter Reuther made his dicker with the Ford Company for welfare benefits and workers' pensions, a new era opened in the United States. This will be our answer to the Totalitarian State. And it will work.

In Washington I climbed those steps and stood for a long time before the statue of Abraham Lincoln. I always do. Of all the statues in all the world, this is the one that moves me most. There he is, sitting so sadly and thoughtfully in his chair: pondering, no doubt, upon the awful people who came after him. He means much to me, for my boyhood was lived among the memories and regrets of the Civil War. Van Wyck Brooks has just written a book about my home town, *Scenes and Portraits,* and says in it that life in Plainfield, New Jersey, was "like a fable agreed upon". And describing how that little old-fashioned town was full of surviving officers of the Civil War (which was nearer to Plainfielders than World War I), he lists my grandfather when he says: "We had three generals . . ."

My American history sat at the head of the breakfast table. It was the old grey-haired man whose house I was born in, who adopted me, and with whom I lived until he died. There is an old photograph of him in uniform, full dress, hanging above my desk as I write this: taken when he was commanding the 1st Brigade of the 18th Division on October 1st 1860. That was five months before Fort Sumter was fired on. Behind his chair was his escutcheon, citing how he had fought in the Duquesne Grays in the Mexican War (where he had collected his limp): how he had organised and equipped a brigade of infantry and artillery for the West, and joined General Sherman in October 1861; how he had participated in the Buell campaign in Tennessee; and how he had defended Nashville in 1862—the sword which Nashville gave him hung over the fireplace mantel in his library, with its gilded scabbard and the emerald-eyed eagle on its hilt. I grew up hearing nostalgic talk at the dinner table; the old United States was embodied in such phrases as "In the Cumberland Gap . . ." or "Beyond the Alleghenies . . ." when he was yarning of days long before the Civil War, of his own boyhood. It was these pictures that he left in my mind: this was the heritage that *he* handed me—blood-love for America. There was an *aroma* about that old gentleman. While he lived, the past lived. But he did not really talk much. There was a strange silence about him—as in the lines of Stephen Vincent Benét's poem of the Bronze Book at Gettysburg, on Cemetery Ridge:

Pickett came
And the South came
And the end came
And the grass comes
And the wind blows
On the bronze book
On the bronze men
On the grown grass,
And the wind says
'Long ago
Long
Ago.'

DARK
SOUTH

In Washington the Negroes invited me to a little gathering. When I asked how things were going with them they were silent, and looked towards an old man. He thought for a while, and then replied: "Well, sir, I'm afraid I have to say that things are really worse for us—here in Washington—than they were twenty years ago." For the benefit of Europeans, I think I should say that Washington, in the District of Columbia, had more restrictions, based on colour-prejudice, both by local laws and by custom, than any other city in the United States. Dr. Ralph Bunche refused to take a high post in government there because he was unwilling that either himself or his family should be subjected to such embarrassments. But this informal talk I had in Washington, the Capital of the United States, was not a hate session. In New York I had asked the head of the Civil Liberties group to give me the names of a few people I might see, and a few situations I might look into, as I drove through the South. "I don't want the 'professional' Negro," I said, "the politician. He may do a lot of good for his race, but——" I found it hard to say just what type I did want to meet and hear talk about his own people, so I said: "I wish you would give me the names of one or two Negroes you yourself *admire*." He smiled, and at once gave me the name of this man.

He was a judge, a venerable old man. There were only seven or eight of us all told, having coffee and cakes; and among them was a Negro schoolteacher, a motherly old person, and the first Negro girl who had gone to Smith. The others were men, one or two of them graduates of Tuskegee: young, eager lawyers and, of course, worshippers of the old judge. He was very careful in what he said. I did not mention it to them, but I was weaned on a coal-black Negro mammy and raised by Negroes; our gardener, old Abner, had a free hand to give me a thrashing whenever he caught me, if he was lucky, in the melon patch (and his hand was heavy); and I grew up before the big range in our kitchen, listening to Rhodie, the cook. *Those* Negroes I loved. But to have mentioned it to these Negroes in Washington would have been fatal: they wanted none of that!

Perhaps the most interesting person there was the girl who had been the first Negro to go to Smith. Smith is a college for white women, and a very good one. She had just graduated. "How did you find things?" I asked. She smiled, a bit plaintively: "Oh, they were too kind to me. *Too* kind." The other Negroes all nodded with understanding. "They couldn't help it," she said, "but they could never let me be 'just one of them'." This young girl was very pretty, and, quite obviously, very intelligent; she had *chic*, and I think that the Smith Year Book, citing the achievements of the graduating class, must have given her rave notices. The schoolmistress had a more distressing story to tell, but she told it without rancour. She had engaged the entire first row of the balcony over the telephone, for her class of young Negro girls to see *Macbeth*. "But when we got there the man in the ticket office said that the balcony was all sold out." She smiled: "It was, of course; sold to *us*. When he saw that we were all coloured he refused to let us in. Don't you think that is a bit hard? Just think what it means, after all the interest they have been taught to feel for his great works, that no Negro child here in Washington can see Shakespeare performed on the stage."

I love every mile of the Tidewater Country of Maryland and Virginia. I passed many a place I should have liked to own. Only trouble was, someone else had them. Most of these were Northerners, come down to enjoy the salubriousness of the Old South. When I passed over the red Rappahannock, just a few miles from where they caught Booth, I felt peace descend upon me. (That bridge is above tidal water, of course: the river runs red, liquid and mud here.) I love the mouths of the rivers opening up into the pearly sunsets of the Chesapeake—the James, for instance, with the reeds flanking its riffled flow. I was at war with myself at that time, and every scene like this, with the peace it brought me, I accepted as a blessing.

My return to the United States the previous autumn had been early enough for me to get some duck shooting. This was down on Currituck Sound, then the finest duck and goose grounds on the Eastern seaboard. The man who had been put in my blind (hide, in the King's English) to be used as a retriever was half-Indian and half-parson: and all duck. When some swans came sailing low, unsuspecting, over our heads, he gasped "Kill 'em! Shoot 'em, Mister!", and actually groaned as I let those beautiful birds go past. To shoot a swan was not only highly illegal: it would have been sacrilege, considering the way wild life was being exterminated in the United States. (We are restoring the duck and goose population now, with most hopeful results.) "Do you local people down here kill swans?" I asked him sternly. "Mister," he replied without a blush, "we kills *everything!*"

The reason why he felt so ruthless about the swans was that all up and down the Atlantic coast rich men were buying, or had already bought, practically every bit of salt marsh. The locals, therefore, felt they had a grudge; they believed, and they were right, that they were being cheated out of their heritage. Therefore they opposed all game laws with a blind misunderstanding. And because of this I suspected (it couldn't have been anything else: it was so big) that the roast goose we were served on the night we arrived at Currituck, at my friend's duck-lodge, was a swan thoughtfully provided for us by this local minister of the Gospel. We got along splendidly.

It is flat, sandy country here, mostly water, with the waves of the Atlantic pounding along the treacherous coast. East, and running south, are the famous Hatteras Banks: a spit of sand projecting down from Virginia through North Carolina, seventy-five miles long, at most two or three hundred yards wide, and with few places more than two or three feet above a spring high tide. It is peopled in scant patches by the descendants of ships that have been wrecked in the dreaded Diamond Shoals: Graveyard of the Atlantic, as these diamond-shaped waves are called—you will see them leaping up and down even on a calm day, for the downcoming Greenland Current meets the Gulf Stream here and sheers it off toward England and Scandinavia. The ribs of old sailing ships are strewn along these sands. When I went down them last, to the big Hatteras Light, I passed a big steel cargo ship that they could not get off. It had just gone ashore. There was no road whatsoever in all those seventy-five miles down the Banks: you had to hunt for the hard sand. And I hope to God there will never be a road—such precious solitude should be preserved. Nor was there a motorcar on the Banks, more than two or three months old, with any mudguards left. The salt and flying sand from the wheels had rusted and cut them off. A more buzzard-like collection of cars I have never seen. West of this low sand-spit lie Pimlico, Albemarle, and Currituck Sounds. And if you love the sound of wild geese clanging in the sky, this is a country that will make you tremble.

My unregenerate padre was a marvellous duck-and-goose caller. He could talk to them. He had a big, wild cry for the open distances, and a little low, chuckling, inviting line of talk for when they were circling—making up their minds whether to settle or not. One day, so wild that only the pintails were up, we saw a long string of Canada geese going south at what seemed a good mile off. The padre put his hand to the side of his mouth: *"Aa-oook! Aa-oooK!"* he called. *"Aa-ook!"* And lo! . . . the line wavered . . . one goose fell out . . . he came straight at us . . . lower, lower, headed for our canvas decoys, which were bobbing so treacherously on the wind-whipped water. The goose set its wings. . . . *"Aa-ook!"* called the padre.

"Shut up!" I hissed.

When the goose was inside thirty yards, I stood up and dropped it.

"Say, *Mister!*" said the padre, after his yelp of triumph, when he was climbing back with the goose into the skiff. "Why did you tell me to shut up?"

"Because he was getting close enough up to know you were not a goose."

It took me a couple of days to get him friendly again.

My own feelings were strumming inside me strong, as wild as the winds that were emptying Currituck Sound. The Sound is so shallow that when the wind blows from its head only a few strips of water, in the deepest parts, remain. Often the water is a good quarter-mile from where you sit in your skiff in the reeds of some island, behind the rushes you have built around you for a blind. At such times you can smoke and be happy, you need not feel taut or nervous: any

birds that will be moving will be flying over those inaccessible strips
of water. And far across the empty Sound you will see thousands
and thousands of V-necked Canada geese, emperor of all our wild-
fowl, following the white line of the Atlantic surf on their winter
pilgrimage to a warmer clime. I don't know why they should always
speak of the geese, especially the Canada geese, as *honkers*. Their
cry is vastly different: a lonely searching, almost melancholic cry—
Aa-ook! Aa-oook! It sets your blood coursing.

And now I must make a confession. My desire to kill things has
finally petered out. The original fine frenzy has gone. Thirteen years
after this shoot I have just been talking about, I went back to the
United States to stay with this same old friend. We had been at
school together, and after he had left the university he went off into
the legal world, entered Wall Street, made his pile, became one of
the governors of the New York Stock Exchange, and retired to a
two-thousand-acre farm on an old slow-flowing river in Virginia.
Here was a man who, you might say, had more money than he knew
what to do with—except that he did know. This farm of his is paradise: and he has a thousand acres of salt marsh which is commonly
accepted as the best duck and goose sanctuary on the Atlantic coastal
lowlands. It is all tidal. Going out in a skiff with an outboard motor
among the creeks in the marshes and on to the 'flats' in the beautiful stretches of the open bay, we estimated that we must have put
up over five thousand ducks and geese one afternoon: pintails, of
which I think the drake is the most beautiful bird that flies; mallard,
black ducks; ten white snow geese, with their black-tipped wings;
a lovely little flotilla of wood duck, which *live* there; and Canada
geese—I am not exaggerating—by the thousand. It was a sight never
to be forgotten: the green necks of the mallards rising against the
grey deadwoods; and those wonderful Canada geese, their brave
breasts shining in the sun as they stood in rows along the muddy
shore of the quiet river and creeks—just sunning themselves—before
they felt the call, and would one day circle higher and higher and
head north. And then people would hear their note in the cities of
New York and New England all the way up to the Arctic tundra—
Aa-oook! Aa-oook!—and they would reach their breeding grounds.
The Canada goose can be a model for man: he mates for life. In the
misty sunsets we sat on the old colonial-pillared veranda of my

friend's home, listened to the clanging of these strings of noble geese as they came in over the acorn-oaks, and watched them drop into his fields of soya beans—beans he had grown, and left, just for them. And during those sunsets I found the richness of my own country— of what it could mean—more moving than I have ever found it in any book about the United States or in any scene there. If that country was sanctuary for the goose and duck, it was also one for us.

Driving down through North Carolina, I got myself into the middle of a chain gang before I knew it. This was in the swamp country, where the road runs on for mile after mile, built up on dykes or wooden trestles, or carried on steel-girder bridges across incessant rivers of swirling red mud. The swamps are blackwater. For miles there is nothing on either side of you except this dismal swamp: a dark wilderness of cypress with their buttressed trunks standing in water and their upper branches so dripping with the sad grey Spanish moss that even in the daytime the water beneath them is black as night. I was making time, and I shot past a road gang without noticing them. It was only a mile or so on that I was struck by the thought there was something peculiar about the two white men I saw standing on either side of the road: each had a shotgun draped over his arm. And this was not the shooting season—for animals.

"Don't they ever try to escape?" I asked one of the guards, nodding toward a Negro who was almost invisible in the depths of the swamp. "Not with this," he answered, patting his shotgun affectionately. "This has got buckshot."

Then he added: "We lock 'em up in cages at night."

The camp itself, when I finally located it in the middle of a wide clearing in the pine woods, looked more like a modern poultry farm than anything else. It was macabre. There was the chicken run, and there were the coops. But the chicken run was an eight-feet-high erection of buffalo wire, and the coops were the notorious steel cages, in which eighteen convicts, in three tiers, spent their brooding nights.

And down at the far end of the convicts' 'run' was another little enclosure—with four bloodhounds.

"Dawgs feelin' kind of playful today," said the Superintendent as he let me in. "Just brought their mother back to them. Finest tracker

I've got. You ought to see a photo I've got of Bell in action—when I was running down a nigger trying to make that swamp."

"Bell", who leaned up against the wire so that I could scratch her liver-coloured nose, was about half the size of an English blood-hound, and without those terrifying bloodshot eyes. Nevertheless, I was just as glad to meet her under present conditions, and not as some struggling, sobbing creature trying to make his way through the undergrowth to the sanctuary of that dismal swamp. The Super-intendent, despite the fact that he wore breeches and boots, looked more like a Sunday-school teacher or a storekeeper than a man who had eighty convicts in his charge. He was awfully pleased that I liked his "dawgs".

The thing that struck me as so extraordinary was the way the bloodhounds and the convicts, when they were in camp, were always face to face. There was nothing but this web of wire separating them. The convicts' washing-trough was dead against the dogs' wire. And during the hour of sunset, when the first lorry-load of convicts was brought back, the bloodhounds stretched themselves playfully up against the chicken wire and watched the Negroes wash. The faces of the Negroes and of the bloodhounds who might one day be baying after them were less than a foot apart. Neither Negroes nor bloodhounds seemed to mind. In fact, I saw a huge buck Negro put his hand through the mesh and pat one of the hounds. "*He* wants a friend," said the Superintendent.

"It's funny," he said, speaking of his inability to tell whether a convict was or was not of the escaping type. "Some of them will try it on the very first night they are here. Others will wait five years— till just when they've got only a couple of days to go to get their freedom; and damn' if they won't try it *then!*"

He told me of one case, a five-year man with a month to go, who made a successful break in 1932. He had just been caught by the New York police. After he had been tried in New York, Carolina was going to extradite him. He could be given two extra years: "But hell," said the Superintendent, "some of them don't even know why they're *in* here!"

Most of the Negro cases could give no clear idea of why they had committed their crimes. "Ah doan know. . . . Ah just felt that-a-ways. . . ." And one I asked, Toots, grinned and said to me: "Ah doan't know. . . . Ah reckon Ah didn't have nuffin' else to do that night. . . ." Toots had broken into a chemist's and didn't even know the money was in a cash-register. The only clear-cut impression I could get from the Negroes in this convict camp was that they were infinitely happier than the white convicts. But whether that should go to their credit or not I cannot say.

The white convicts presented a blank and silent wall.

All the convicts have to be inside the camp before sundown. They are brought back in motor-lorries with a white man (and the inevitable shotgun) watching them from the tailboard and the driver's seat. Then they march in two files into the enclosure, throw their hands aloft, and permit themselves to be searched. Two white guards go along behind them "frisking" their bodies. "Hack-saws," explained the Superintendent. "They try to saw themselves out of their cages. Especially on windy nights when they think the camp guards can't hear them."

With the Negroes this performance did not affect me. But when the lorry-load of white men was brought in, the air became ominous at once. There was something sinister about the very way they walked into the enclosure—a tone given, perhaps, by two old lags, whose grey faces could have been spotted a mile off. They flung their arms aloft with sullen defiance as they felt themselves being frisked; and the instant they had finished their dinner they walked directly to their cage, as if anxious to be locked up. It struck me that the white men were infuriated by the Negroes: not by Negroes *qua* Negroes, but by the fact that these coloured people could sing and dance and endure durance vile much better than they could. I feel sure this was the thing that made them so bitter.

The Superintendent had brought out to me a white boy who was working in the office. He had a banjo, made from a tin pie-plate, and with steel wire for strings; and these were stretched up a hickory shaft which had no frets. The white boy had made it himself here in the camp. He was serving five years for having hit a friend with a moonshine bottle during a drinking bout. "Chain gangs seem to run in that boy's family," the Superintendent said to me aside. "His father was killed in a chain gang. Down in Georgia—trying to escape."

As the boy played, two Negroes did a soft buck-and-wing dance in the camp's sandy yard. They danced with the happy aimlessness with which they lived. The black and white stripes of their convict suits had merged into dirty grey. There were eighty other convicts, in attitudes of studied indifference; and around all this, of course, was the eight-foot wire enclosure, with two white men armed with shotguns watching from the outside.

Behind the convicts stood the six steel cages into which they would soon be marched and locked up for the night. They were made of diagonal steel strips, and were the size of the vans in which a travelling circus moves its animals from town to town. These cages were on wheels.

"Now, Toots," said the Superintendent, when the dancers had stopped shuffling, "let's hear your quartette."

"Suh . . . Ah . . . Ah can't *get* mah quartette."

"What's the matter—ain't they *here?*"

"Yessuh, they's——" Toots suddenly saw the humour of that remark and guffawed. "Yessuh, dey's here, all right."

And so they were—with shotguns covering them.

"Well then," said the Superintendent, "don't be so damned bashful."

Toots came back with his quartette (there were actually eight). "Yessuh, here we is." "Sing!" said the Superintendent. Toots closed his eyes. "Y-es . . . y-es. . . ." He began to sob. Then the nine Negroes swung into the lament: "Y-es . . . y-es . . . we gotta GO— and find Jesus . . ."

The sun was setting over the camp. Once the Negroes had started singing they forgot us. So did the other Negroes in the wire enclosure. They moved up to the singers . . . "Oh, yes! . . . y-es . . . we gotta go—and seek Jesus . . ."

Listening to that, I knew it was hopeless to try to form any opinion on North Carolina's experiment. The Negroes could be happy, and free from this world, under any conditions. This was on the edge of the "deep" South. In Georgia, not so many miles below us, the men on the road gangs had chains; in North Carolina there were none. In the Georgia camp they told me "We put our hard cases out on the roads—murderers and all the rest of them—and we are not taking any chances that they'll ever escape." In North Carolina the guards had the right to fire at any time when it looked as if a convict was even intending to make a break.

"It's not healthy to try it," said the Superintendent.

I am sure that if he had not stopped them those Negroes would have been singing yet. "When they sing to each other," he said to me—a peculiar note of wonderment and respect in his voice—"why, God damn it, it seems to me as if they could sing for ever!"

The sun sank over the camp, the Negroes and the bloodhounds. And that is one sunset I shall remember all my life.

The Georgia camp was horrible. It housed hundreds of convicts, all Negroes; and they were behind a big stockade, like a concentration camp. Yet, although I had been allowed to take all the photographs that I wanted in the Carolina camp, the Georgia Superintendent stopped me after I had taken a few shots of the Negroes leaping down from the trucks and holding the shackles on their legs. "One day," he said, "*some* of these niggers will be allowed out. How'd you like to come on a photo of yourself, like you just took, on a newspaper page? I'm not going to ask you for your film. I'm just going to beg you, as a gentleman, not to use those photos publicly." I never have.

There were some evil cases there. One was the "Black Dillinger". "Want to see how I'm taking some of the hell out of him?" said the Superintendent. He took me into a huge building like a drill hall, which it probably had been, where the Negroes lay in rows, like fish on the counter—and, like a catch of fish, they were all 'strung': a steel wire had been passed through the shackles on each man's leg. "This is it," said the Superintendent, standing before a horrible specimen of Negro. "This is the goddamned son of a bitch. Look at him!"

"Now you see that pail," he went on. "That's what they piss in at nights. You see we got this nigger strung six niggers from the pail. Now if he wants to relieve himself, he's got to disturb six other niggers. They was afraid of him, at first. Not now! Take a look at his face. . . ."

I did. I saw that it was all sores and open cuts. "That's *chains!* Yes, sir, they sock him with their chains. You're almost tame, aren't you, you black son of a bitch? *You* won't shoot any more people in the back."

I went down through the sharecropper country: the sandy country of the jack pines, west of Albemarle Sound, where on the one-mule farms in tumbledown shacks we had, at that time, a form of peonage, an American peasantry living in greater squalor than anything I have seen in the Balkans or in old Russia. Lost one wet dreary sunset, I came to an old cross-roads store, and pulled up there to have my car filled. "Can you tell me where I am?" I asked the young man who came out to serve me. "Mister," he said, with savage emphasis, "you're in the country that God forgot."

That sounded interesting, so I followed him into the store to get some cigarettes. There it was: the same old smell of lamp-oil, lard and slabs of salt sow-belly dangling from the ceiling like white stalactites. This young man had been fired from the U.S. Navy for hitting an officer out at San Diego. His father—an ex-sharecropper, he told me—owned this store, and had all the wretched sharecroppers in that region working for him. "And he's the meanest son of a bitch in these parts!" As he punched the till before closing up shop, the young man stuffed a handful of dollar bills into his pocket, informing me happily "I'm paying myself double. What the hell; why not? My old man's got a pencil that writes twice when these poor croppers around here come in at the end of the year to square accounts with him. Not one of them can read nor write—they ain't got a chance on God's green earth to get away from him. They're *always* in debt!" I spent the night with his family; and he was right about his old man. The next few days I wandered about among the wretched croppers. And now I am not so sorry that I abandoned the idea of writing *Created Equal*. It might have been good documentary evidence for conditions at that time; but the whole scene has changed. The age-old economic war between the Industrial East and the Agricultural West and South has been reversed: it is the farmer who is on top these days. Now that the world is hungry, food is king. Even these oppressed sharecroppers have a Union.

From there on I lived the rest of that return to my native country for myself, or for what was left of myself. I was tired of writing about others. The Old South can be salubriously backward in many places. Southerners love their land, their melancholy swamps, bayous and rivers: it suits something gloomy in their nature, for they all seem to be haunted by the past. I am fond of rivers and any sort of running water, and wherever I could I usually looked up the local fishermen, talked about bait and catfish, and drank. No masonic order has a wider brotherhood than that of the fish-hook: with the help of it I have even made friends with Frenchmen, which is saying something. It was comforting, with all my stuff in the car, to lay over in any place that appealed to me. Down on the Scuppernong River, at a little farming and saw-mill town called Columbia, where they have the statue of a Confederate soldier leaning on his musket in the main square, the proprietor of the one and only hotel began to address me as Negley after we had finished the last of his jug of moonshine. "My idea," he said, when he had removed his little finger from the crook of its handle (they pour it ritually by resting the jug on their shoulder and bending forward over the glass), "we-all need more of this stuff. This town's dry. But I'll give you a small boy, and he'll show you how to get to a store—that's on the other side of nigger-town—and if you give the man there five dollars he'll tell this boy where he's got a gallon hid in the woods." I drove out through the shambles of nigger-town—they have one of these slums outside every town in the rural south, just as they have in Africa—and another small boy that had been put in the Ford with us came back from the bushes toting a heavy jug in a wicker basket: it was one straight gallon of moonshine, made from corn-mash, about the colour of carbolic acid, and just as deadly. "Now," sighed the curly-headed young hotel owner, "we'll get to work on this. Come evenin', we'll have some poker."

There were four of us: the hotel man, a minister of the Gospel, myself, and a miniature salesman. Interesting man, the last. He worked among the crackers and hillbillies. He made photos of them, and took them back to whatever city he worked from; there they transposed the photo on to a china-faced piece of metal, and then painted it. They were pretty awful. Wish I'd had one done of myself: it would have been a worthy souvenir of that night. I put the jug of whiskey down on the floor and sat beside it, where I should not have so far to fall. The company did likewise. "Now look here, Preacher," said the sporty young hotel man as he began to shuffle: "none of your miracles. Don't you go and try to pull any of that 'loaves and fishes' stuff—we don't want no five aces to appear in this here deck."

"Sir, I do not have to cheat at cards," said the parson, a lanky, saturnine man, the local Cassius. "I can take all the money you've got without having to demean myself." The parson did not drink, and he won all our cash. Along about two I felt that I had had enough: I felt as if I had swallowed a wildcat. I had almost gone to sleep when the hotel man was at my door: "Neg—got any of that whiskey left?" I told him to come in; the jug was in the empty fireplace. "I'm afraid I'm going to die," he said. I turned over and over, and fought for sleep. At four he was in my room again. "Jug's in the same place," I told him. "I know," he said. "Now I'm afraid I'm *not* going to die!"

I had *Anna Karenina* along with me on that trip; and *On a Chinese Screen*, in Cape's Travellers' Library, so aptly named, for I have carried copies of them all over the world with me. Maugham's urbane style is very soothing on a morning after, and with *Anna* I could almost read myself out of this world. At that time I could still find refuge in a decent book to escape from a hangover; now I read the back numbers of every magazine we have in the house, even the advertisements, with *The New Statesman* top (for all that this stimulating periodical, not infrequently, makes me murderously pro-American). . . . When I tottered down to the drug-store below this lazy hotel beside the slow-flowing muddy Scuppernong, I could find nothing but *True Confessions*, sex and saxophones, and banana splits. It had never heard of a pick-me-up. I was miserable. When we did meet for breakfast—fried deep sea oysters and scrapple—the young hotel proprietor was good company: we had some grand talks about "what the hell we are all headed for!" "Trouble with this country is, too many people are working for somebody else—someone they'll never see. And all the pleasure of running your own show is being squeezed out of this country." And he related how the big cannibal chain-store companies were forcing the local butcher, grocery store, and bakers to sell out to them or work for them as managers. "And then," he said, "all this bull-shit about rugged individualism!" We also discussed the great truth that no American boy, or at any rate no healthy one, is born with the money-urge: that is forced on him by his parents, the environment, and their experience of the American way of life. He had been to his State university—"Didn't do much but whore around"—and was frank to admit that he had automatically stopped reading books the day he left it. But, on the other hand, he was a very wise young man, and he had an astonishingly fine taste. There was a house near the hotel, just where you come off the low wooden bridge, which, he told me, did not have a nail in it. It was built just before, or just after, the American Revolution: 1776; and the whole structure was put together with hickory pegs. It was almost a museum piece, standing there by the quiet river, and he loved it. "Look at it! Compared to some of the goddam rickety peach-crates they're putting up now!" The sawmill across the river whined; and as we sat on the bridge, watching the river flow beneath us, he gave me his final verdict: "Any way you look at it, fornication is what makes the world go round. That's one goddam pleasure they can't take away from us."

And I worked. I don't want to appear facetious about drink, or hypocritical. I lost *Created Equal* because I was drinking. If I had been cold sober I might have had the book of my life. My story in this present book is not that everybody is out of step but our John. Drink has always taken all the guts out of me: I have never got a drop of inspiration, or courage, from a bottle. In fact, drink has made a coward of me on one or two occasions that I should be only too glad to forget. But I do not intend to condemn drinking—for those who can stand up to it. I think drink has been responsible for some of the greatest deeds of mankind; and I'm not talking about the Dutch courage variety, I'm talking about grandeur of ideas, about an imagination that can lift one out of the ruts of conventions. I've often wondered if Columbus hadn't had a few drinks when he first got the idea of sailing west until he found a passage to the East Indies. Drink may have been responsible for the discovery of America. Who knows? But there was one thing I did know, and much to my sorrow: we fevered mortals have lost the vitality of the freebooting Elizabethans or the horse-riding Georgians. So our alcoholism is not due to the fact that we are drinking more than they did: man himself is a weaker vessel, with an inferior capacity for holding liquids. Like others, I have lost several friends through drink, but I would rather have the few that are left than all those who quit. And I knew that my only way to save my self-respect on this trip, now rapidly dwindling, was to work. I 'holed up', which is the right way to put it, in a cheap little theatrical hotel in Atlanta, Georgia, one used by an almost extinct type of American travelling salesmen; and there I pounded away at my typewriter from breakfast to midnight. Sitting down in the lobby while they did my room, I got some terrifying side-lights on U.S. life below stairs. There was a broken-down vaudeville troupe there that was disbanding at Atlanta. Sitting in one of the row of rocking chairs that faced the hotel's plate-glass window, I eavesdropped into a handful of human tragedies, and then went upstairs and wrote it. This was the story, the only one, that I sold to the *Manchester Guardian:* Jim Bone bought it for his precious two-column feature, when I showed him the way the American theatrical bible, *Variety,* had played it up. The only act of that troupe that had gone over was their performing fox-terrier.

The square was a restful place, sad with live oaks, the Spanish moss dripping from them as if mourning. On the other side was a café inhabited by the bookies from the Florida race-tracks. I would sit there eating those delicious little Charleston deep sea oysters, when my stomach could stand solids. The reason may have been gastric, but I have seldom been so full of pessimism. Nowhere in the South had I found what, foolishly perhaps, I just hoped might be there—and what must simply come if we are to have a way of life that we can actually enjoy living: a large area, with contented people—medium-sized people—living on the land. But I found nothing but wretched sharecroppers; or, if a man got to any size, he was a hard-faced creature who talked—well, as if he hated the land. He was a business man, not a farmer: we Americans are disinheriting ourselves from the good earth.

A few more miles, through Georgia; and then, down by the border of Florida, I turned the car. In New York I checked in at the Brevoort, repacked all the stuff I had left there, and sold the car. When I was decanted from the ship at Southampton . . . meteor lights flamed through the sky of my mind at nights, torn faces laughed at me; I was lost in some great city, every road led me away from where I wanted to go—the mountain was slipping, falling; I could get no toe-hold . . . falling, falling. In the mornings I lay in terror, waiting for the pubs to open. What if this was Sunday—not till twelve o'clock! What—what—if they were not to open at all! I made myself shave; but I swayed on my feet. . . . Then, thinking of the only thing I *could* think of that might save me, I packed my trout rods. The healing rod.

I was soon in Norway.

IN NORWAY

In the log cabin beside the river at Gjendesheim I woke in a room of bare scented wood, washed in the crisp air, and then walked up the hill to a breakfast of fried trout, goat's cheese and a jug of milk. I fished the heavy river until tired, then lay in the sun and watched the pines. I love getting back into old clothes and boots, and when I am in those again, down around bed-rock, I am in the right mood, and usually the right place, to plan against that perpetual antagonist we call life. I love Norway, where the water from the glaciers pours off the plateaux in foaming falls amid the soft airs of farming valleys; where the rivers are white with rapids, and then blue, green, peacock-coloured, as they swing beneath the snows around grey bouldered points shining in the sun; where you see salmon in the ice-green pools, resting for the next jump; and where you can watch the conventional Englishman standing upright in his skiff, and casting—cast, cast, cast, cast, cast—all day long (and he can have it). For myself, I like prowling up and down a river, enjoying the sights and the day as I go along; and a half dozen small mountain trout will suit me perfectly. Though I must say this: when the locals wish to compliment you in Norway, they say "Why, you cast like an Englishman!" I fished that year below Gendin Ridge where

Golden eagles seem to float
And fall away like motes in sunlight.

I always feel I am getting back to something decent when I return to Norway. I have known the country ever since the winter of

1914, when the line from our ship split a cask of valuable fish-oil at Stavanger, and, in the resultant cursing from the pier, I first heard Norwegian in its pure form. I have returned there many a time, as I had now, for a moral wash and brush up—to make a fresh start. And walking among the juniper, feeling the crunch of crisp reindeer moss, and thinking such thoughts as you can think only on the roof of Norway, I shed the shibboleths and got back to some of the instinctive values. For a few weeks I felt absolutely right with life.

I sometimes think that the Norwegians have the finest set of values of any people I know. To absolve them from the charge of priggishness this may seem to imply, let me state that they also have the highest rate of children born out of wedlock of any country in Europe. For they take full advantage of bodily pleasure, as you can see in the happy expectant faces of young men and girls as they hitch-hike in country Norway with a rucksack on their backs—even if that happiness is only temporary; though most of those trial marriages seem to work out. But sometimes I feel that there is something missing in this set of values: the Norwegians seem too handsome, too healthy, too happy. And then I think of a country like Spain. . . .

I read *Pan* again, and bits of *Growth of the Soil,* beside the river at Gjendesheim: little knowing that in three or four years I should be back in Norway again with the war on, and that Knut Hamsun's admirers would be sending his own books back to him. The postman used to arrive at his house with a cart in the morning. But now, with that particularly Norwegian good nature, they have restored him to favour. I know of no people who live less on hate.

I re-read much of Ibsen again in the clean air below Gendin Ridge —and found the meanness and pettiness of his characters unpleasantly out of place in that Norwegian atmosphere. I like to read the writers of a country while I am in it, the way I first met the great Russians during the last years of the Romanoffs. But from the Russians I got nobility and bigness; from Ibsen's characters I got the taint of smallness, meanness, pettiness, timidity. I have often wondered—everything I have read about Ibsen has increased it: his own letters especially—I have often wondered whether he *was* such a great ironist: did he know that idealism pushed to its extreme limits can be absurd? I don't think he did. I think that in loading the dice for Dr. Stockmann, Ibsen loaded the dice against himself: he himself believed all that nonsense. I asked a friend of mine who had known Ibsen in his last days if his Norwegians were real. My friend smiled:

"Our stage is small. But aren't we all like that? If you scrape away the self-satisfaction and sanctimonious hypocrisy of Victorian England, what have you got? The most money-conscious people in Europe—Napoleon was right—and a class structure reeking with unworthy distinctions. We have no class of hereditary privilege in Norway. Our rewards are so small—Chamberlain is the only title the King can bestow—that it looks as if we had made a great to-do about nothing. But there *were* Norwegians like Ibsen's in Pastor Mander's day—when we all lived in holy terror of Public Opinion. Now, as you have seen for yourself, we are the least church-ridden people in Europe. That is a great advance. That Lutheran conscience is no longer permitted to rob us of the joy of life. Perhaps we have reacted too far from the spiritual. But now our young people can be natural: 'too happy', as you claim, lacking that—whatever it is?

"They say that you must not judge an artist's work by the man: we have to, with Ibsen. Something inside him—he was a mean man, suffering from 'craven timidities'—made him afraid of the other face of Norway. In the meanness, the smallness, the cowardice of Dr. Stockmann's brother you find the anger of his own remorse."

My friend spoke of seeing Ibsen during the last two years of his life, "drunk all the time": coming in to take the same table at precisely the same hour in the Grand Hotel, Christiania—"You could set your watch by him!"—and sitting there moodily until he had put down, every day, precisely the same quantity of alcohol; then getting to his feet and making his way out without a nod or word to anybody. "At the end he was a child again, playing about on the floor on his hands and knees with toy railway trains." But what the outside world did not know, he went on, was that Ibsen was haunted all his life by a ghost: by the picture of himself walking down the streets of Bergen with the girl he really loved, and running away as he saw her irate father bearing down on them. . . . In late years, when they met again, and he was the Eagle, he asked her why they had never fulfilled their love: she answered him "Don't you remember? . . . the day you ran away."

This "sick conscience" of Ibsen's undoubtedly made him shrink from flesh-and-blood Norwegians. "That is why Knut Hamsun and

Strindberg attacked him. And Bjørnson, whose daughter married Ibsen's son, and who should have known Ibsen better than most people, said contemptuously: 'Ibsen? Ibsen is a pen, not a man!'" That was why, concluded my friend, the Norwegians of his day did not care much for Ibsen, and why Ibsen lived most of his life out of Norway.

Yes, it was wonderful to be back in a land where people were not obsessed with the idea of being big. But, as my friend said, Norway is a small stage. Much as I envied some of the lives I saw around me, I knew I should be living in a fool's paradise if I tried to make myself believe we could have lives like those in the United States—except in the matter of their values. We could learn a lesson from them there. The Scandinavians form a very small part of the American population, but have made a finer moral impact on the United States than any other people. Without their ever having striven for it, the term Scandinavian is synonymous in America with a capacity for hard work, a stubborn strength of character, a passion for independence, and a determined straightforwardness in all business affairs, such as have made us call these rock-like individualists (who can be very hard to handle) "square-heads". And there is no question in my mind that these virtues have been stamped into the Scandinavians, and the Norwegians especially, by both the beauty and the hardness of their country. In the United States it takes courage, and a great deal of intelligence, to stay small; you do it in the face of public opinion and of an overwhelming economic competition. In Norway they can't help it: especially the farmers. Only four per cent of the land is cultivated, even cultivable; the rest is rock, forests or barrens. And this rules out the monster-farm that would drive the small man out of business, as has happened—until very recently—in the United States. A man has to be intelligent, with both his head and his hands, to get a good living out of four acres. Other than the mountain-peasant civilisation of old Austria, I know no life on the land that can compare with the Norwegian. And these smallholders are most definitely not peasants.

See one of their little four- or five-acre farms in the rosy glows of sunset; or, better still, see it in the warm rays of a long Northern afternoon, when the entire family is getting in its hay. The man is swinging the short-bladed Norwegian scythe, which cuts close; so close that the green slope, where he has passed, is as smooth as a country lawn. His wife and daughter are collecting every blade of grass, sweet with clover, and hanging it to dry in rows on long wires. The beautiful little Norwegian fjord pony, plump, biscuit-coloured, even strawberry, with its high, arched neck, is standing proudly by, with a baby playing at its heels. When the baby grows up he will go to sea; but before that he will have received the same education as the son of the Prime Minister, for education is identical for every-one in Norway. From that wandering around the world he will come back with the pleasing sophistication that is so typical of the Nor-wegian, and, as there are no class-barriers, without subconscious re-sentments. And after he has seen life in foreign parts, the chances are that he will return to the farm when his old man slows down. There it will be: the little white house with the flower boxes at its windows; the red barn with the road sloping up to its loft; the net-shed down by the rocks at its foot—and a boat bobbing on the fjord, for this fisherman-farmer will harvest a large part of his season's crop, cod, mackerel and herring, without losing sight of the smoke of his house. Such a holding—even its loneliness—conditions the people who live on it. Some of these small Norwegians are among the best-read people I have ever met. It was good to be back with them again and to have the thought, odd as it may seem, that in the pain-ful evolution of my own country we Americans might, in time, regain some such affinity with the land, and be allowed to live small. For bigness is our curse; and unless we recognise it we shall be increas-ingly emptied by the things we make, and never find our way out of our present maze of purposelessness.

Not that every Norwegian farmer is small! Along the long lake at Lom; all up the great, open valley of Gudbrandsdal; and on the eighty wonderful miles of the east side of Trondheim Fjord, there are some of the loveliest farms and farming towns you will find any-where on earth, with a beautiful civilisation. I have slept in two houses in Norway where I was afraid to smoke in bed: every article in the house—glass, china, paintings, furniture—was such a museum piece that I feared some careless act of mine might destroy it all.

I spent a lot of my time wandering in those mountains and brood-ing on what it is that a man really lives for. If you do not have the money urge, if you do not want the house with the two-mile drive, if you do not want a motorcar bigger than the Jones's (and to hell with the Joneses) it is not so easy to answer that question. Money is liberty: give me enough to let me wander about the world freely, and you can have the rest. I wasn't worrying my head about the morals of living decently—Christ gave us a pretty good set of rules two thousand years ago, if only we had ever obeyed them—I was wondering how to live a decent life under the circumstances. And that is not so easy as it sounds. Power, position, pomp—I wanted none of those. Shall we fall back, then, on the myths—on rugged individualism, for example? I had never believed in that sort of nonsense since the day I stopped playing Indians. If the individual is very rugged, God help someone else—there is the whole story of colonialism. And not at all a nice story. I am tired, too, of being told, as if it were a revelation, that the solution of our problems lies not in any change of political parties or in a new ideology, but in ourselves: "The fault, dear Brutus . . ." has been preached for a long time. That was the essence of Thoreau's mouse-trap philosophy. And so what?

I sometimes think that if life has taught me anything, it is not to believe all these people who make it their business to tell you how to live. Priests, politicians, philosophers; and especially the ideologists. I have seen them all go wrong: always preaching contrary doctrines. And if there is one common denominator I have found among the Intellectuals of this world it is—heartlessness. Looking back, my own life seems to have been a constant beat to windward: to break through the barrier reef of other people's minds. Those dreadful fixed opinions, which have wrecked so many lives. I distrust the Interpreters.

Back in England again, I bought an English Ford—gallant little bus: it is with us yet, though I expect to fall through its floor any moment—and my wife, son and I drove to Vienna. At Salzburg I ran into my publisher, Victor Gollancz: he was there for the Festival, and deliriously happy, as who wouldn't be? In Vienna I went to the Café Louvre to pick up old threads, and, without the slightest warning, stepped right back into the world of journalism. Fodor, the man who knew more about Central Europe than all the rest of us put together, was sitting at the same old table and reading the same old papers.

Over coffee he said: "The daughter of Stephan Radich is here in Vienna. She has just escaped from Yugoslavia by sliding down a mountain—without a passport. I think you should see her." We had her and her husband to lunch at the Bristol the next day.

Stephan Radich was the Croat deputy who was shot on the floor of the Yugoslav parliament in 1928. A Parnell among the always-quarrelling Serbs, Croats and Slovenes, he wanted a Croat king and a Croat flag—he had even demanded, as next best, that Woodrow Wilson should insist on an independent Republic of Croatia. (And this must have been the only bit of crazy self-determination that Wilson turned down.) Radich's daughter and her husband were now working, as only Balkan plotters could, for such a Republic—under the Croat national hero, Dr. Matchek. She told me that if I went to the back room of a certain small eating-place in Zagreb—and she wrote its name in my notebook—a man would come in who would have some interesting information to give me, and that he would then take me to Dr. Matchek. "But how will he know me?" I asked. The handsome young woman smiled: "You just say what day you will be in Zagreb, and you will be recognised. I shall send word on today." At this cloak-and-dagger stuff my nine-year-old son's eyes popped wide open, and I date his journalistic career from that lunch.

It all worked out. "What men considered sacred and important", wrote Tolstoy, "were their own devices for wielding power over their fellow men." Well, here I was right in the thick of it: here was the mental atmosphere of a madhouse. The man who picked me up in that Zagreb café was Dr. Jellassich, and it did not need his pallid face, with the lines of suffering on it, to prove his tale. He had only just come out of prison: the Serb police had tied his hands and feet together behind his back, and, bent like that, he had been beaten until he urinated blood. Dr. Matchek himself had been liberated from a Serbian prison only a short time back; he, too, had been roughly handled. Dr. Jellassich told me how Mussolini had tried to remove Dr. Matchek: because Matchek wanted independence from the Serbs, but not as a lackey of the Italians. The latter had therefore subsidised some Belgrade police and Serbian terrorists to murder him; but, instead, the peasants at his village, Kupenich, twenty miles outside Zagreb, had killed all the seven terrorists with scythes, sickles and flails. For this Matchek had been imprisoned. A good story out of that *Prisoner of Zenda* world; and I drove out to Matchek's farm.

Here, the prospective interview took an unexpected turn. Matchek was not there when we arrived; and some of the gay and husky Croat kids, playing with my son Dan, got him into a swing and swung him so high that, at some twenty feet, he came out and dropped like a plummet on his stubborn head. A bump like half a lemon began to form; and when Dr. Matchek came across his fields, with an armed guard on either side of him, a peasant with a rifle, all he seemed interested in was that bump on my son's head. He was a kindly, scholarly old man, and we sat by the soft glow of an oil lamp in his farmhouse. He seemed peace itself. I have seen many national figures in my years as a correspondent, and here again I saw the strength that comes from simplicity. But, to my crude American mind, he oversimplified. I protested somewhat to that effect when he began talking about a Croat passive-resistance movement: I said it would not work. "Why not?" he asked, with a confident smile. "Because it won't work against the Serbs." I spoke of my talks with Gandhi in India—how I had told him that the civil-disobedience plan he proposed would be all-powerful, provided he could get all his followers to obey it implicitly; how he had replied that he could not control the Chittagong terrorists, who, so most people thought, were ruining his *satyagraha* campaign; and how, in my own opinion, he knew very well that passive-resistance was only an incitement to violence—which he wanted: it would focus the eyes of the world on India. "Beat me, you brute!"—so would Mother India shriek to Britain, and the British would be ashamed. As they were.

"Your adversary must have an Achilles heel," I said to venerable Dr. Matchek, "his conscience! What you propose wouldn't work one day against Mussolini."

Matchek gave a short, humourless laugh; then he frowned: "But that's just the very person we should have to use it against!"

So there you are. Here in this year of our Lord 1936, with all the trouble then brewing in Europe, was a patriot who wanted to add to the existing heap of nations still another one, with its own army, diplomatic corps, police, top drawer of bureaucrats, and so on and so on. What the Croats, the Croat man in the street, would gain from it all was beyond me. But Dr. Matchek was willing to die for it. And the shooting of Radich in the Yugoslav parliament in 1928 had led in direct historical sequence to the murder of Alexander, to the gallant Mihailovitch, fighting to prevent Yugoslavia being overwhelmed by Ante Pavlich's "Ustasha", and—to Tito. While we were talking, Matchek's house was being guarded by eleven armed peasants; and, as we drove away, one of them stepped out from behind a tree and covered us with his Steyr carbine. It was my son Dan who got the most out of that interview: when he returned to his English school in the autumn he wrote a paper: *Dr. Matchek and the Croat Separatist Movement*. It was full of good stuff.

Our old lake in Slovenia had gone. The tourist agencies had found it. A horror of a new hotel had been built in one year. It was full of fat, prosperous Czechs. The Saint James and the Holy Ghost had been taken over by Prince Paul's general staff; but Madame Yuri and her household of happy bare-legged servant girls welcomed us back as members of the family, and Josef resumed reading my newspapers, and letters, over my shoulder. The atmosphere of this little place was still very *White Horse Inn*. Madame Yuri always asked us to make out our own bills: she said it saved her the bother. And I resumed fishing. But when I went up to the Savitca at the head of the lake for some sunset casting, I found two surly soldiers standing guard over the lovely water where, on my previous visit, I had taken eleven trout one sunset, all over a pound. They pointed their rifles at me, jabbering in some excited lingo. I mentioned this to the Flag Captain of Prince Paul, Regent of Yugoslavia, who was then at his hunting lodge, ringed by soldiers.

"Oh, yes!" said the Flag Captain, smiling. "His Highness understands you had some wonderful fishing on the Savitca when you were here before. He read your article in *The Sphere*. . . ." That article had been entitled *Poaching a Regent's River,* so I knew I had had it. Prince Paul, who was married to the sister of the Duchess of Kent, was supposed to be sentimentally pro-British; he spent much of his time, when in London, in the Tate Gallery, and his little hunting lodge at Bohinjska was full of all the British glossy weeklies—the *Sphere, Tatler,* etc. I got the impression that this Flag Captain and his brother officers had been rather pleased with my article and were not so keen on Prince Paul, whom later during the war, the British were to intern in Kenya. And I was sorry that they did not know that again, on this present visit, I was poaching Prince Paul's stretch on the river Sava after dark, right below the hunting lodge where he was living.

He was so angry I had poached his river that he refused to give me an official interview at Bohinjska. But, anyway, the lovely lake had lost its charm—as had much of Europe, for me. A paranoiac in Berlin; a swaggering braggart in Rome; every new nation in Eastern Europe become a snake-pit of demented diplomats by Woodrow Wilson's right of self-determination; Spaniards murdering each other —a million dead (twice the number killed in the U. S. Civil War), and ninety per cent of them shot behind the lines; the new Poland, which might have been the most glorious thing to emerge from the Peace Conference, but in fact another madhouse of quarrelling nationalists, whose utter lack of statesmanship (these charming people!) was to bring on the next war; *and not one great spiritual leader in all Europe*.

We drove to Belgrade along the Sava; then back across Bosnia and Herzegovina; settled down finally in that little walled relic of Venice, Budva, on the border of Albania. Ate sea-urchins. Swam. Lay out in the sun. And I planned to leave Europe. The *shell* of Europe still remained: Chartres and the Louvre were still there; France was still fresh as a lettuce in the spring—but the Europeans were making Europe a very unpleasant place. I wanted fresher air.

I thought of the trade winds. How pleasant it would be to lie in a deck-chair and watch the white wake trail astern—watch the flying fish spin their silver flight to zip into the beautiful cobalt waves. . . . I would get the captain to let me go up on the bridge for that most beautiful hour at sea: the hour, well before sunrise, when you watch the light of a new day coming into this world . . . and, more than likely, the officer on watch and I would have one of those chats that you can have only in that hour: when men can say things to one another they would never dare admit to in the garish light of day: you have been so close to the truth. . . . I thought of the desert, and of all the peace that many fine Englishmen have found in it. . . . Where should I go? What should I do? I thought of Richard Burton, making his own rules for life:

"Do what thy manhood bids thee do,
From none but self expect applause;
He noblest lives and noblest dies
Who makes and keeps his self-made laws."

But had that worked out, even for that great man? Where had he been, what misfortune had overtaken him, when he was found in his dilapidated condition in Buenos Aires?

BELOW THE
RIO GRANDE

"History's three greatest fools: Jesus, Don Quixote, and I," moaned Simon Bolivar, as he lay dying near royalist Santa Marta. He knew already that he had liberated the Spanish Americans from Spain, only to have them become victims of their own generals on horseback. It is not widely enough known, at any rate by South Americans, that Bolivar (who dreamed of a *United* America) did not want the new States to become Republics; like George Canning, he wanted them to adopt monarchical constitutions as an assurance of internal stability, and to maintain the link with Europe. If that had happened they could not have developed into the twenty-one human cock-pits they are today, and that weird isolation of the Latin American mind from Europe might never have come about. The Spanish Americans love cock-fighting, and with the exception of Mexico, which has not been in the news lately, they have been enjoying cock-fights ever since Bolivar's day—both with birds and men. Revolution is the national pastime below the Rio Grande.

I had intended to go to South America ever since I studied to become a civil engineer with the specific dream of building bridges in the high Andes. But when I left my university at the end of my junior year and said goodbye to Edgar Marburg, our Dean (he was perhaps the greatest bridge-builder in the world), he smiled: "Negley, I wish you would make me a promise. Promise me—for the sake of humanity—that you will never build a bridge." So I ceased to picture myself slinging trestles across the Andes.

My actual going was the result of a chance talk. Webb Miller, of

the United Press, had returned to London with a nervous breakdown, after watching the Moors and the Tercio, the Foreign Legion,
machine-gun their prisoners, including women and children, in the
streets of Oviedo. He had been machine-gunned himself, lying flat
on the bottom of a truck as he dashed into the town; but that was all
in the game to Webb Miller. This veteran newspaper correspondent,
who had covered every war since the U.S. fracas with Mexico in
1912, and whose book, *I Found No Peace,* is a record of mass mur-
ders, sat there in the Boltons (when I obeyed an agitated call from
him to "Come around at once!") at four in the afternoon, still in his
pyjamas, a bottle of whiskey before him and the tears streaming
down his face. He spoke of hands uplifted, pleading, as in that
painting of Goya's, and of a woman hugging her child to protect it
from the bullets. . . . "That cooked me. I cracked right then and
there."

We talked all that dreadful afternoon of Spain and Spaniards, a
country and a people we both loved deeply; and I said what an
extraordinary thing it was, the awful misconception about Spaniards
in the United States—as if the Conquistadores had never existed!—
where we had the idea that one Texas Ranger could lick any ten
Spiggoties (everybody below the Rio Grande) with one hand tied
behind his back: whereas the Spaniards are probably the most fero-
ciously brave people who have ever slaughtered one another. "I've
often thought," I said to Webb, "that I should like to wander down
the Andes." Then something popped inside my head: "Which, as a
matter of fact, I am going to do. As from here."

Webb smiled through his tears. "Well, if you do I'll get my crowd
to commission some articles from you." The head of Webb's service
rushed over from New York; Webb, one of the bravest, straightest
correspondents who ever lived (he died, stepping out of a railway
train before it had reached the station, in the darkness of the Blitz),
was finally persuaded to go to the Island of Rab in the Adriatic, to
recuperate. And he telephoned me the very morning I was leaving
my London house to take the boat for Barranquilla, in the Republic
of Colombia, that the job was mine. I had forgotten all about it; and
it was not till I reached the coast of South America that I realised
I had sold my liberty.

When I saw the frigate-birds sailing over the three warships of the Venezuelan Navy—about the size of steam yachts—which were rusting at their anchors in the harbour of La Guaira, with the inevitable buzzards wheeling high up against the snow of the Sierras as we were saluted by bugle-calls from an equally obsolete fort, I wanted to rush below and tell my steward to put my stuff ashore right then and there. For here was *Nostromo!*

One of the toy warships was troubling my mind. With her thin, twin stacks and ram bow, she aroused dusty memories. I felt I ought to know her.

"Why, she's the old *Cuba*," said an Englishman, leaning over the rail by my side. "Sunk in the Spanish-American war. Back in 1898. Raised, reconditioned, and sold to the poor Venezuelans by your Secretary of State, Philander Knox."

Philander Knox! Already the South American picture was coming into focus. Philander Knox, American Secretary of State: backer of U.S. "Dollar Diplomacy" in the Caribbean, in Central and South America: sold on the Big Brother policy, and wielder, when these things didn't work, of the Big Stick, under a much-perverted Monroe Doctrine—here was one reason why the South Americans are not in love with us. It was a misinterpretation of the Monroe Doctrine that had brought U.S. Marines into Haiti and Nicaragua to help them settle their domestic difficulties, usually on behalf of New York banks. So it was not unnatural, in view of such memories, that the United States had been unable to reach more than polite sentimental agreements at the Pan-American Conference at Buenos Aires, and that no American Secretary of State has been able to get much further since.

(Many years before I had been in Barcelona when the Catalans were throwing stones at Columbus, on the waterfront, for having discovered America. This was just after we had called the first Pan-American Conference—in Cuba: last of the rich and lost Spanish possessions! The pillar on which Columbus stands is very high. Few of the stones reached him, if any. The futility of the whole performance struck me as symbolic of the exasperated feelings smouldering in the bosom of all Spanish Americans about their northern Good Neighbour.)

"The South Americans are still waiting," said that Englishman, my self-appointed interpreter, "to see what sort of line the Americans will take after Roosevelt goes out."

"And we," I replied, "are still waiting to see when the South Americans will be able, if ever, to agree upon any question of importance among themselves."

I mishandled that trip. I did, to some extent, what everybody else did—played up the comic-opera side of South America. The series I wrote for the United Press was very poor indeed. And yet, although I have never been on such a round of drinking in all my life, I would not have missed that South American experience for all the gold of the Incas.

Sitting under the stars on the walls of Cartagena, once sacked by Drake and Morgan, now scene of the evening promenade—two carriages abreast can be driven along them—I thought what a pity it was that we always have to write about these countries in terms of their politics. Yet you can do nothing else with the Latin American republics. They *are* their politics—each one with full steam up, ready to blow its top: each with a strong personality, trying to hold down the lid: each, at the same time, quarrelling with its neighbours. We had had a graphic little incident, one night, as a sort of side-show in the melodrama of their feuds.

There is a little *cantina* outside the walls of Cartagena, down by the docks, where the musicians, a *mestizo* with a guitar and a *sambo* rattling two calabashes, perch like parrots on a shelf along the wall; and the girls carry Gillette blades in their breasts, encased in ingenious little holders made from flaps of inner-tubes, which they use with astonishing alacrity in case they think you are going too far— free of charge. And in that *cantina* sat two British sailors. . . .

They, or their counterparts, had been sitting there for two years —ever since the Colombians had bought a couple of brand-new destroyers from the British navy, with which, they hoped, they could flatten out the Peruvians (after the necessary training) to settle a boundary dispute as to who owned what along the Putumayo River. The destroyers still lay at anchor in Cartagena harbour; and by the time the sun sank behind the mangrove swamps and coconut palms they were hot enough inside to broil a chicken. Hence Bill and Jock, telling me how bloody bored they were, and both looking as innocent as a new-born babe. As one of the señoritas brought our drinks, with her flashing eyes and the demure little spit-curls on her apricot cheeks, sailor Jock lazily turned her around and gave her a playful little slap on the bottom. She did not like this—in public—and she gave the proper yelp.

"'E's 'armless," explained his pal to me—and oh, how bored he was!—"'E don't mean nothink by that—*everybody* knows Jock."

And then they poured out their grief . . . 78 of the original 278 British sailors were still manning these destroyers, waiting for the Colombians to use them, or for the League of Nations to settle the dispute at Geneva. I pointed out that Ecuador and Peru had been having a similar dispute over who owned some territory at the head-waters of the Amazon—with one side arresting or shooting soldiers of the other—for 106 years ("Christ!" said Jock): ever since a Span-iard, operating from Quito, had crossed over the Andes into what is now the Oriente. Bill and Jock took this information stoically. Or so I thought. Then Bill, who wore his hat perched on the bridge of his nose, got up, walked over to the cash-register, and pulled its handle backward. Whether he thought that would reverse cash-receipts I don't know; but the Jamaican Negro tending the bar, a King Kong by the way, said to me almost frantically:

"I can't make these sailors out nohow! I've known these two for years—they comes in here and they drinks up their pay every night —and when they goes broke I give them chits—but they don't never have nothing to do with no girls. I just can't make 'em out!"

"Maybe," I said, thinking of sailors I had seen in other ports, "they get drunk before they can get that far?"

"Yes, Mister. I guess you're right." Then, while he was still clutch-ing the handle of the raped cash-register, I saw his eyes open with horror. He was staring at Jock. Jock had removed his hat—he wore it perched on the extreme back of his head as only a British sailor can—and had taken something from it. He had pressed his lighted cigarette against this object, which was now sputtering. He threw it among the dancers. . . . Hell broke loose.

Like the self-guided missiles which can hunt their own targets in the stratosphere, that rocket zipped around the dance-floor. The bar was full of the local police—for what is the use of being a policeman if you can't get free drinks?—and these charged like wild buffaloes among the screaming señoritas, who were trying to climb up the walls. The *sambo* with the calabashes fell off his perch. King Kong, the Jamaican Negro, waded in—then leapt back behind the bar, and fought off all comers. I don't know what is the length of life of those rockets, but this one's seemed eternal. It was whizzing around like a fiery snake in a forest of legs, belching its trail of sparks. It hit a fat Colombian beauty in a place where no girl expects to get a rocket— and the Jamaican Negro, trying to save his establishment, squirted two soda-syphons on the floor. The Colombian police attacked it with truncheons. And it was finally beaten to death.

Jock stared at it indifferently. He had done the thing he had come there to do. Now he turned to our table, folded his arms, and went quietly to sleep. None of us were locked up in the *callabose* that night. I don't know why . . .

At Cartagena I met Mr. MacWithers. He was a gold-miner who turned up after a mysterious journey by mule and aeroplane from the suffocating jungles of the Choco, over on the Pacific slope, where he had been one of the hydraulic engineers for an American concession. This, he told me, would probably be the last time he would ever try to get back to New York. "Been trying it some twenty years now. Every time I get to the coast, I get drunk. Drink it all up. Bust. Then I got to go back and work some more." I thought, as we sat there creating our own breeze by rocking back and forth in the chairs of the Hotel Americano's patio, that if he didn't make New York this time he was just about one drink off from becoming a tropical tramp. His blue eyes had been bleached by the sun until they were now the colour of watered milk; he had cut off his patchy hair (I suppose to preserve it) at half-inch height, wherever any remained on his melon-shaped head; his damp, sallow face looked as if he had coated it that morning with a thin layer of candle-grease—and he had a mean sense of humour. Mighty mean.

This was embodied, mostly, in a collection of newspaper clippings he kept in an enormous black wallet, whose bulge almost deformed his right hip. "*That* shows you," he said, "what the Church still thinks it can do to the women of this country." Mr. MacWithers had been to a Hallowe'en party in Cartagena, the previous November, that had led to an excommunication.

The Church (this was one of Mr. MacWithers's sore subjects) was still trying to dominate the women in the Americas below Panama; and, up until the advent of the present López government, the Republic of Colombia had been more under its domination than any other of these Latin American republics. The Church was fighting a tenacious battle to keep things that way. The women were its last stronghold: they still put on their black mantillas to go to Mass. The village priest still dictated the mode and manners of social life, and what the priest no longer did consciously was still being done for him by centuries of tradition. And in this priestly enclave a crude American oil millionaire had decided to throw a Hallowe'en party at the Popa Club—a most respectable institution, very much like the Century Clubs in the small towns of the United States: Mrs. Grundy's club.

"It was a dud show," said Mr. MacWithers. The women had sat in an uncomfortable jumble at one end of the hall, the men, by themselves, at the other. The oil man had put on a curious little cabaret, with a few girls shrouded in sacks hopping about in what was supposed to be a Dance of Witches. When that was over, a few brave couples proceeded to dare all the proprieties by taking a timorous turn on the dance floor themselves. "But everyone was a perfect gentleman and lady. It was just damned dull."

Why the Archbishop of Cartagena, the next morning, should ponder the idea of excommunicating everyone who had been at that party was beyond comprehension, said Mr. MacWithers. But he had; and it was only after the lengthiest argument that he was persuaded to select one particular participant as a scapegoat. He selected the most important figure present—a former mayor of Cartagena and one-time Governor of the Province. Him he excommunicated. Mr. MacWithers, ordering two more Tom Collinses—which were made for us, with fresh limes, by a happy, expert and very busy little *mestizo* boy—handed me the newspaper clipping of the open letter the Archbishop had written to the press:

"This grave affair regarding the ball at the Club de la Popa has been resolved favourably . . . the real culprit of the disorder has now been discovered. . . ."

"That's where the Archbishop lets the cat out of the bag," put in Mr. MacWithers. "The ex-Governor was a Liberal; and in these countries a Liberal is a man who wants to separate Church and State. Go on. . . ."

"This sympathiser of the cannibals in Spain, this black heart who seems to desire that similar crimes should be committed among us, this depraved gentleman, in addition covered the ladies of Cartagena with ignominy by saying that the time would come when men and women would smoke equally, drink cocktails together, and dance the rumba. . . ."

The Archbishop then concluded:

"This unnatural being without conscience, who has always been a repugnant scandal, deserves an outstanding censure. We therefore excommunicate Señor X for the inhuman sentiments that fill his soul and for his infamous conduct, shown in the recent incident. . . ."

"What gets me," said Mr. MacWithers, "is not that the old Bish. could believe all that nonsense—and he sure did throw the book, didn't he!—it's the fact that he knows damned well that the *women* will believe it. That's what you're up against down here: the Dark Ages."

"Well, for me," I said, ordering two more Tom Collinses (I have never known such refreshing limes as those of Colombia), "I prefer priest to rumba. . . . I'm not at all sure that when these South American johnnies burst into the Machine Age they are going to have such a very good time. Here's death to all Progress."

The early Spaniards built their capital of Bogotá at 8,500 feet up in the Andes because they wanted to put themselves beyond reach of the English pirates. It is, with the possible exception of Lhassa, the most inaccessible capital in the world. You can fly up to Bogotá in a couple of hours from Barranquilla on the Caribbean; but that will break you if you have any luggage. Otherwise, you can go up the long Magdalena River, eight days in a stern paddle-wheeler—always provided that you don't get stuck for a week on some sandbar; and even then you have another day, crossing the mountains by rail and motorcar—provided, again, that there has been no landslide. Or you can go up to Colón, through the Panama Canal, and then by steamer down to Buenaventura, which is known, correctly, as the "ass-hole of the Pacific". I took this route.

I have often thought what a pity it was that we correspondents did not go more to the women of foreign countries for our information. The female mind is freer from clichés than the male. It is less under the spell of the politicians. It is less inclined to take things for granted. Often I have thought what a fine thing it would be if some practical woman could be put in to clean up all the man-made mess. One felt that a woman would put that house in order with the ruthless efficiency with which she handles her own domestic affairs. Yet, in practice, it does not seem to work out that way. In Soviet Russia, after the first burst of speed, the women seem to have fallen into the background of national affairs—and they were a nuisance while they lasted. In 1928–29, when I spent a year back in the U.S.S.R., Lenin's widow, Krupskaya, was placed in charge of the publication of foreign books; and she made herself about as idiotic an overseer as could be imagined. In order to prevent the pure Soviet mind from being corrupted by these sordid pictures from the Capitalist world, this lumbering and humourless female dictated that each book must have an *ideological preface*. (Comrade Artsky, censor and ideological prefacer, writes that "Robinson Crusoe was typical of the English adventurers, who never refuse an opportunity to exploit a primitive race in order to put something in their own pockets". Poor old Friday; you never thought about that, did you? [But that is what the Africans are saying, not without reason, about the British today.] Of *Gulliver's Travels*, Ideologist Cohen writes: "Swift was the man of the rising bourgeoisie which was struggling to master the other classes. We must not be in sympathy with his feelings. As a bourgeois he doesn't exist for us. But we may feel touched by his protest against the exploitation of the poor. . . .") And, to return to the West, a long experience of hospital matrons has cured me of any delusions that women make either kindly or efficient administrators.

We had a little 104-lb blonde on our boat going through the Canal who made even her Captain tremble. "Beautiful but dumb," he said to me, despairingly. "But tell me—*is* she so dumb?" When we were coming into Gatun Locks (they are a fifth of a mile long, and a man standing in a control tower, half a mile off, merely manipulates a knob to close the 600-ton leaf gates behind your ship, whereupon you rise eighty-five feet) I asked her "Well, Sweetie, what do you think of the Panama Canal?" and she replied "Oh, *I* think it's *cute!*"

Later, when the process was reversed and we were being lowered in Pedro Miguel Lock, and the red stacks of a big Royal Mail boat appeared in the twin lock beside us, going up, Sweetie said: "The power of the water must be awfully strong to lift that audacious big thing!"

You could not invent that girl, and only a country as virile as the United States could have produced her. Beautiful but dumb indeed: with that weird sort of innocence so typical of American girls abroad, even in the most indecent places. She looked like Jean Harlow. In fact "Don't you think I look like Jean Harlow?" she asked, as she lay in my bunk pressing her baby lips against mine (but there was nothing doing there: she had harnessed herself in a chastity-belt that was as impregnable as a Chubb lock). "*Don't* I look like Jean Harlow?" "Get the hell out on deck," I ordered, frenzied by the tropics and her close-pressed femaleness. "Or else tell me what you are going to do with that big black Packard?"

The Packard: that was what had been worrying the Captain—and me. She was taking it to Peru. It was brand new. "I told you," she said, "I'm going to drive it from Callao to Lima." "Yes, I know that —but I also told you that it is only eight miles from Callao to Lima —and you are going to drive that great big black car there all by yourself?" "Uh-huh." She took my cigarette away from me: "Now give us a *real* kiss. . . . And don't you be goofy."

"Captain, you can have her," I said, after Sweetie had bullied us into showing her some of the night life of Panama. From the sanitary interior of a motorcar we had let Sweetie take a quick look, as our open-air taxi drove through the notorious Coconut Grove; about as innocent a name for the red light district as the tropics could furnish. It was a stifling night. Most of the houses in the Coconut Grove had not only their doors but their windows open . . . "Well . . . !" gasped Sweetie. "I never! Look at those people—in *there!*"

The Captain looked, and punched the driver: "Make it snappy! I'm in a hurry." The girls sitting on all the verandas waved to us. "Why—Captain!" cried Sweetie, cuddling up to him. "They all *know* you!"

The skipper's hand was trembling—he had been the first to take a ship through the Panama Canal—as he stood there in his singlet, pouring another steadying four-fingers of whiskey. "Tell me—could, could any girl be as dumb as all that? Not to have known where we were!"

"She knew," I said. "Captain, that girl is one of the most deadly of her species." "Well," he said desperately, "in New York her father asked me to keep an eye on her. I'm afraid I am going to lose that eye." "But are you sure it was her *father?*" I asked him. He jumped. (Where are you, Sweetie? And what did you do with that big black Packard? Was it true that you were going to Peru to work the badger game?) Just think what I might have learned from Sweetie—about South Americans.

At Buenaventura it rains some time in the day, every day in the year; and the collection of rusted tin roofs is as grim as anything I have ever been forced to look at. "We had a lovely fire here, two years ago," said the young English shipping agent, "but some bloody fool put it out." We were watching one of the weirdest fashion-parades I have yet seen in any hotel lobby. In a humidity in which a fish could have swum, conspicuously well-dressed girls, and young men in spotless white, were promenading—and all stalking one other. It was so obvious, so blatant, that I said it was like the start of a cock-fight: the birds watching for an opening. "Which is exactly what it is," said the desperate young Englishman. "The girls are looking over prospective husbands. The men are stalking a rich wife."

He explained that, awful as it was with the mud and the rain ceaselessly pattering on its tin roofs, Buenaventura was Colombia's marriage mart. If the young girls were forbidden to see anything of the young men, after dark, in the big cities, and could see little of them in the daytime except when sitting on a park bench with a *duenna,* they could see quite a lot of each other at a bathing resort. The beach was beating the Church in the Republic of Colombia; and every year, for the short season of a few weeks, comparatively wealthy mothers took their daughters (or the daughters dragged their mothers) over two walls of the Cordilleras down to Buenaventura on the Pacific—to catch a foreign diplomat, if they could.

"They aren't hunting us poor damned English, German or American clerks," said this young man bitterly; "these girls are stalking some man with *position!* Lying on the beach, they can usually see what kind of man they are going to bed down with. The man has a more difficult job: *he's* sizing them up to see what they have in their bank accounts."

Among the many things left on the dock at Buenaventura by the big Grace liner before she continued her long voyage down the West Coast of South America was a pretty young Colombian girl and her new Austrian husband. They stood among a pile of bags and trunks that bore the labels of every Ritzy hotel in Europe. The young Austrian, in this spatter of tin roofs and mud, looked as if he had eaten something that had disagreed with him. They were facing a very real revolution in South American life. The exchange restrictions that some of these Republics had put on (to save their currency) meant that even people with the means to live abroad could no longer do so: Colombia, for instance, had put a tax of 23 per cent on all sums sent out of the country. The result was that thousands of well-to-do Colombians—and how they love Paris!—were coming back. And this girl knew what it meant. The handsome young Austrian aristocrat did not.

"I know exactly what it will be like," she told me, as our train squirmed up through the jungle towards the distant Andes. "Nothing! I shall do absolutely nothing! On the *hacienda* I shall sit around all day—after a short time, in a dressing gown. Kurt, who likes horses, will ride himself to death for a time. But he'll soon get over that. There'll be week-end parties, and we shall ride over for them to other *haciendas;* but this is all we shall have to say to each other: 'I wonder what it is like in Paris today? Don't you love London in May? Remember? . . .' Things like that.

"Then we shall go up to Bogotá. In Bogotá I shall play bridge all day. What else? Kurt will go to the Jockey Club—he'll play baccarat. We won't entertain much in the evenings, because people don't do that in Bogotá. And all the nice frocks I've worn in Paris will be no good to me up there—it's too cold, 8,500 feet, you know—and there aren't sufficient fires in the houses. . . . They think they are unhealthy.

"We'll go to the movies, of course. Now that I've married I can do that at any time. If I were a young girl, my young man could take me without escort to the six o'clock movie: for the nine o'clock performance he would have to take my father or brother along with us.

"And what shall we talk about in Bogotá? We shall say: 'I wonder what it is like in Paris today? Don't you remember London in May?'

"You see," she said decisively, "we can't change the life here—it's too strong for us. Therefore, this system of sending us abroad to be educated, to Paris or London, is all wrong. When we are forced to come back we both talk and feel like expatriated Europeans. We shall never forget what it was like in London and Paris."

SOME STRANGE
COMPANIONS

I took with me no good books on modern South America. There are none. I took, instead, the two best books that have ever been written about the Spaniard in the Americas: Prescott's *Conquest of Mexico* and *Conquest of Peru*, which I had read off and on for many years. The three volumes of the delightful little Everyman edition were on my bookshelves. So was *The Purple Land*, which I had packed, and a very poor book on Bolivar. Beside them today stands *The Naturalist on the River Amazon*, which, alas, I met only when it was pressed affectionately into my hands (his affection was for the book) by the United Press correspondent in the Argentine, just as my steamer gave her hoarse *baugh*, and we passed out into the red River Plate, and I said goodbye to South America for ever.

It was not until I was back in Europe that I read *Green Mansions*, and found what to me is the most beautiful of all Hudson's books, the nostalgic story of his youth in the Argentine: *Far Away and Long Ago*.

My own little Odyssey down the Andes, for so I think of it as I look back, now also seems far away and long ago. If I met Calypso, she was in the guise of a bottle of gin. And I saw Cyclops on many a mad night. But once, in Quito, I woke up to find a human head being dangled before my face—this time *real*. It was one of those heads shrunk by the Jivaro Indians to about the size of a large fist; an enterprising Indian had sneaked into my bedroom to sell it to me, for there was a fine of $400 if you were caught with one of these hunting trophies in Ecuador. The Government was trying to discourage the sport. From my yell, I should imagine that the Indian is running still. . . . I went to South America with the deliberate intention of going the limit. I had abandoned all hopes of propriety. I took a thousand dollars from the royalties of the *Transgressor*, and made the rest irrevocably over to my wife, so as to save the family from disaster. There has not been, nor ever will be, a woman like her in my life. I had an idea that, somewhere along the road down, I could take a hold on myself and pull up. Foolish man: I had no idea how inevitably the small Andean fevers, and drinking double-whiskeys at 9 a.m. at 9,000 feet (Quito), can turn a man into a Tropical Tramp. I have met several of them—unpleasant specimens, and not in the least romantic: that is only in books.

I needed the money I got from the U.P. as their South American correspondent; and, obliged to be more or less on my toes when I interviewed the South American Presidents, I did not let myself go entirely. I undoubtedly robbed myself of some highly interesting and irregular adventures, and if I had gone broke in South America, a thing I had rather looked forward to before the U.P. stepped in, I might have written some really good stuff. But I worked.

It was a good thing that I had no books on modern South America. That saved me from being deflected by other people's opinions. I got my data first-hand—from the American Consular reports, which I picked up at consulates and embassies along the way; from talks with angry politicos who disliked their present government; from prolonged bouts with American mining engineers, etc.; from drunks in the *cantinas* with some of my broken-down countrymen; from the Presidents of the countries themselves; from the foreign colony living in the capitals—and, at the very start, from two of the best men I could have found. One was the American Ambassador at Bogotá, a career man, among the best in our service. We were no longer sending out the "garter-snappers", wealthy U.S. business men (with an entirely mistaken idea of the gaiety and abandon of diplomatic life) who had been made ambassadors just because of their huge donations to the political campaign funds: we were sending out the very best men we could find to try to straighten our tangled relations with these touchy Latin Americans. The other man was an Englishman. Every time I called upon him he was in bed (he had a fever, he told me: he certainly looked like it): and this brilliant eccentric, of a type such as it seems only England can produce, gave me some ironic pictures of certain people in the Andes. His information was a little too hot for my newspaper service, but, if I had had the opportunity to use it, would have been invaluable for blackmail. He was as good as Scotland Yard.

I stuck to the beaten track, except for the five hundred miles of new road that had just been completed over the Andes, from Popayán to Quito. An amphibious and aerial journey, this—we were slung by steel cables over foaming torrents, and paddled across wide, high Andean rivers in native dugouts, past six volcanoes in a row with their peaks lost in the clouds. . . . Picturesque, but unexceptional. I admire the explorers, I revere some; but I did not try to emulate them. One look at that steaming coastal jungle, and I knew that it was not my cup of tea. I found it fascinating enough work to explore the South Americans.

I should like to call attention to a cardinal truth. The Latin Americans are petulant at the way big American business interests have been exploiting their natural resources. They are painfully in the right about that—though the United Fruit Company has probably done as much good for Guatemala as it has for itself—but they do not seem to realise that what the U.S. big business corporations have done to them is not one half of what they have done to the natural resources of their own United States. (Take Teapot Dome; the rape of the national forests and parks, at this very moment.) Nor do we Americans seem to realise it sufficiently. But there is another side to the picture, and one that suggests what is coming: I mean, the inspired actions of Big Business *outside* the corruption and stupidity of politics. The huge Weyerhauser lumbering interests have just planted a million or so acres on the Pacific slope with trees—*which are not to be touched for eighty years*. For patience (from Americans!) I think that can be taken as an all-time record. I talked a little about this when I interviewed the South American Presidents. I got some fine replies—even fireworks.

These hot-headed dictators are dramatic personalities. Like their South American statuary, they are grandiose and prancing, driven by passionate dreams of power and glory, which, as a matter of fact, they often fulfil. (Ronald Firbank could have written about them beautifully.) Their dreams come perhaps from their Spanish blood:

their daring from their memory of the impossible feats achieved by the old Conquistadores. In 1929 Captain Urbina, a Venezuelan political refugee, captured the Dutch fortress of Willemstad, on Curaçao, with only a revolver in his hand: not a good story to tell the Dutch at dinner. Then there are the liberators of undying memory: Bolivar, Sucre, and the *creole* adventurers who broke the grip of Spain. These heroes are to the Latin Americans what the Elizabethans are to the English. The modern leaders may look rather comic when you pick up a newspaper and see one of them riding at the head of his barefooted troops: they do not look so funny as seen from the business end of a revolver. When you meet them face to face, with some idea of the people and the problems they have to deal with—the illiteracy, the poverty, the fiery ambitions of rival would-be dictators, more often than not backed by Wall Street—you can't help but like them. If they have one common denominator, it is, strange to say, charm. Their simplicity can take your breath away.

When I asked "Bloody" Benavides, President of Peru—he had earned his sobriquet as far back as 1912 from his way of Maxim-gunning the Opposition—how, even in the South American way of reasoning, he could justify his statement that Peru had a constitutional government, considering the facts that he had just cancelled the last elections, which his opponent had won hands down; that he had abolished Parliament and was now ruling by decree; and that his Cabinet, as I sat there talking with him, was made up of four army generals, three colonels, and three captains of the regular navy—little pint-sized General Benavides tapped his chest and croaked: "A strong man was needed: I am he."

I had been warned that if I asked that question the interview would end forthwith. On the contrary, Benavides, who was the only man in the Presidential Palace not dripping with gold braid, slung one leg over another and set about educating me on the subject of Dictatorship: how such a thing as a free vote in illiterate South America, with only small groups trying to seize power at the top, would be as farcical as the same thing in Soviet Russia. (I could not go all the way with him: the other man I wanted to see in Peru was Raul Haya de la Torre, the young Peruvian aristocrat who was backing the APRA—the pro-Indian movement—and was 'on the run' at that moment, with both myself and the police looking for him.) Every President threw the Communist Menace at me; and only in Chile was there anything at all in it at that time—and in Chile only because of the awful wretchedness of the workers. This talk in the Palace at Lima was beside the fig-tree Pizzaro is alleged to have planted. I had passed his statue on the way to Benavides: there he was, sword uplifted, on his charger, in green bronze—and for a second or so I stood in awe before him. Peru still trembles to Pizzaro. And in the Cathedral, in a gold and crystal cabinet, I saw his alleged heart: looking like pressed caviare. . . .

When I asked Dr. Federico Páez, the Dictator of Ecuador (for that, with delightful frankness, was his official title), whether it wasn't true that he had been put in by the Army and that he was being kept in by the Army, he replied: "Of course. And as long as I pay the Army I shall stay here. But I told them that unless they let me do what I wanted I should go home." I love that 'go home'. "What do you want to do, Mr. President?"

"Get rid of you foreigners. I want you to give us our country back. I want Ecuador for the Ecuadorians." (Do you hear *Nostromo* there?) Ecuador had a population of only two millions—two-thirds as many as Chicago—and nearly all its public services, such as railways, electric light and power, streetcar companies and most of its biggest factories were owned and operated by foreigners, chiefly English and Americans. "Have you any programme of social reform, Mr. President?"

"Yes! The Indians! They form ninety per cent of our population. The Indians of Ecuador must be given a decent life. Why! Do you know that on some of those big *haciendas* over in the Oriente the big landowners think they have the power of life and death? They use it, too. When a big estate is sold in this country, the owner imagines he can sell the Indians with it! I am going to tame the big landowners."

You never see an Indian smile—in the Andes. They have no reason to. The man whom General "Bloody" Benavides spent a morning trying to make me describe, in my articles for the United Press, as a "monster from Moscow" *had* been to Moscow. But, having seen it, he was no communist. This afore-mentioned Raul Haya de la Torre (still alive and kicking) might have become almost a living Christ to the oppressed Indians of the Andes. He had gone into hid-

ing the night before I arrived in Lima: Benavides' police had shot
two of the Apristas, and almost got him. His movement was to restore
an *Indian civilisation* to the Indians. It was one of the most interesting cultural, political and psychological movements ever to appear
on the sad continent of South America. He finally gained sanctuary
inside the confines of Colombia's Embassy at Lima. Never venturing
from its grounds, he lived there for five years. He had been to Oxford, and passed his time giving English lessons, reading, writing,
and taking up cooking as a hobby. Bored with this incredible situation, the Peruvians finally allowed him to "escape" (in April 1954)
and he is now in Mexico, free once more to dream and scheme.

One of these Presidents, I confess, led me up the garden path. This
was General "The Horse" Ibáñez, then an ex-President in exile.
When I ran him to earth in Buenos Aires he was living up a back
street, almost incognito. It was a friendly tip from the bartender of
my Ritzy hotel that led me direct to him. He was then plotting his
counter-revolution, and buying the arms and ammunition with which
his forces were soon to fire, at point blank range, upon the university
students of Santiago, who had barricaded themselves inside the
city's telephone exchange. But his first act, after he had made me
explain myself at his door, was to open a little mahogany box on his
desk and take out two passports.

"Mine and my wife's," he said with a philosophical smile. "I applied for leave to go back to Chile two days ago. The Chilean Consul sent them back. I cannot go home." He almost wiped a tear from
his eye as he pointed to a photograph of three children on the wall.
"Mine. They are in Chile. I cannot bring them here. The exchange
is against us. I am too poor." Heart-rending.

I wish I could write that I knew at the time he was buying those
field guns. I didn't; any more than I knew that one day a man named
Juan Domingo Perón would seize power in the Argentine; that he
and his Evita would back this very Rightest Horse; and that after
two unsuccessful attempts General Carlos Ibáñez would again become President of Chile, which is what he is as I write. He is hard as
nails. Communism got started in Chile earlier than in any of the other
South American Republics, as I have said, because of the incredible
wretchedness of its working classes. They have a name for themselves, these tatterdemalions; they are the *rotos,* "the broken ones",

and you could see them any day in the Calle Prat, main business street of Valparaiso, squatting before the office of *El Mercurio,* Chile's biggest newspaper, which was owned, if memory serves me, by the Minister of Finance. It is said of Ibáñez that when he was in office in 1927–31, and had arrested a quantity of communist, or alleged communist, agitators he put them on barges to be towed by destroyers to Easter Island, 2,000 miles out in the Pacific. *"Tow them under!",* they say, was his order. No communist reached Easter Island, anyhow—not of that lot.

Anything less like a prancing dictator than Dr. Alfonso López, at that time President of Colombia, would be hard to imagine. With his horn-rimmed spectacles he reminded me of Harold Lloyd, as he led me briskly to a file in the Presidential Palace, pulled out a ledger, and slapped the long list of loans which, he said, New York banks had "forced" upon the South American statesmen. These loans stank to heaven. The carpet-bagging loan-salesmen raced each other to get there first, then rushed back to New York: where the banks, with their bond-annexe, retailed these loans to the American investing public, leaving it to hold the bag. They were still a live issue, these loans, in the Republics below Panama: at least, the Americans who were left holding them hoped they were. "And you have ruined us!" said López. "These loans have corrupted the morals of South America's politics." He was a banker himself; and all I could do in reply was summon the most innocent smile I could put on, and say: "Well, Mr. President, the—ah—South American politicians took the money." Under López, Colombia was fast becoming the most advanced republic in South America: under Laureano Gomez, four Presidents later, it was fast becoming the most reactionary.

Dr. Eduardo Santos, who became President after López, asked me to lunch at his attractive house on the outskirts of Bogotá, where his beautiful blonde wife gave me a knowing smile when he declared that no Presidency could tempt him from his enviable position as owner-editor of *El Tiempo,* the *Manchester Guardian* of South America. His wife's smile made me think I was talking to the next President of Colombia. Back from Africa in 1939 I was walking down the Rue Duphot in Paris, on my way to Prunier's for my ritual daily lunch of *moules en coquille, sauce Remoulade,* with two goblets of Chablis, when I saw a slight, dark man and a lovely blonde woman coming towards me. . . . I took off my hat. "Do I," I said, "have the pleasure of saluting the new President of Colombia?"

She gave a squeak of joy. "You do—you do—I told you he would take it!"

DOWN THE
ANDES

When in the company of Spaniards I always feel that I am a better man than I know I *really* am. There is a nobility about the Spaniard, with his feet in mud and blood and his head in the stars. I felt nothing of the kind in South America. It is an exasperating continent.

The three 14,000-foot walls of the Cordilleras divide the Republic of Colombia into practically four separate countries. Bogotá lies behind the second wall. These sky-scraping ranges are so high that the sun never gets over them until midday. Their western flanks are always cloaked in morning shadow. Seen from the coast, they show the sharp, jagged silhouette of broken blue glass—hall-mark of Colombia. When the sun does get overhead, it blazes down into valleys of surprising beauty. Silver rivers curve through the feathery green of bamboo forests and scarlet cachimba-trees. The cattle lie in white clumps on the green plains. Faded tile roofs of old *haciendas*, some of which have been there since the Spaniards' day, show as pink rectangles on the velvety green of lesser mountain slopes. Strange birds, found nowhere else in the world, not even in South America, undulate and hover over fields of rice and sugar-cane: birds the size of a sparrow, with only one ribbon-feather in their tail, about the width of a typewriter-ribbon and a foot long. They shed it after the mating season. As I was wandering through the bamboo forests of the Cauca Valley one day, thinking how like walking on the bottom of the sea it was, with those green sprays of bamboo clumps arching to cut off all sky from over my head, a long line of scarlet parrots passed me, a hundred or so of them, just like a line of scarlet fish

. . . White ibis slowly rise from the dead trees of stagnant swamps. A minute speck appears in the sky: the condor, taking in all the Andes in his glance. East of the last Cordillera, south to the head-waters of the Rio Negro and the Amazon, an area larger than France, lies a vast waste of jungle and plain in which you can find some of the most savage Indians and white men in the whole of South America.

Immediately your train has pulled out from the rust of Buenaventura beside its yellow river in the mangrove swamps of the Pacific, it begins a sixty-mile squirm through jungle so dense, dark and sickening that human beings rot in it. The word rot is in no sense an exaggeration, for the Negroes living in their wretched hovels of bamboo slats and banana leaves, among this stifling vegetation, are so eaten by yaws, and by hook-worm ulcers which seep into their calf-muscles and jerk their heels up permanently, that it is painful to look at them. Their black feet swollen to clown-like dimensions, they hop about with one shoulder held up by a stick. It is such human catastrophes that assemble in the clearings and beg you to buy something from them, wherever there is a railway station. No wonder they call this jungle "green hell". Every man, woman and child walks about with the inevitable *machete* in hand; for without that cane-knife there is no way of passing through this misanthropic under-growth, which shuts off for ever any possible glimpse of the hot sky. Steam. Vegetation that is obviously gasping and straining for air. Every tree with some creeper crawling around it and trying to choke it, so that you can't even tell tree from parasite. Lianas swinging in loops from tree to tree, like nets, and catching everything that falls from above, to begin another life where orchids grow a hundred feet above the spray of palms. Monkey world. Cactus, that occasionally has the affrontery to push out brilliant flowers of scarlet and yellow in this reek and rot of steaming shadows.

The conversation of Kurt, the Austrian aristocrat, took on, during this part of our road to Bogotá, a brilliant, fragile quality that was too much like the forced gaiety a brave woman puts up on the night before an operation. And a Dutchman in the train, who had been sent out to Colombia by an English Church organisation to find a spot for a colony of fifty refugees from Hitler, stared at this green hell and remarked: "I think I better go back to Yava!" (Java).

I shared an asthmatic motorcar with him over the 10,000-foot Quindío Pass. This wall of the Andes was drenched in mist—a good thing, perhaps, as it prevented us from seeing how far we had to drop if our frolicsome Colombian driver missed a turn. I'll swear he had two wheels over the edge at least a couple of times. And at 10,000 feet, where the high wind blew the mist away, showing us that even at that altitude there were still green forests, with purple flowers growing two hundred feet up in the trees, the Dutchman informed me:

"I shoot a elephant in Yava. He vos a mad elephant."

The unreality of Bogotá lies in suddenly finding yourself in a city of purring limousines, with shops not so much inferior to those of Piccadilly or the Boulevard des Capucines, after the emotional and geographical gamut you have run to get there: and in confronting, side by side with this luxury, files of resentful-faced Indians—bandy dwarfs, pattering barefoot through the traffic, and bearing anything from a packing-case to a grand piano on their backs. This is the city in which the riots and killings of 1948 reached a maniac ferocity that shocked even South Americans. And even as I write, on June 21st 1954, there is a photo in *Time* of eleven dead and thirty wounded students lying before the Presidential Palace in Bogotá, below the windows where I had had a whiskey-and-soda with that genial man, President Alfonso López. Firing on students is a pastime in South America.

And yet Bogotá was called, and with good reason, the Athens of the Andes. Everybody writes poetry in Bogotá, mooding under the cedars. Playing billiards in the Jockey Club was like being back in London. The young men there, sons of the immense landowners, had nearly all been to good English public schools, and then to either Oxford or Cambridge. The marker called the shots in English. Or rather, I think I should say that it was like being back in old Petrograd—at the New English Club on the Morskaya, playing poker with the young Russian bloods. Or, as some of these charming young Colombians were so archaic about their estates, it might remind you of Chevalier's in Moscow, that snowy night Olenin drank farewell to his comrades and set off in his sledge for the snowy Caucasus: except that, so far as I was able to find out, none of these big *hacienda* owners in South America ever had the heart-searchings about their duty to the peasants that so tortured the old Russian aristocracy. In fact, now that I come to think of it, the talk in the Jockey Club must have been identical with the talk at another Club—at the one whose immense plate-glass windows stare out on the river Arlanzón at Burgos, in Old Castile: heart of the Falange.

There was a young Colombian landowner in the Jockey Club who had just founded a political party, the *Derechistas*, which, his friends joyously informed me, was to the right of even that arch-Catholic reactionary, Dr. Laureano Gomez. When I asked him what his programme was, he smiled: *"Fan-tas-tique!"* It was he who told me I should be mad if I did not go up to Popayán and see Colombia's "perfect poet", William Valencia. "He is the one thing in this country we can be proud of!" He also told me they were taking bets that I should be unable to get over the Andes at this time of the year, in the rainy season: point being that the Andes are made of mud, and that mud slips; and if the rains are too heavy, and there happens to be an earthquake tremor (there is about a tremor a day in the Andes), the mountainside just slides down. I saw that very thing up outside Ipales, which had just been flattened by an earthquake; there was a gash in the mountain and a slide under which an entire village had been buried, men, women and children: some three hundred human beings interred for eternity. They were not going to try to dig them out. It was an imposing grave. So I shipped my heavy stuff by rail to Popayán; flew over the cloud-decked Cordilleras in a little German plane with two Dachshunds and a pilot smoking a big cigar under the NO SMOKING! sign; and hired a car at Cali. . . .

During the following days I came much nearer to the Colombians —days on the *haciendas*. I found a composure, once you got them off politics, that you would never expect from the South American temperament. I stopped at one *hacienda* in the Cauca Valley (paradise!) that had been in the wife's side of the family since the days of early Spanish rule. She believed, and it may have been so, that she was a direct descendant of the Conquistadores. She was of pure Spanish blood—first requirement for aristocracy in South America. The low buff ranch house had oil-paintings in its dining-room of the Archbishop of Quito in 1726, and of other stern-faced prelates, all members of this family; and of the young patriot, also of this family —his statue now stands in the main square of Cali—who was shot by the Spaniards in 1810 when he tried to lead the revolution against them. The leather backs of the drawing-room chairs had been tooled at Cordova in Spain. . . . And over coffee the Señora, who was then packing to spend a year in her Paris apartment, told me how terrible it was with the servants "these days": the Indians just would not work! A neighbouring *haciendado*, who had ridden over, pointed to where the blue peaks of the Andes reared above us in a thunder of clouds:

"*They* live up there," he said, "the Indians. But they are in another world—mentally. We just have no contact with them. When I was young I tried to get an old chief to teach me their language. 'Why should I?' he asked. 'Then you will know our secrets.'"

They drove me over to see that great gentleman General Alfredo Vásquez de Cobo, who had begun his astonishing career as an attaché at the Court of St. James when Queen Victoria was on the throne. He was a large man—very large—with an air of ease, foreign travel and good cigars. Standing beside him were the two direct descendants of Louis XIV of France: the nephews of Don Carlos, the Spanish Pretender.

"You must try my sugar!" he said, putting on his old straw hat and leading us out to his mill. It was, like his home, a most modest affair. Indians and Negroes were grinding cane with a water-wheel, propelling wooden cogs. They were boiling down a sweet called *Penula*—special delight of the peon and aristocracy. "You must give me a good write-up about this," said de Cobo. "It will increase my profits!" I told him I would cable New York at once. It tasted like a cross between maple syrup and butter-toffee; and its crunch was delicious. He led us back to his tiny two-storied ranch house: the descendants of *Le Roi Soleil* rushed to pull out his chair. The faintest flutter of those bullfroggy humorous eyes, and they were off to obey him.

It was General Vásquez de Cobo, then Minister in Paris, who, when he heard how "that Peruvian fellow, Vigal!" had ridden into the town of Leticia and imprisoned its Colombian Governor, dropped the portfolio and donned the sword: bought two steamships and a battery of French 75s: press-ganged Colombians wherever he could catch them—in Paris, London, Monte Carlo: sailed across the Atlantic to Para, up the Amazon, up the Putumayo River, and—"I let drive at those damned Peruvians!"

His 75s outranged the Peruvian artillery, but that fellow Vigal had decamped. Instead, a Peruvian aeroplane flew over one of his steamships, the *Highland King,* and dropped three bombs. De Cobo closed his froggy eyes as he told us "I prayed to Heaven!" He put his hand a foot above the floor: "They were no higher than that over my head, and then—*boom-boom-boom*—they all fell harmlessly. . . ." He saw me smiling. "You are sceptical? You do not believe in Divine Intervention?" "Indeed, Sir, I do—or I should not have met you." He loved that, and pounded his knee. That fine old gentleman knew the secret of living. Simplicity, simplicity, simplicity.

The great poet, Valencia, was different. He was ill, and sent word into Popayán for me to drive out to his *hacienda.* A young engineer in Cali who was courting one of Valencia's daughters (and omitted to tell me that he had been forbidden to set foot on the property) offered to direct me. This might have accounted for the poet's air of almost painful dignity as he came out, wrapped in a camel's-hair dressing-gown, to greet me. He looked enough like Shakespeare to make no difference. The Colombians talk as if there were no difference. Before discussing anything at all poetic or political he purposefully conducted me into his study, where I noted in succession a signed photograph of d'Annunzio; a letter from Hindenburg, framed with a silver medal he had given Valencia; the last letter of Simon Bolivar, written from his death-bed—this under its own private light, like a painting in an art gallery; a case full of glittering decorations and ribbons conferred on Valencia by foreign governments; and a glass statuette of Gandhi, sitting impishly on the poet's ink-well.

He led me through a long darkened hall, with a floor of old polished parquet and chairs of ancient tooled leather bearing the Valencia coat-of-arms and brought over by the Counts of Valencia to this same *hacienda.* We went out on to a small veranda overlooking a little stream; and there Valencia sat himself down on a couch covered with black panther skins—he understood the effect!—and began to talk of the Europe he had known so well: the Vienna of Franz Josef, the Germany of Nietzsche.

He told me how, to get in to talk to the great philosopher, he had disguised himself as a servant. Nietzsche was old, Valencia was young; they formed a friendship, the poet told me, that had had a great influence on his life. But the superman had not materialised. Valencia looked around him now with the hopeless air of wondering why it was—why no man in Colombia could call a stop to this madness that the Liberal government called Progress, and why he should be told that if he failed to cultivate his vast estates (they reached out of sight to the wall of the Andes) he must let someone else do it. There were three conspirators in Popayán, he told me, who he *knew* were in the pay of Moscow. Anarchy! madness! death!—that was what was coming.

"They have let the tiger loose," he said weakly, plucking at his little grey goatee. "And they have put it into the hands of children."

Politics poison all our lives. The instant he began to talk about the Colombian government, this great literary figure became quite childish. He saw a communist behind every bush. I no longer heard the voice of a poet: it was the voice of an angry landowner, disfigured by hate. But there was not the least doubt that he believed what he said. He was the perfect type of the old pure-blooded Spaniard of the Andes, still living in a world that had ended with that last letter of Simon Bolivar's on his study wall.

Mountains have stronger personalities than mere mortals, though it is hard to define their distinctions. Riding horseback across the Western Caucasus, where I spent days in forests in which no major tree had ever been felled, and there were glades of azaleas and lilies, I always had the feeling that the mountains were as old as time, and covered with the dust of Asia. As I fished some clear stream in the Canadian Rockies, all the world seemed as fresh as if I had come there on the first day of Creation. In the Andes I never had mountain-feeling. The constant sense of unreality you experience in crossing them comes from their everlasting greenness. At altitudes above 10,000 feet you expect to see rock-masses, but flowers and forests grow in the Andes to above those heights. When you look down into the valley at the two towns of Pasto and Tulcan, one in Colombia and the other in Ecuador, both lying at 9,000 feet, this valley below you is bright green, and the tall trees in the mist-drenched pass have wild, spikey pineapples growing like fungus in their branches, other queer spines with reddish flowers, and clusters of purple blooms, like wild azaleas, a hundred feet up along their limbs. This is sultry rather than imposing. In the Andes I have never felt the *wisdom* of mountains.

The five-hundred-mile road which had just been completed between Popayán and Quito was, except for chance landslides, as easy to get across as any mountain highway in Canada or the United States. The warnings I had had to listen to, down in Cali and Bogotá, of the two bridges which had been swept away were nonsense—there never had been any bridges. We crossed the Rio San Jorge in thirty-foot Indian dugouts. . . . We had three nuns for company: they were taking a weeping novice up to some convent in the Andes. The old Mother Superior wept herself as the girl said goodbye to her family. Even the driver was moved as we watched this young Indian girl clutching her father in their farewell kiss. But her tears were not over renouncing this world—from what I had seen, and was to see, of Andean nuns, she was going to take a very active and useful part in it. The Mother Superior was a German. She was much intrigued by my case of trout rods and asked me where I intended to use them. I replied "Wherever there are trout"—a logical answer that made her laugh out loud.

Quito provided me with some grand drinking companions. The best of them was an ex-regular British army officer with a little toothbrush moustache: Captain Erskine Locke, who had just knocked out two of his front teeth against his diving helmet when he had tripped, walking along the bottom of a lagoon with André Roosevelt. Twice a week, when the railway train got up from Guayaquil, it brought iced prawns from the Pacific. At 9 a.m., when the bar opened, Locke and I sat there most mornings eating prawns—strips of fresh, uncooked fish lying on little platters of red peppers and rings of onion; and for lunch we had a marvellous fresh salad of alligator pear and beetroot on beds of lettuce. All downed with a pinch-bottle of Haig & Haig.

Locke was leader of the Andes-Amazon Expedition, and had just returned from a trip on which, trying to get around a spur of the Andes, he had fallen and broken all his ribs on one side when he hit a ledge. He had watched seventeen of his Indian porters desert him; but one, one only, took the risk of climbing down to him, and nursed and fed him on that ledge until his ribs stuck together again

—whereupon Captain Erskine Locke, and that one noble Indian, went on; over into the steaming unmapped jungles on the far side, in his quest to find the Phantom Indians. . . . When he eventually got back to Quito he gave the War Department his maps, which showed that theirs had some rivers on the far side of the Andes running the wrong way—and had been *persona non grata* with the Ecuadorian Army ever since. Some years later, when I was one of the first to appear on the very-experimental British television at Alexandria Palace, I took Locke and the Jivaro Indians as my offering. Locke's father and brother happened to be in Selfridges that day; and I got a letter from his brother: "You can imagine!—my father and I were looking at the screen, and there you were—talking about Erskine! How is he? Where is he?" I had to write him that I did not know. Locke came halfway down to Guayaquil "for a farewell gab" with me, as he put it—he was to go off on another trip around the headwaters of the Amazon—and during the war I read in the *Times* "British explorer dies in Ecuador. . . ."

It was André Roosevelt who came into my room at 8 o'clock one morning, gave me a prod, and said "The President of Ecuador awaits you!"—for it was at this ungodly hour that Federico Paez liked to give his audiences. André and his equally inspiring wife had just made what I believe was the first movie ever taken under water—the time Erskine lost two of his front teeth. They were all out of the same bin, these people: at the word *adventure* they would shy like a horse, yet that is what they were living. One could feel at home and at ease with them. They had made their choice, and put money and 'success' below getting the best out of life. Their talk was young. To be in such company was like a renewal. We had all seen enough of the greed, cruelty and ignorance of man not to care what the 'preachers' said. I knew then, down in the Andes, that I should find what I was after.

I caught a dirty little steamer at Guayaquil, that former pest-hole of yellow fever and still an uninviting prospect of mud, rats, mosquitoes, bubonic, and flying cockroaches two inches long, and went down the Guayas River through the floating islands of water-hyacinths. There the "bends" hit me, and I curled up like a shrimp. It was to be a year before I ever felt healthy again, or was without a low fever.

I had been in South America some time now, and it was nearing Easter—carnival-time. And our ship stopped at every port. After the green, steaming jungle of Colombia and Ecuador, the coast was just one long burning desert from shortly south of Guayaquil to Valparaiso—about two and a half thousand miles. At Paita, where we were to unload 900 tons of tin and steel pipes for the oil concession, we were told that the town was in the middle of a religious fête. "And that means," yelled down our gloomy chief officer to a man on a lighter, "that we've got to lie in this —— port all day?" "Sure," yelled back the white boss of the stevedores. "These people got to live and eat and play just the same as you do, don't they?" We all hoped that our weary Wallace Beery of a first officer would shout back "NO!" but he just said "—— all South America!" I went ashore, got tangled up with a religious procession, found my stateroom steward, plastered, in a *cantina,* and woke up the next afternoon to see that our ship was keeping pace with the derisive pelicans . . .

I got some fishing in the Laja River in southern Chile—my first fish was a 6-lb rainbow; my next, 5½—such as I never dreamed could be in this world. And then I crossed the Andes again. So eventually I got to railhead in Patagonia; crossed the drought-stricken plains, with their horror of dried hoof-marks around each dead watering-trough; ran down General "The Horse" Ibáñez in Buenos Aires; and between Rio de Janeiro and Casablanca, on a slow boat, completed my articles and began to shape them for a book.

It is practically impossible, they say, to write a good book about South America. I was not, as my own book showed, the exception that proves the rule.

CRACK-UP

After a few months back in Europe I decided to go to the Institute of Tropical Medicine at Hamburg. There were several low-grade Andean fevers that were still puzzling the doctors at that time. My case was complicated, for it would be very difficult for them to tell which of my complaints was due to altitude and which to alcohol. And it was a German doctor himself—I met him at a cocktail party at the American Consul-General's—who said: "Once you get into the hands of the specialists they will regard it as a point of professional honour to find something wrong with you—and, of course, one can always find *something* wrong with anybody! We are a thorough lot, you know." So when I was shown into my room in the *Hotel Vier Jahreszeiten,* looking out on the lovely Alster, I said to myself "This is the place for me!" And I sat down to finish my book on South America.

The fresh breeze inspired me (not that the book showed it), and I wandered about that fine old city, trying a different place every day for my lunch; sat in the beer halls; ate shrimp mayonnaise; listened to the *Lieder* singers; and in the evenings usually went to a little cabaret I had found on the Grimm Strasse, where there was a sailor with an accordion who loved playing *Wien! Wien! Nur du allein* . . . as much as I liked hearing it. It brought back the old Europe. Returning early in the morning from an all-night session, I found the proprietor of the Four Seasons on its door-step. "You have lost your hat, Mr. Farson?" "Yes, I usually lose my hat when I'm drinking." "Would it be impolite to ask you where you have been?"

"Not at all. I've been down in a little place on the Grimm Strasse, overlooking the Canal." "The *Grimm* Strasse! Mr. Farson—you are lucky that your hat is all you lost on the Grimm Strasse." He then told me what I already knew: that the Nazis and the communists regarded the Grimm Strasse as a favourite fighting-ground—I had already, one midnight, seen two groups of dark figures flailing away at each other: though who was slugging whom, and for why, I did not stop to find out. "Yes," I said. "It's a *gemütlich* little night-place . . ." And I hummed *Wien! Wien!* for him. "Oh, I know, I *know!*" he said. He put up a protesting hand: "How that song brings back the old days. . . ." We agreed that we should never see that Europe again.

In his position he had to be professionally jolly about the Nazis, but the doom that was hanging over Europe saddened both of us. I think he took it for granted that I knew how he felt. At another cocktail party given by the U.S. Consul-General I again met the German doctor who had warned me off tropical specialists. He regaled the party by telling us how the German girls were having the face of Hitler tattooed on their breasts. "And if they are very enthusiastic, some of the young ladies will have Goering on their other breast." That brought the house down.

But, alas, he went on, those breasts would not always remain as firm as they once were. "So I told them it would be rather unpatriotic of them, if . . . well, you know." When the laughter had died down, he said "So I remove the Führer." He was a very amusing man; and, getting him into a corner, I showed him a ghastly anchor tattooed on my right forearm. I had found it when I woke up one morning in the Canal Zone: a gaudy little affair, with a red stock, done with the electric needle. "Could you free me from that?" I asked. "Per-fectly! Nothing at all. Come to my surgery." And he gave me his card. I went there at four the next afternoon, taking a pretty German girl I had met at the party with me. He gave me a local, took his scalpel, and in a jiffy cut a shape out of me about the size of a magnolia leaf and as thick as a banana skin. He then put in six stitches, and handed me the removed bit of myself in an antiseptic little bottle. I dropped the bottle down a street drain when the girl and I had walked around the corner. I returned several days later to have the stitches taken out. "Well—ta-ta," he said. "Goodbye. I hope you have some good goose shooting."

I had intended to go up to Schleswig-Holstein. What day I saw the doctor, what day I left Hamburg, I don't know: those last two weeks in Hamburg had been a shambles. I haven't an idea how it came that I should be there, but, changing trains, I found that I was headed for the Harz mountains; and, feeling suddenly sick, I hurriedly got off at the station the train was halted at: Quedlinburg. And there I felt too ill to go on. My German is weak, so the only thing I could think of was to tell the taxi-driver to take me to a *Nervenarzt*, a sanatorium. I wanted a bed! *"Ja! Ja!"* he answered instantly and with glee. It was a long drive. Finally the car turned down an avenue of pines . . . and there I began to shiver from the chills I knew so well. I had a violent infection. Streptococci.

I lay there two days. By then my arm was bloated. A doctor was hastily summoned from Quedlinburg. He drove me immediately there, to the hospital, in his car, and operated on me at once. This time I was split open like a kipper. Just below my elbow, almost down to the bone, was a cut over four inches long when I saw it at the first dressing. It looked, with all its gaudy colours, like the Grand Canyon of Colorado. I came out of the anaesthetic on the table as they were finishing the operation; the mask was clapped back on my face. And then—I still can't be certain why they allowed this to happen—I came out again on the table while they were bandaging. "So!" said that bloody butcher, smiling down at me. He was a German ex-Navy surgeon, and one of the hottest Nazis I ever came up against; but he did have some lingering sense of humour, if you knew where to look for it. He laughed and pounded his fat knee when I told him how I had woken up in the dark the first morning, to hear a chorus of voices singing beside me: "I thought I had at last got to Heaven! Heavenly Choir, you know." Then—suddenly—his preciseness got the better of him: "But that is their church! The nurses' chapel is in the room next to yours." I had not known it, but I was being nursed by nuns. And those nuns were very good to me.

I stayed in that hospital a little over two months. The infection had not been successfully drained by the cut. The gland in my arm-pit began to swell, and it looked as if I should have to have another operation. Meanwhile, I was learning a lot about Germany: I saw two Germanies inside that very hospital, every day. Apart from the rather astonishing fact that in this boastfully pagan Germany the nuns could still continue with their duties, the former head of the hospital had been allowed to remain at his post. He was not a Nazi. A slight figure, almost painfully unassertive, one would have thought he would have been unable to hold his own, even in normal times, against the overbearing type which the Nazis had put in; but he managed it. I saw this play between the two men every time I went to the room where they did the dressings. This room was where the out-patients came to have their wounds dealt with. I saw a bull of a German there, a Quedlinburg butcher, who had nearly lopped off his own thumb with a cleaver. It was a ghastly sight: the flesh had rotted, and, for a time, I could see the bone sticking out of it. The non-Nazi surgeon turned his head away when the big ex-Navy surgeon did that dressing; but the butcher himself never winced. I sometimes even wondered if that bovine man was not insensitive to pain: there was something so 'low' about him. All meat. I sat on a stool, and the Nazi surgeon clipped me: *clip-clip-clip* went his shining scissors, clipping away the proud flesh. I felt that if that blond beast of a butcher could take it I must take it also; but it had me at the breaking point several times, for during these agonising few minutes the Nazi would talk about what Hitler was doing for Germany—"*We* shall . . ." etc., etc.—and as he boasted he would go through a pantomime, as if he were Atlas bearing the world on his shoulders. "Look here," I said to him one morning, when I felt I couldn't stand this much longer—I still can't be certain whether he put me through it on purpose—"I wish to God you wouldn't talk politics when you are dressing me. Come in to my room and do it." He just laughed. Then I did faint: I fell off the stool, and woke up to find they had put me back on it—and that the big ex-Navy man was patting me: "Kein Wort! Kein Wort!" he was saying. A few days later, when I was already on the table waiting to be anaesthetised for my second operation, he came into the theatre, gave me a cheery nod, took a look where they had prepared my upper arm the night before—and then began to *feel* it, with unwashed hands. "You're all right," he said. "That thing has gone down. I shan't have to operate."

For one big reason I was grateful to have reached that hospital. My last days in Hamburg had been disgusting. Anyone who has ever fought against drink will know what I mean when I say that I loathed seeing the daylight come into my room. A thing I never do unless I am desperate, I slept with the blinds down. I never knew what time it was when I woke up; I never wanted to wake up. I wanted to be out of this world: sleep was the only way I could escape. My bedclothes were like sheets thrown in the laundry basket; in the paroxysms of my nightmares I had twisted them all over the bed. My clothes lay wherever I had flung them before falling into bed—I even woke up fully dressed without even having had the decency to take my shoes off. My suit-cases were a revolting mess: books, clothes, suits, all piled in confusion. My typewriter, untouched, was a constant reproach to me. While I had been finishing the book I had hardly taken a drink. For this, through life, has been my saving grace; I can't write one word when I'm drinking. When I was writing happily, the proprietor of the *Vier Jahrszeiten* and I had many pleasant chats; now I saw that he was trying to avoid me. Perhaps the most humiliating day I have known in Germany was when my baggage was being taken out of the lift as I was leaving, and I saw him standing by the desk; he turned and walked into his office. That was terrible.

So now, I thought, if there was anything in me at all, some solid bit of strength somewhere, I had better set out to find it. I was tired of making a fool of myself, and I was beginning to get frightened. There was no question of any 'cure', of course, while I was in this hospital: but here was the spot where I could start to make a comeback, to put it crudely. For I intended to do just that; and the fact that I did intend to do it was, I knew, the most hopeful decision I had taken for years—*if* I could hang on to it: I couldn't use my right arm at all, for it nearly drove me mad if I put it down and let the blood rush back into it. I asked the nuns if they could get me a stenographer. The special nun who had been detailed to look after me, because she spoke fair English, said there was a "very nice and pretty young lady" who visited the patients. She came in. She *was* nice, and very pretty in a faded way, but there was a dulled look in her blue eyes that made me wonder what had happened to her and why she should go in for such "good works"; and she produced a frowning little *fraülein* who took down every word, dash, dot, comma and full stop, meticulously, but whose special frown, at

times, let me know that she did not agree with what I was saying.
A friend of mine had written me, while I was still at Hamburg, to
remind me that I had promised him an article for his magazine: I
sent him this one, called *What's On Your Mind?*—a semantic study of
the tripe embodied in all political slogans. I am sure that the frowning little typist reported that I was a fault-finding foreign journalist.

When I was able to get up and go for a walk, the Visitor, the
"nice and pretty young lady", asked me to have coffee with her.
Quedlinburg is a lovely old city. The Thousand Year Old Capital,
the Germans call it—walled in 922 by Henry the Fowler. It had a
charming little Opera House which the biggest singers came to from
Berlin; its mediaeval city hall had an elegant little restaurant in the
basement, with spotless linen, proud but friendly waiters, and some
of the best food I have had anywhere in Europe. A beautiful castle,
church and convent looked down on this delightful old city from
their green hill. The Visitor belonged to an old Quedlinburg family,
and had a few of her friends to the café. Among them was a German
whose father owned some of the immense seed-farms along the Harz
mountains. Fritz was a delightful chap, one of the very best.

He was an S.A. man; but when I asked him, after I got to know
him better, why he never wore the Brown Shirt, he laughed: "Oh,
I haven't got time for all that damned nonsense. I'm too busy. I told
them to go and parade by themselves." "Don't they ever hold it
against you?" "Not a bit. They know how I stand. We have all grown
up together." I never could tell how Nazi he was; but that he was
almost exalted by the way Hitler was making a new, strong Germany there could be not the slightest doubt. He made me a member
of a little *Stammtisch,* a puzzling cross-section of Quedlinburg, which
included an old grey-haired professor, head of the schools for that
city (definitely not a Nazi), a young engineer, building a big steam
laundry in the town (very Nazi indeed), and another young landowner (much like Fritz in his nationalism): and I never left a session
of those talks over bottles of Moselle with a clear conviction of what
the group stood for. I don't think they knew themselves—I am talking about the inner struggle which must have been developing in
many Germans between pride in a reviving Germany and a full belief in National-Socialism. One late afternoon, when Fritz and I were
standing before a lighted bookshop window, a smart young man in

the black S.S. uniform came along. "Hel-lo, Fritz!" he called, seizing
him by the arm. One of his own arms was in a sling. Fritz nodded
at it and laughed: "So your head was too hard to break—yes?" The
other smiled and said: "I was leading when my car went off the
road." Fritz told me afterwards that his friend had just come out of
hospital: he had been driving for the S.S. in an Italian competition
when the smash occurred. "He's a Baron," laughed Fritz. "That's his
castle you see on the hill beyond my father's farms. He's my best
friend."

There was snow on the ground. One of the reasons we had been
lingering before that lighted bookshop window was to enjoy the
warmth we could feel, even if vicariously, through its heavy plate-
glass. The illumination had been made especially sunny and alluring,
for there was a Colonial Week on in Germany; and this window was
full of nothing but books on Africa—with cardboard cut-outs showing
Germans leading head-safaris through the African bush; German explorers reaching the Great Lakes; German big-game hunters sitting
on the top of dead elephants . . . daring, virile, dauntless Germans:
supermen. There were books on German West Africa, East Africa;
and on men like Karl Peters. . . . I noticed that at least half a dozen
German authors had written about Peters. "Tell me," I asked Fritz,
"do you really want your colonies back? Do they mean so much to
you? How serious are you in your demand for them?" "To be honest,"
he said, "I don't know. Some of us do. Von Epp. People like that.
Anyway—we're going to get 'em." He slapped me on the shoulder.
"You will, like hell," I said. He laughed: "Let's not argue about it—
you and I." He pointed to the window. "But tell me—wouldn't you
like to go to Africa?"

"I think so. I think that's where I shall go," I said.

So it was when I was standing in the snow before that enticing
window-display in old Quedlinburg that the idea first came to me.
There was the road. It is rather ironic that it should have been German propaganda that caught me. And the road had a big gap in it,
a dark abyss, before I could ever get to Africa. I used the rest of that
winter and the spring, most of which I spent in Munich, trying to
learn as much as I could about just how serious the Germans were
in this matter of getting back their colonies. It brought me no further
than what Fritz had said: "Some of us. People like von Epp. . . ."

But at that, I found that the Germans knew more about their colonies, even though they had lost them, than the average Englishman knows about his—or cares. Yet I did not go to Africa to investigate and write a book; while I was staring into that window in Quedlinburg I saw myself leading a completely new life. I wanted to break with everything.

The surgeon who was not a Nazi was waiting for me one afternoon outside the hospital in his little two-seater Opel. He took me to a café packed with cadets from the big flying school outside Quedlinburg, the biggest in Germany. How these young men kept human shape after the number of cream-puffs they ate is beyond comprehension, but they were some of the smartest, most physically fit young officers I have seen anywhere. Their perfection was something to think about, considering that we all knew what they were going to be used for. And they knew it, too: there was a dog-on-the-leash eagerness about every one of them. "Pity, isn't it?" said the non-Nazi surgeon. "Yes," I said, "it's a damned shame." That was all we needed. In this indirect manner he could always say what he wanted me to understand. He told me he had been a doctor in the big Naval Hospital at Kiel. "We had a special ward there for cases from the Far East—from Kiao-Chow, you know. We had some very bad cases from there. Syphilis. It seemed to be almost a syphilis of its own: we used to call it Black Syphilis. And we kept those men apart from the others." He went on to tell me of the various treatments they used; how even a Wasserman test could not be trusted to reveal syphilis— "The spirochetes can linger in the *walls* of the arteries, you know, and a blood test could miss that." He told me how he had given the 'malaria' treatment for syphilis; how they got the serum from Vienna; how it had to be kept at just such-and-such a temperature, otherwise it would go off; and how he himself had killed one or two patients.

"But there was one case," he went on, "that I shall never forget. This was a colonel. He walked in looking the very picture of health —I have seldom seen such a fine figure of a man—he was really a beautiful man, only fifty years old. He just said that he 'felt queer inside'. We asked him his history: he said frankly that he had had syphilis out in the East, but had been cured of it years before. It seemed almost unnecessary to take a Wasserman on him but we did of course. We always do. And the next morning when I went in to see him he was *dead*. There he was, not a blemish on him—dead." "Syphilis?" "Oh—*yes!* He was all rotten inside. . . . I have never seen such a case."

"It was strange," he went on. "So perfect outside—and so——" He looked around the room. "And sometimes, you know, even a nation can be like that."

He had a friend who was a German U-boat ace—the Commander who wrote *The Sunken Fleet,* about when the Germans sank their ships at Scapa Flow. He took me up into the Harz mountains to see him. This former hero, a famous ace, had a Jewish wife and two children. The two children could not go to the Quedlinburg schools. The U-boat man was writing articles, mostly about the seafaring life, and mailing mimeographed copies all over the world; he had a good market, he told me, in South America. He got a few pesos in this way. They were living in the game-keeper's shack of a big estate. There was no rancour. They gave us coffee and cakes—the two children were very excited, as if the cakes were a treat—and as we drove away the doctor said: "A little hard to believe, isn't it? A fine man like that—finished."

I went to live in a hotel in Quedlinburg, going to the hospital every other day for my dressings. The hotel was perfect: nowhere in England or the United States will you find hotels of such excellence as you used to find in the small cities of Germany and mountain Austria. One day the Nazi surgeon asked me to dine at his home. "I'll be in my Surgery when you come." I went there and found two surly-looking types I had seen in the out-patients' dressing-room at the hospital. He was very rough with them. As he led me back into the house to introduce me to his pretty blonde wife, he said, quite casually, "Nasty types, weren't they?" I replied that they did not look very pleasant. "Yes. I sterilised them." "You—*what?*" "Yes. Didn't spoil their pleasure. But *they* won't breed any more. We've got to keep our blood clean." When I asked him where the two rough-looking characters came from, he said "Oh, they're just Poles. They came here to work in the seed fields. Well, they won't plant any of their own seed."

Fritz's home was a haven. The golden-straw harvest-crown still hung on its porch. "We have a harvest festival every year. All our own workers, the horsemen and foremen; we have them all here and we dance and drink. We have hundreds of Polish girls on our farms —you should have been here!" He gave me a wink, for which his wife reprimanded him. They had just been married, and they sent me a picture of their first-born the next year: just a week or so before war started. "And we will now have some more of Atlas," said Fritz. Atlas was a pig they had killed, and that we ultimately ate from blood-sausage to hoofs. Fritz loved a good hock; and we drank most of his cellar.

When I wasn't drinking with Fritz I was drinking in the hotel. I began to drink in the mornings. The bookshop in Quedlinburg had a row of Tauchnitz, and they got me some of the English translations of the German overseas propaganda, about the moral right to have back their colonies. As if morals, about anything, could have concerned me much then! I should have returned to London, but I made the excuse that I wanted to get my arm soundly healed before I left, and that the hospital was so conveniently near. This was inertia; I was like a chip in an eddy. The hotel was very comfortable, too comfortable; I didn't bother to get up, I just ordered the wine from the waiter and drank it in bed. I didn't go out to see Fritz any more. I soon began to skip dressings. At any rate, these were now trivial. I always carried some dressings for my leg. And getting out as far as the chemist one day, I bought bandages, gauze, cotton, and a big bottle of hydrogen peroxide. When I thought my arm was getting a bit smelly and sticky I put on a fresh pad. Then reading ceased to mean anything to me; I did not have even that excuse left. The eddy swirled round and round; and I drifted, in agony, until I could get enough drink in me to doze off in a torpor again. Then I got so that I had to steady myself with the back of a chair, which I pushed before me, to cross my own room to the bathroom toilet. I knew this could not go on. One morning I telephoned Fritz and told him I was going to Munich. "Wait a minute," he said. "I'll be right over. But why Munich?" When he came I told him I was going to try to reach Professor Bumke. He asked: "But why such extremes? All you have to do is to stop."

"Ha-ha! *Stop?*" I said. "I can't."

That was the point I had reached. I knew it. I was lucky to have such a good friend. Fritz helped me pack, and when he went down to the desk to look up trains I asked him to have them send up my bill. I took quick advantage of his absence to have a good stiffener of cognac. This was a bottle of Martel that I kept on hand for when I came out of my nightmares at three or four in the morning. It would have been awful, lying there in the dark, to wait for the wine-room to open, and I could not begin telephoning for drinks before they had even started getting the breakfasts. Even I did not have enough gall for that. This was a fresh bottle; I did not bother about a glass, but took three or four full swigs and had it stowed in my little handbag when Fritz came up. I was shocked when the waiter appeared with my account to see the ghastly part that just drinks made up. I showed it to Fritz: "There you are. I have been on a liquid diet, you see. Pretty awful, isn't it?" He was stupefied: "Well, a *Bummel* is a *Bummel*," he said, shaking his blond head; "but this. . . ." I told him he need not say any more. He telephoned his wife and they drove me to the station. They walked along beside me as the train slowly pulled out, and the last I saw of those two good souls they were standing at the end of the platform waving their handkerchiefs. Then I pulled my head in and swayed along the train until I found the dining-car, whereupon I sank down. . . .

How, or when, I reached Munich I don't know. It was morning when I woke up in the *Vier Jahreszeiten*—there is a hotel of that name in Munich too. I was lying on the bed, fully dressed. My bags, all of them, were stacked beside the table. Feeling that I hardly dared expect such luck, I opened the handbag in which I kept my pyjamas and shaving-kit, and found the bottle of Martel was still there. Anyone who has suffered the misery of heavy drinking will know the feeling of *power* that gave me. I was safe. I got a glass from the bathroom, poured it half full, and sat there sipping it neat. I did not intend to dirty this nest the way I had the *Vier Jahreszeiten* at Hamburg. I would put up a good show—not that I could possibly tell whether my sly drinker's artfulness ever fooled anyone. When the cognac had given my nerves the peace I wanted I went across to the bed and pulled the bedclothes down, rumpling them to show I had slept in it; I then got into pyjamas and bath-robe, dumped the other suit-cases upside down on the floor, took out about two weeks' back laundry, made a list of it, and tied it up in a shirt. I collected my books and put them in piles on the table with my type-

writer—they would look impressive—and then rang for the maid. I
watched her furtively when she came in, but her face gave no clue.
For all I could tell, she had not been "on" the night before—there
was a gap in my memory from almost the moment I had got my bottle of Rotwein in the dining-car, after Quedlinburg, to when I woke
up in this room. And I did not want to have it filled. I was getting
used to these blackouts of memory, and how I got to this room, or
even from the station, with all my bags intact was a thing I had no
wish to shudder about. I had enough to reproach myself with. On
the other hand I might have arrived at the *Hotel Vier Jahreszeiten*
like anyone else. With these gaps I could never know. I have had
gaps during which, my friends said, I had been quite normal, considering the occasion. "You were a bit high, as people do get at such
parties, but otherwise you seemed all right. We didn't notice anything exceptional." They could say that just as easily as "When Knick
brought you home you didn't even know your own room". That could
be disconcerting. It seemed that it was only *after* I had got safely
into bed that I had lost all controls and that this total erasure of the
few previous hours had occurred. I had stayed in this fine old hotel
several times before, the first being when I had taken a few days'
Bavarian holiday from my post in Berlin at Christmas 1930, and
the last only two summers previously when I had come up for a
couple of weeks from writing in Yugoslavia. I love Munich. And like
the old Astoria, at which I had lived for years in Petrograd, the *Vier
Jahreszeiten* was much more than a hotel: it was a way of life. I
did not intend to spoil that life if I could help it. I rang the room
service and ordered three soft-boiled eggs broken in a cup, American
fashion, with coffee and toast, and made myself eat it. Then I ran
the tub full of water as hot as I could stand, put the bottle of Martel
down on the tiles beside it, and lay there until the tension in my
nerves eased a bit. I applied a clean dressing to replace my soggy
one, shaved, and put on fresh clothes. When I went down in the lift
to see the manager I may have looked like someone who had had
a night out, but so did many another man in the Munich of those
days; and I had no compunction in asking him to put me in touch
with Professor Bumke, and in telling him why. He showed no surprise, but merely picked up the phone-book. While he was talking
it occurred to me that he must have had others in this room on the

same quest, and I later confirmed this. But when he put down the telephone he said with genuine sympathy "The Herr Professor is in Venice. They do not know when he will return." That was a blow.

I have never had the D.T.s; but I must have been in their ante-room, one or two nights, there in Munich. I passed through purgatory. The only thing stable in my near-deliriums was my resolution that I would let nothing muddy my slate in this hotel; that one resolve was like a life-line. The manager knew of course, because I had told him, that I had been drinking my head off. The desk must have gossiped about the size of my drink-bill, and had probably been told not to worry about it. *I* had to keep going. I made myself bathe and shave and go out. I knew from experience that I was always better on my feet, and the streets would fill my mind with other things beside myself. To get the mood of the times, remember that this was only a few months before the Munich Conference: Daladier was to make his home at the *Vier Jahreszeiten*. That famous old place had been the setting for many actors, and acts, in the Hitlerian tragedy. I stepped very carefully out of the lift around noon; once out in the street I did not have to be so careful. Munich was a city that had always exhilarated me; I can't say just why (perhaps it was the wind from the snow?) but, in Munich, I have always felt a sense of extra life—and the desire to do something good, some really worth-while writing: things that would last. It has always appalled me that the *Führerhaus* could have been at Munich. I steered past it . . . its interior evil seemed to shame the big bronze eagle whose noble wings stretched along its brown face. I walked the streets trying to force myself to be interested in the passing crowd. Every day I made an attempt to slow down my drinking. If I came to a hotel I would enter it and sit down on a chair in its lobby as if I were waiting for someone. One day I entered one of the big hotels where the giant-like General Hoffman was at the desk, impatiently waiting for his key—a bear of a Teuton in his grey field coat with the scarlet lining —with the little capering Austrian General, Schwartz, red stripes down his breeches four inches wide, prancing around him, over-obsequious. In my daze, I was back in Moscow again, watching some play at the Art Theatre or Meyerhold's, where the Russian actors were caricaturing the prancing Poles. When Hoffman went up in the lift, everyone in that lobby breathed more easily. I lunched, when I could bear eating, at any other restaurant than the hotel's; and to pass the afternoons I strolled through the Museums, or sat in the Pinakothek staring at the Van Goghs or Toulouse-Lautrecs, both of whom should have been a good warning. I had once lived in Arles, in that square with the horse-chestnuts, where the little hotel fed me on meadow-larks, their *specialité de la maison,* in a shabby building near where Van Gogh had cut his own ear off to give to his girl in the whore-house; and I had spent many a pleasant summer sunset walking along the canal to his famous draw-bridge. To sit there in Munich and think back to those carefree days was rather painful.

I could no longer face the heaviness of my once harmless drinkings in Munich: evenings in the smoky old *Hofbräuhaus,* where one watched the waddling old women-waiters cheerily carrying six tall mugs of that heavenly brown Munich beer in each hand, and where all Bavaria drank in company. I had to have hard liquor to eat its way through the haze of my mind. And I drank alone.

By now my money was running out. If it had not been for the two advances on my South American book, which now came in, I should have been in a tight spot. But to get the New York draft changed into aski-marks, with the German bureaucracy making all the trouble they could, was enough to drive me crazy in itself. I kept sober enough to accomplish that, cashed most of it, and gave it to the desk at the *Vier Jahreszeiten;* for with those needless fears that all heavy drinkers are subject to, I did not know whether my credit was still good there or not. Then I began to feel too unsure of my ability to stand up even to try the streets any longer. Also I had begun to realise, as I had before—even out in British Columbia—, that this trying to force yourself to be interested in your daily surroundings usually defeats its own purpose. I saw no reason to fool myself; the best thing to do was just to hold drink at bay. I was doing this one noon in the American Bar of the *Vier Jahreszeiten,* chatting with a cheery young landowner, when the manager came in smiling. He nodded: "The Herr Professor is back."

Bumke was the "specialist" whom the desperate Russians had flown to Moscow in the hope that he might save, or at least help, the dying Lenin. They had tried to keep it a great secret. I did not know he had been to Moscow until weeks after I had been in his hands; and then it was his chief assistant, not he, who told me. Bumke was not the talkative type of psychologist; for which, even then, I had sense enough to be grateful. The only time I did get him to talk about Lenin he merely made a face, said he did not like him, but was quick to add "he had one of the most interesting minds I have encountered". Nor did I know that, back in 1930, when I had gone down to Leipzig and had sat behind the back of Hitler's shiny double-breasted blue suit—the time he was defending the three young Reichswehr officers he had been accused of corrupting (that famous "heads will roll in the sands" speech, so badly reported by foreign correspondents who had not gone near Leipzig)—I did not know that the central figure of the seven judges of its Supreme Court, resplendent in their scarlet and ermine, whom Hitler was jabbing his finger at, was Bumke's brother, the most distinguished jurist in Brüning's Germany. All I knew when I was ushered into Professor Bumke's private study was that I had reached him at last. And only just in time.

In this first judgement we made of each other, which, of course, meant so much to me, I saw a slender little man, grey, with an air of great learning. He had none of the affectations of the near-great, but got down to business at once. I think he saw in my face that I knew I had come into good hands. I believed in Dr. Bumke from the first moment I saw him. He made me undress completely. He directed me to stand facing a window and pulled up a chair and sat behind me. There had been a premature spring in Bavaria, or an exceptionally late fall of snow; for there were some pink blossoms on a fruit tree in his sunny garden, glistening with snow; and I shall never forget my feelings, my forlornness, as I stood there, staring out at that fresh growing life, so beautiful and gay under its clean snow, and thought of the dirty mess I had made of my own life. Of all things, beasts, flowers and man, man, as exemplified by myself, was surely the most detestable in the universe. Bumke was touching my back lightly with a feather—making me say *"Ja"*—to test my reactions: to see, I suppose, what nerves had already been destroyed by alcohol. He was very serious. He did not speak much English, and his French was even worse than mine, if that was possible; but there was not very much that he did wish to say to me at this initial interview—except to tell me that I was not at all well, either mentally or physically, but that, so far, it looked as if no irreparable damage had been done. He asked me to get dressed, and to take the chair before his desk. He sat there looking at me. Behind his eyes I saw the question of just how serious were my intentions. I knew that this was the most important thing in our interview; I knew that this great man would not waste time working with material that would not take the strain. But that, of course, was not a thing that I could *tell* him: he had to decide that for himself. He asked me how long I was prepared to stay, and I replied that I would leave that to him. "I am serious," I said. He pressed a button on his desk, and a young girl came in. Bumke spoke for some time to her. She turned to me:

"The Herr Professor asks me to tell you he is sorry he does not speak better English. He says he will try and help you. He asks me to say that, so far as he can tell—that is, up to the present—there is nothing that cannot be put right." She looked at Bumke, who had here made an interjection. "Oh, yes—he hopes you understand how ill you are?" I nodded. "Very well, then." She stood up. "And now, if you will allow me, I will take you to the office." I shook hands with Bumke and walked out. "We have two Classes here," she said, brightening as soon as she had got out of the room. "The First Class and the Second Class rooms are just the same. But the food is—ah—a little different." I gave her a dim smile. "The Second will do for me," I said. "I am not very much interested in food at the moment." "This is a State Hospital," she went on. "Now I shall have to ask you about money. Professor Bumke, it does not matter with him—you and he can speak about that at any time—the charges are . . ." I was able to make satisfactory arrangements at the desk—a doctor there shone a light in my eyes and wrote something down on a card—and I gave them my passport. Then I was led down to the ground floor; two heavy oak doors were unlocked, and I was taken into a long corridor.

"This is Sister Cecile," said the young girl, introducing me to a nun. "Sister Cecile is our Matron." She left us. I faced a dignified old lady whose grey eyes were clearly taking stock of me. She smiled. She opened the door of a room: "This will be yours," she said. I walked to the window and saw, over some bushes, that it looked out on a courtyard. Some men in grey suits were slowly moving about in the yard. I had left my stuff at the *Vier Jahreszeiten* and told the Sister I would now go back and get it. But this, I at once discovered, did not mean simply walking out of the door. Not at all. Both doors were locked. I had signed in; now I was locked in. Sister Cecile smiled when she saw what I was thinking, and said she would phone the office for permission. "That is quite all right," she said when she returned. "What time will you come back? After lunch?" "Yes," I said, grudgingly. But it was not lunch I was thinking about. What I had in mind was a few last drinks. I packed at the hotel, told the valet to take care of most of my stuff, and had my typewriter and one bag sent down to the lobby. Then I went into the American Bar and sat there until late in the afternoon. It was not a good start. Yet those were the last drinks I was to have for eighteen months.

I did not know how unbalanced my own mind was until one day I received a letter from a friend in Vienna, saying: "Do come here. It would be much more sensible. That place you are in now really will drive you mad." I decided to go: the lure of this friend, the Prater, and all the fun we could have in Vienna were too much for me. I was already dressed and packed when Dr. Bumke's chief assistant (I shall call him Goetzen) came to give me my morning injection. I asked for permission to go out, and to have my passport back from the office so that I could go to the bank and cash some money. Dr. Goetzen, whom I had come to like very much, began to argue: someone could go to the bank for me, etc. I did not know that he was fending me off, playing for time, so what he said struck me as just so much nonsense. "Look here, Dr. Goetzen, you just don't know what you're talking about. You don't know a damn' thing about foreign exchange." Then I found myself practically yelling at him. "Please!" he said, getting up. "I'll be back in just a moment." I followed him out into the corridor, but Sister Cecile was already locking the door after him; and she turned to me now as patiently as if she were addressing a child. "Just you sit here," she said, patting one of the wicker chairs in that grim corridor—and I was to know the number of paces it measured from one end to the other before I left it—"Mr. Farson, please. . . . Dr. Goetzen will be right back."

Instead, Dr. Bumke unlocked the door and came in. It was the only time that I saw him show the least sign of emotion. He looked worried. "Mr. Farson, you live in London—but you are really an American, yes?" I told him I was an American. "You have my passport right here in your office. Dr. Bumke, I have been trying to get Dr. Goetzen to give me my passport—so that I can go to the bank to get some money. But he says——" Bumke nodded: "Just a minute, Mr. Farson." And then he, too, went out and locked the door after him. He was gone half an hour. I did not know what was going on; afterwards, I learned that he had been talking to the American Consul on the telephone, probably preparing the ground to restrain me. By the time he returned my fit of anger had cooled off. I followed him obediently into my own room, where I took the bed and he sat on the chair. He spoke slowly, picking every word:

"Mr. Farson—your—your mind is in grave peril. You must believe me. I do not want you to ask me for permission to leave here. If you go to Vienna, why, Mr. Farson . . ." He shook his head. "No, you must not go. No, Mr. Farson. You are in a condition now where I can help you. Please, do stay here." I nodded. I looked out of my barred window to where the schizophrenics—and they had five hundred of them—were sitting, or walking about, in the courtyard. I began to untie my tie. "Very well, Dr. Bumke, I will stay. I'm sorry. Now I shall stay here until *you* tell me to go." He just nodded and left me. I got into my pyjamas and bath-robe, and a little while later I lay face down on the bed, bared my buttocks and let Dr. Goetzen give me the injection. When he had finished he sat down and had a smoke with me. "You had Dr. Bumke worried," he smiled. "Now tell me about all the intricacies of foreign exchange. . . . Perhaps, one day, I shall have use for that; because, as I have already told you, I was once an art student in Paris . . . and perhaps, one day, I shall want to go back—perhaps I shall get tired of this thankless job, trying to help people who know so much they will not let us help them. Now, this question about aski-marks—I suppose that is enough to drive anyone crazy itself, yes?" He then bowed and left.

I only had these injections while Dr. Bumke was cleaning up my body. I don't know what they were. But, for the layman, I can say that the syringe had a barrel-diameter of at least one inch, that the barrel was at least four inches long, full of a liquid that looked like port (and I often wished it was), and that pushing the needle into me was fun neither for me nor for the doctor. When a student-assistant of Dr. Goetzen gave it to me one day, he leaned on the needle and groaned. But it worked. One day when I was sitting in that same wicker chair in the corridor opposite my door I fell asleep. When I woke up I felt a sense of ease that was almost ineffable— as if all the tensions inside me had suddenly been let down—and while I was enjoying this drowsy languor of a peace I had not known for years I was aware that Bumke himself was standing there looking down on me. He was smiling. But even his smile was brief and cryptic: it seemed as if the last thing he wanted was for anyone in his hands to be friendly with him—the reverse of the feeling of dependence some psychologists try to establish, so that they can take the place of 'the father you never had'. . . . After that day, I had no more injections.

The corridor had eight rooms. These were for Professor Bumke's private cases. I saw only three of them. I had to avoid the first by stepping quickly aside, for he would have walked straight into me. He was a scarred, weatherbeaten man of about fifty, wearing plus-fours and a grey Tyrolean jacket with the usual stag-horn buttons. This was a German ex-major, who had been treated in other hospitals and institutions for shell-shock: he had been buried by a land-mine. He had eyes like grey marbles, and he never moved them. When he wanted to see something at one side or the other he turned his whole head. It was macabre. Let us say that the corridor was thirty-six paces long. Every day, all day, he paced that corridor from end to end. When he reached the door at either end he did a smart military about-turn, stamping his feet, and then marched to the other door. He marched—that is the word. Five of these cases I never saw. I did not know the existence of the sulfa drugs then, so I thought that the urinal I saw the other nun taking out of the room next to mine every day was filled with blood, whereas its colour was the result of this man being given sulfanilamide. I was to get to know that myself, but not here. However, that little man with the twisted face—I caught a glimpse of it by accident through his door—was not with us long. When I came out into the corridor one morning there were several women weeping, and men with red eyes and swollen faces; and shortly after they left. We were asked to return to our rooms, and the body was removed. I never knew what was in those other five rooms. I never saw a man come out of them. But they were occupied. The only other case that I saw, and he was tragic, was a young man, all too obviously "not there", who watched the door through which Bumke came in every day; and who, the instant he saw that handle turning on our side of the door, began to straighten himself up and put on the appearance of being normal. Bumke always had a word or two for him. But Sister Cecile, with whom I soon became able to say what I liked, shook her head and told me that he would soon be "sent away". . . . I thought about what "sent away" might mean.

CLINIC

People who know me well, well enough to realise what a hold drink had on me, often ask what Professor Bumke did for me—or to me, as some like to put it. My answers never satisfy them. To the layman it all looks too simple. The facts are that after I had been with Bumke for only a few weeks he allowed me to go out into Munich whenever I felt like it; and that for eighteen months thereafter it never even occurred to me to have a drink, though eight of those months were in Africa, and spent as often as not in the company of men who took their sundowners every night as a daily ritual and prophylactic against boredom and the tropics. It is my firm belief, moreover, that if I had not been suffering from idiotic overdoses of M & B, which I ate daily to hold down an infection in my leg during the four months it took me to drive across Africa from the Indian Ocean to the Atlantic—and from a bad case of malaria, picked up in French Equatorial Africa—I should never have taken another drink in my life. Not once was it a question of will-power.

Just keep in mind that I did stop drinking—it was as easy as falling off a log—and that Bumke was the man the Russians brought to Moscow to save Lenin. They had the brains of all Europe and the United States to draw upon, yet they took this physically frail little man, who just hated their guts. And as my own experience may be of some use to others, I am going to give it. I *know* Bumke had something. The Vienna school said he was old-fashioned. Having undergone some of their *pratique* (as exemplified, I must say, by rather feeble practitioners), I regard their condemnation as the

greatest tribute they could pay him. This is how that great man handled me:

Bumke began with what, it seemed to me, the orthodox psychologist, especially the psychiatrist, leaves to the last—the present. He
confined himself to my relationships with the world around me. He
did not dig into my past so to provide me with an alibi. He gave
me no excuses. In explaining myself to him, I had to explain myself
to myself. That is what my family and friends found too simple; they
had never been put through this particular course of thinking. To
me it was a most revealing experience; a dual diagnosis, whose chief
reward was that it confirmed me in so many things I already knew.
If you think that over, for a moment, you will see that it meant a
strengthening of the mind. It was similar to, though not identical
with, being confirmed in one's religious faith—that last resort for
help, which has saved many a desperate soul. Though I think Bumke
was an agnostic: we never discussed religion. Bumke brought me
face to face with modern times, as I had seen them and gone wrong
in them. Does that sound too simple, even now? It might. It easily
could—*if* you miss the cardinal fact that the reason why so many men
take to drink is that their daily lives are not interesting enough to
hold them steady. Plain boredom, emptiness, the absence of things
one can fervently believe in: these, I think, are responsible for more
of today's alcoholics than all the phantoms of our past. It is the *present* that makes us crack up. And to find an alibi, an excuse for yourself, in the past, is, it stands to reason, a deflection from a straight
attempt to solve your present. Why is it that so many highly-strung
people, after they have had their own little demons brought to the
surface and "rationalised", are so much weaker than before their
rescue? They have been turned about and face the wrong way—
away from their problems. Bumke was not in the least concerned as
to whether my boyhood had been unhappy (it certainly had not);
he knew that I was having a miserable present—and that I realised,
at the back of my mind, that the only way I could come to the surface
again was on my own power. And Bumke stuck to that.

Perhaps I am simplifying it all a bit too much. When I first came
in there I asked Bumke if he thought I should write. He said no:
it would be better to do nothing for a while. Until the day I fell
asleep in the wicker chair and felt that ineffable ease (the day he

said there was no need to go on with the injections: he had finished
driving the alcohol out of me) I was never allowed to step outside
that corridor. But the next morning, when Bumke came in, he asked
me when I would like to take my exercise. I could take it when the
courtyard was free from the schizophrenics and the congenital idiots,
or I could take it with them. I chose the latter. He nodded, and left
me: that, of course, was what he wanted. I sat on a green park-
bench and watched them shuffle past me, many with their faces horribly torn by their nights of madness. Some of them were chasing
the pigeons, trying to catch them with their bare hands: the pigeons,
it struck me, being about the only normal creatures in that paved
yard, where the faces of those who were too maniacal to be allowed
out looked down on us from the mural of barred windows. By the
fish-white foreheads and weather-brown faces of these lost ones, you
knew that many of them were peasants from the alpine districts. A
lot of people go mad up in the snow. . . . A Mongolian idiot sat
down on the bench beside me. He had a head twice normal size.
"Buch? Buch?" he managed to utter, touching the one I had in my
hand. "Yes—book," I said. Then he pointed to my cigarette and stuck
his finger in his mouth. I did not know if it would do him any harm,
or was against the regulations, but I gave him a cigarette and lighted
it for him. I know how *I* feel when I can't find a cigarette! His smile
almost killed me. That peasant boy fastened himself to me: he took a
fancy to me. And one day he almost scared the life out of me. My
room was on the ground floor, in a corner of the buildings, behind a
flower-bed and some bushes. Its fancy white-painted trellis, at the
window, was made of steel. I was batting away happily at my typewriter one morning when suddenly I felt a shove—and there was
that boy, pulling the bushes apart and trying to push his ghastly
head through the steel trellis. He wanted a cigarette, that was all.

Above me was a little mouse in a private room, or cell: he used
to trot up and down all night. Then I would hear the heavy boots
of warders running along the corridor, the sounds of a scuffle, and
a piercing little squeak. He had been given an injection to knock
him out. I have called him a mouse: for so I always saw his little
face, with its long nose, peering down at us in the mornings, his web
belts drying on his steel trellis. All the windows to the left of my
side of the yard had faces at them, and these faces were always

changing. For this was the most important sorting-centre in Germany. My feeling grew, from the easy indifference with which even pleasant young Dr. Goetzen spoke of them as human rejects, and Sister Cecile's glumness whenever I asked her where they would be sent, that some of these unfortunates were being sorted out for death. And every night there was heavy, muffled singing from the top floor on my side. When I asked Goetzen why anyone should want to sing in such a place, he gave me a sad smile: "It's their bath. We put them in a pool of hot water, and let them lie there: to cool off in their own juice, so to speak. With a great majority of the cases that does bring relief. And then, they have company. You could say that it is a form of community singing."

He asked me for a copy of my *Transgressor,* and told me Bumke was reading it, or had read it, in a translation from the Norwegian edition by his pretty niece. It was banned in Germany. And when they wanted to publish *The Story of a Lake* I would not sign that paper saying that I had no Jewish blood in my ancestry. I did not want my German friends, for I did have a few good ones, to think I would sign so disgusting a document. "You seem to have got about quite a bit!" said young Dr. Goetzen affably, lighting his cigarette. "Tell me, if you had your choice, which country would you prefer to live in? Which did you find best?" "Best for what?" I asked him gloomily. "There are so many things. . . ." I told him I had found several places in the world where I wanted to stay and live all my life. I did not tell him that I lay there, night after night, thinking about British Columbia and my cabin out there on that lonely lake. I wanted to get clear away from all people—from the world of today. I had come to hate the word civilisation. I never knew how much of these talks was for his benefit, as giving him a chance to reminisce, and how much for mine, as giving me the chance to talk myself out; but at first I was too desperate, too insanely dissatisfied with my own condition, even to discuss myself. Was this a form of the psychiatrist's couch? It might have been. Goetzen sat there smoking, being pleasant, which was company; and I was not at all displeased to listen, sometimes rising to the point of even putting in an inner shot of my own. His tales of *la vie de bohème* in Paris were excruciating: he was so damned serious. "When I wanted to paint. . . . Then I became interested in this. . . . I often wonder which was right.

. . ." "The world has lost a great artist, and I have got you," I said.
But I could not have had the heart to joke with him like that in my
first weeks of black gloom. When I did come up near the surface,
and saw daylight overhead, I found young, charming Dr. Goetzen
sinisterly interesting; and I felt that if I was supposed to bare my
soul to him, it would be interesting to find out what was in his. This
likeable young German, this most intelligent young German—of
Hitler's day—was the very type of German that has puzzled the
world ever since there *were* Germans. He could never quite get over
the chance remark of mine you may remember: that in the company
of Spaniards I always felt I was a better man than I knew I *really*
was; nor could I ever make him understand it. He was on his home
ground if we discussed the Prado; he could talk all morning about
Velásquez; but the Spain of El Greco and Goya was beyond his
perimeter. I tried to make him understand the loneliness that is the
grandeur of Spain. "There is a nobility in the Spaniard," I said,
"which I think comes from his poverty. Take a Spaniard of La
Mancha . . . or of one of those mud-villages west of Toledo . . .
where there is not a word of lettering in any street, no shop signs,
nothing . . . where you can hardly tell the men from the soil, they
are so close to it . . . dust of Spain themselves. You will find a bigness
in those Spaniards who are hungry from the day they are born until
the day they die, a generosity and a dignity, that you will find nowhere else in Europe. It's a question of to *be*, and not to *have*, I suppose. . . ."

"Ho!" he laughed easily. "Spain is five hundred years behind the
times. We have to change all that—that poverty. Spain is out of date."

"Perhaps. But what about being ahead of the times? Take your
own lovely Bavaria." I told him that of all the places I had known
Bavaria had once been the country where I had been sure I could
spend all my days. "Do you remember the wonderful old life in these
mountains, the life of the jaegers? Do you remember all the peace
and tranquillity of the Prince-Bishop country?" I told him how I had
first come on Bavaria: sailing my own boat across Germany, being
pulled up the Main, and then pulling that 26-foot yawl myself—like
a tow-horse, for weeks—over the Fränkische Jura mountains, to get
down to the Danube, Austria, and the Black Sea. "Do you remember
that old Europe?" I asked him. "Don't you wish—sometimes—that

things could be like they were in the Kaiser's day—instead of all these damned Brown Shirt parades . . . ?"

"I am too young to have known the Kaiser's Germany," he said quickly—and uncomfortably. "But it is useless for you to go on looking for lost worlds. A man can't live in the past, you know." "Can't he?" I retorted. "Then why waste days in the Prado?" He had no answer to that.

But these talks were very pleasant. They did bring back the "taste of life". He obviously gave Bumke a summary; for Bumke often began to talk, when he came in, at about the same point Goetzen and I had broken off. Bumke was always pleased when he saw me hard at work; and good Sister Cecile used to come in, when she had gone off duty, for a chat. Now and then she would bring a little plate of sugared cookies and eat them with me as I had my coffee. "I prayed for you last night. For that——" She nodded at the paper in my typewriter. "What are you writing?" Sister Cecile was unmistakably of gentle birth, if one dare use that expression: and for twenty years she had been in this corridor, going back only to her Convent for her yearly fortnight vacation. "You have seen a lot of life," she said one night, smiling. "Too much."

"And you, Sister Cecile, have seen far more than I have. Right in this corridor." She nodded thoughtfully. Some mornings when she came in to see me she looked stunned; as if her nerves had had more than they could stand, in one of those five rooms with the locked doors. The other nun was a peasant; heavy, pink-cheeked, bursting with femininity. Even her nun's habit could not suppress it. Her smile was worth a lot; and she always smiled when she prepared my medicinal bath for me, as I invariably asked for tar: it made me think of the pine woods, I told her. She was a mountain Bavarian.

My friends and family, to explain the miracle, think Bumke must have hypnotised me. If so, he must have done it by telepathy, or by proxy. But that explanation so radically misconceives Bumke's philosophy that I won't even bother to brush it aside. Bumke *was* a philosopher; and—the two do not always go together—a very sophisticated man. He knew a lot of the world. It was a pleasure to talk with him. I had been to two fools before him: libel prevents me from being specific. One was a bookish type, with all the mannerisms of the second-rate, who asked me to write a candid profile of myself: where I was born, where I was raised, where I had been— until I had the good luck to reach him. "I see," he said, "that you are an escapist." "Possibly," I said. "You go here—you go there—you never stay in any one spot to face your problems," he announced with finality. "Yes—on the surface, it does look like that," I said. "But that's too easy. I'm afraid you haven't noticed that travelling has been an integral part of my profession—I'm a foreign correspondent —to say nothing of the fact that I like knocking about the world." I looked at him. The ease with which he knew at once what was wrong with me could have been alarming if I hadn't known as easily what was wrong with him: he was a portentous ass. "But tell me, just for interest," I asked, "why do *you* think that people climb mountains . . . ?" And I picked up my hat. "I'm afraid I'm the wrong man for you," I said. He afterwards told a member of my family that I had been "very rude". I hope so.

The other was a hearty chap who seemed willing to let me drink all I could hold, and then some. When I eventually landed in a nursing home he pointed at my typewriter, and said: "Just write down on that '*I am going to write a short story today*'." "Why?" I asked. "Will-power! If you have will-power enough, you will write it." He was quite a man. He took me out of London to a gunsmith's grounds, to shoot clay-pigeons. We broke even on the first twenty-five. "Now," I said, feeling life coming back to me, "I'll shoot you double or quits for your fee. I'll shoot you miss-and-out." He shook his head. And I had the empty satisfaction of breaking twenty-one straight. I still laugh when I think that all he thought one needed for writing a short story was will-power.

I did not laugh much at Bumke's. A madhouse isn't conducive to laughter. On the other hand, I knew I was in the right hands; and I woke up every morning with a feeling of expectation. Bumke repeatedly said to me: "You are at constant war with yourself. You must find peace. Unless you can find peace, I should not like to feel responsible for you after you leave." He had said the first day, and I knew it of course, that there is no such thing as a cure. I had not come to Bumke with any such illusion; neither did I expect he would give me additional will-power. I came to him, frankly, for an escape from the physical and mental torture I was suffering at that time.

He had given me physical peace. I could think now, and only a short time back I had felt I could never think again. But, in my mind, I was far from well. Bodily ill-health matters little compared with mental ill-health. An injury can very often be the best thing that could have happened to you—I prefer people (and countries) who have been hurt. "You have had an unusually wide experience of life," said Bumke. "Why don't you give yourself the benefit of it? Be kinder to yourself."

"You mean—get rid of this guilt-complex?" Bumke gave me a weary smile: "More than that—*much* more." He went on to say that I did not let the lessons of life become cumulative: I piled one experience on top of another, but I did not add them up. "Your life should have given you exceptional opportunities to weigh up human values. You should weigh them up now, and apply them to yourself. Nothing but your own intelligence will ever get you out of the dark pit you are now in. You must do it yourself." I knew that I was a great "worrier"; one of the ways I have tried to break myself of that is by trying to live every day as if time did not exist at either end of the twenty-four hours—by trying to take an interest in the very ground under my feet, to shut out everything else, tomorrow and all my yesterdays. If one *could* do that it might be wonderful; but then you have to disregard so many of the realities. I have never been able to bring myself to such a state; nor, upon reflection, do I want to. But Bumke's "You must do it yourself", and his injunction to take the lessons of my own life into account, to give myself peace, did make sense. It did then, it still does; and as I was able to climb out of the dark pit by it at that time, I may be able to do so again.

The nearest I ever came to an explanation of what Bumke did for me I found many years later in *Face of a Victim*, Elizabeth Lermolo's story of her imprisonment in the Solovetsk Monastery on an island in the White Sea. This camp was known as a "political isolater", and was reserved for high State criminals, former Kremlin officials, playwrights, authors, and some actresses who had fallen foul of the party line. Solovetsk was the most difficult prison of all in which to retain one's mental balance. And her fellow-prisoners there taught her what they called "psychological self-defence"—in her case, to exercise her mind constantly, recalling long-forgotten impressions, reconstructing, word for word, stories she had just heard from her fellow-prisoners, memorising names, dates, places. . . . If I fail in portraying what that exercise meant to a mind in trouble, it is because of my own limitations: but I recognise this lesson of the "psychological self-defence"—the way a man consciously *trains his mind to defend itself*. Those last six words contain what Bumke taught me.

If you ask why, when he was such a wonder, my reformation did not last, the answer is, of course, that it was I who failed, not Bumke. And if you ask why, when he was so intelligent a man, he should also be a Nazi, you have me stopped—though I could reply that you seem to know little about the Germany that led to Hitler, and the Germans of all time. In fact it was when I got out into Munich, and saw what was growing there, that, I think, a certain resolution came to me. I was disgusted with this city I had loved, and so I wanted to have no cause for disgust with myself: pride, if you must have it, was what made me pull myself together. I did not want to crack up in Hitler's Germany.

Bumke was a man of immense reserve, outwardly cold; the last man on earth to be a 'substitute father'. But I think he took a special interest in me, even liked me; and I have confirmation of this. In Copenhagen in 1939, when I was lying in hospital before the Germans got in (yes, again hospital; and this time for a sizeable bone operation, in which I had more chiselled out than I felt I could spare), my *Story of a Lake* was published. There was a piece about me in the *Politiken* which said I was in the Sundby Hospital; and Bumke's Norwegian niece came out to see me. "I have written him that you are here," she said. "Tell me," I asked, "what did he really think of me?" She laughed: "Oh, he said that you were a 'character' . . . but he always said that he thought you would be all right." "Well, give him my best." (Bumke was a man to whom you did not send 'love'.) She came back almost the next day: "I've had an answer to my first letter—and old Papa Bumke sends his love to you." She handed me a snapshot he had sent me. Old Bumke—he seemed smaller now—sitting on a bench in his garden: that garden I had looked out on so desperately, as, standing naked in his study, I had stared at that strange sight of snow on the apple blossoms . . . long, long ago. "Papa Bumke has a son in the *Luftwaffe*," I heard the Norwegian girl saying; "and I can tell you one thing—if that son is killed, that's the end of Papa Bumke."

But to return to my time at his clinic. He came into my room one morning, and said that there was an excellent little café, with an open terrace, overlooking the little pond in the park. Why didn't I do my reading there? "They have excellent coffee," he said, with as near as he would permit himself to a secretive smile. "And Munich —the rest of Munich?" I asked. He told me to go where I liked.

At first I thought that this time in Munich was going to be the best I had known. To see it with sober eyes was like discovering a new city. It can be an exhilarating city—had been. Whenever I stayed away from the clinic for my luncheon I ate in the *Vier Jahreszeiten* itself. There was no longer any need to feel embarrassed, or to slink past the desk, wondering what they were saying about me. I could hold my head up. When I had first stayed at that fine old hotel, as a foreign correspondent, before the drink got me, I found its owner standing down in the lobby one noon, and asked him if he could suggest a good place to lunch. "I am tired of always eating at the Preysing-Palais, good as it is." He stared at me curiously: "Are you joking?" I shook my head. "Because, if you aren't," he said with a proud smile, "the best restaurant in Europe is right behind your back." He pointed to a door, with no sign on it, leading off the lobby. This was the little *Walterspiel,* rendezvous for the great landowners of that part of Bavaria. It is small, I don't think it has more than twelve tables, and it was too aristocratic to be *gemütlich;* but its *canapés,* especially the *fois gras,* were—*fabelhaft!* The Germans had the right word for it. But now—I was finding that the Germans had too many words.

I was becoming tired of reading German speeches about what they were going to do to us if the *Führer's* patience was exhausted, to say nothing of those grotesque parades, in the lovely old city, of the bulging Brown Shirts with their fat behinds. Germany began to bore me. Perhaps that is why I refrained from talking about Africa, old German Africa, with Dr. Bumke: I feared that the ensuing rumpus might break up our relationship. I had sent to London for *The Colonial Problem,* the report by a study group of the Royal Institute of International Affairs. When it came, and I had the delight of looking through it, I realised that if I knew that book from cover to cover I should have the experience of some of the greatest men who had ever understood Africa at my command. It became my bedside book at Bumke's.

Bumke, with his lectures in the University and his work on the board that was grading the various categories of insane, did not have much time for me, now that I was regaining some sense. I realised that he only saw me when he thought this necessary, and was using young Dr. Goetzen as a hunting dog: to point when, or if, he saw any improvement in me. Goetzen loved long talks; though whether they were part of his work, or because he was a Bavarian, I could never decide. He knew the old Dôme and Rotonde, and I would speak of the magic springs of Paris: how we sat listening to the bogus profundities of the Lost Generation as the saucers piled up, and how they dragged into the conversation, as their own opinions, the findings of every philosopher they had read or even heard of— having a wonderful time cashing in on their mornings of alcoholic melancholia. I told him what Scott Fitzgerald had said of one of the most belligerent of these deep thinkers (and they could be very belligerent): "Poor baby—et up all its Spinoza!" Goetzen exploded. He had never read *Tender is the Night*. I told him to get it: he would find some good case-history. . . .

I often wanted to get Bumke talking about the degrees of insanity. I should have liked to ask him what he thought of the *Siegesallee* in old Berlin—the Victors' Avenue, lined with what is probably the most ghastly assemblage of statues put up anywhere on earth. (I had been in the habit of passing through that *grotesquerie* on my walk to the office every morning, if it was sunny; and I never could look at that pantheon of German heroes without thinking of the half-mad side of the German mind, so horribly close to both its poetry and its music. That walk 'conditioned' me every morning: it always made me think of the Wagnerian melodrama with which even the most solid German wants to live real life. Always, I had to keep the consciousness of this sinister sentimentality, this appointment-with-death psychology of the German, behind my dispatches; other-wise the people I had to write about would have been unbelievable. That was the Berlin of Sally Bowles, of the *I am a Camera* epoch, of *Eldorado*, that pansies' paradise where even the 'girl' in the cloak-room tried to kiss you as you checked your hat. The most vicious, desperate, decadent capital in all Europe.)

But, of course, I was only interested in what Professor Bumke thought of me. I had stopped drinking. And I had stopped without even thinking about stopping. There had been no resolutions. Never once did I consciously use will-power. It was a question of reason, I suppose, reasserting itself.

Bumke came into my room one morning and settled himself in my arm-chair. He said tentatively, "I think you should go up into the mountains here. Stay there for some time. I think that is where you will find peace." I shook my head. "No, Professor Bumke, that would not do. If I went up and tried to isolate myself in those mountains I should only fret myself to death. I should know I was only postponing the issue. That would be dodging life. I think I'd better face it. I have a job to do, and I think I had better go back to London and get on with it." He said nothing for some time. Then he smiled. "I think you do know yourself. I have done all I can for you. You should go."

But I knew what he meant about the mountains. He wanted me to stay away from old associations. I had been thinking this over for some time. I had already decided to deal myself a new hand of cards. When I returned to England I told Eve that I was going to keep away from the family for some time—I did not know for how long; but that one day we should be together again. She understood. So I went off. I went down to Chichester Harbour to the Emsworth Sailing Club, to which I happened to belong. I wanted the ease of that company, and the peace of just knocking about in a boat—then I could get on with my *Story of a Lake*. That charming little club —most of its members were ex-naval officers—had two admirals on its racing committee who must have sailed with Nelson. To see them standing on the terrace while a race was in progress, eyeing the sea through their old-fashioned one-barrelled telescopes, was to be back in the days when an Admiral of the Fleet had ranked with Lord God Almighty, and life had been a much more straightforward affair.

The daughters of these ex-officers of the Royal Navy were some of the best racing skippers in the club, and properly mutinous. Their motto was: "The three most useless things in a boat are a step-ladder, a bicycle, and an ex-naval officer." Using one of these young ladies as ballast, I got second in a race of Thames dinghies, blanketing a naval commander just at the finish. But for the rest of the time I sailed alone, depending upon the tide, and wrote most of the day. I had a room overlooking the harbour, and one gale almost blew some swans in. I went up to London during the crisis preceding Munich to sign on again with the R.A.F. Then Chamberlain came back with "peace in our time" and "this time it is different; this time he made the promises to *me*". I had already finished my book, writing it in my London club, without taking one drink, which establishes a record. Tony Lind, my hero, watching the absurdities of the statesmen at Geneva, had already expressed my feelings: "If these are supposed to be our leaders, then our little world is bound straight for hell." And so, strolling idly down the Haymarket one morning, I turned into the offices of the Woermann Line, without any conscious decision, and bought a ticket for Walvis Bay. The break had come.

I don't know why I should have picked Walvis. Except that years before, as we lay off the Gulf Stream in a little Norwegian whale-catcher, Olsen, the dean of Norwegian gunners (who had already killed 2,300 whales in the Antarctic) said to me: "Know what? Place you ought to go to is Whale-fish Bay. Dot's where de whales go to make love." The beauty of the sunset evoked memories, and he described the performance of Leviathan: the male charging through sluicing seas at the female, then turning on his side—"One rap! What the hell fun they get out of it, I just don't know!" I did not see the whales making love. But I am glad I entered Africa by Walvis Bay.

AFRICA

*"The only spiritual phenomena are good intentions,
and we all know what portion of the universe is paved
with them."* William Temple

I had come out to Africa, as I have said, to deal myself a fresh hand
of cards; and one morning, as I lay in my blankets watching the red
ball of sun rise through the vlei grass, I knew that my luck was running strong. I wanted to be nowhere else than where I was, I needed
no more than what I had with me, and I could not have wished for
better company. This was peace, perfect peace.

Our fire had died during the night and the buck had moved up.
I watched a little springbok jumping within twenty yards of us.
Pronking, the Boers call it, when this graceful little gazelle springs
straight up into the air for sheer joy, the joy of just being alive. My
rifle lay by my side. We needed a buck for the pot. I knew that as
soon as we stirred to get the coffee I should not get within 300 yards
of one on that treeless plain. Yet it was worth more to watch that
dainty little animal at such close range, and to see all the fun it was
getting out of life on this glorious sunrise, than to have a shot at it.
It was only when I reached for my cigarettes, and my elbow showed
above the grass, that the buck saw me. After that I had the dawn all
to myself. This was on the 'flats' above Etosha Pan in upper South
West Africa, a hundred miles north of the last settlement, where some
of the greatest concentrations of game on that continent still remained.

As I lay there in my blankets, thinking over my turn of fortune and
watching that immense blob of blood-red slowly lift off the earth—
there was not a cloud to catch any glow or reflection in that lonely
sky—a bird, about the size of a chicken, shot straight up into the air

from the grass beside me, turned over at the top of its rise as if shot, and crashed back to earth. This surprising bird, which the Boers call the African Nightingale because it has no song whatever, claps its wings together behind its back as it shoots upward. Otherwise there was no sound—only the cries of the plover and the curlew from along the pan. It was beautiful. . . . I lay there thinking of life in the cities, of the millions of people in them living lives they did not like; and I wondered by what right we imposed our way of life upon the African when we had made so little a success of our own.

I could not have picked a better place for starting in Africa than Walvis Bay. There they all were, in that ghastly little hole: the heavy, brutal, hairy-armed German, obsessed with his myth of Nordic superiority; the 'English' civil servant and his wife (she was the worst) dominated by the idea of being gentlefolk, and pining away at Walvis because they could find no one to be snobbish to—chief pleasure and official perquisite of British colonial life; the green-eyed Afrikaners, always looking for insults where none were intended, and unpleasantly certain that you were going to write something nasty about them (with reason). Then there was the mute mass of native Africans, South Africa's "Black Diamonds", the continent's richest and most inexhaustible natural resource, but treated by everybody as if the whites were annoyed just to see them alive, which they were; for the white South African, both 'English' and Afrikaner, is afraid of the black man and his terrifying vitality: he won't die! And a desperate settlement of Coloureds ("Some of those bastards try to pass for white!") was there too: they hated everybody, themselves most of all, and stung themselves in their misery as a scorpion does when wounded. Shores of Hate.

So this was to be the end of Livingstone's dream—that the black man should be made an outsider even in his own country? And by what white men! It does not take long to see that when the white man is holding the black man down in the gutter he is down there with him. We call the black man a savage. Before I sailed from the Gold Coast the next year, I knew, with plenty of evidence to prove it, that the black man had an equal right to reverse the charge. It all depends upon who does the talking.

The Archbishop of Canterbury has just laid it down that though all men are equal within the love of God they are not within the sight of God. Who gave His Grace the superhuman power to make such distinctions between what is going on within God's love and sight? The assumption is odious. In that beautiful dawn at Etosha Pan, I was with men who were sure of no such divine guidance.

The man lying beside me, the one in candy-stick pyjamas, was Major H. C. (Cocky) Hahn, Native Commissioner of Ovambaland. He had been up in this country ever since 1915, when he had ridden over as a Mounted Scout for General Louis Botha, that marvellous old Boer Commando leader who hit the Germans in South West Africa as if they had been struck by lightning. On this morning—without one soldier or one policeman—Hahn was governing 117,000 Ovambas over 20,000 square miles of territory, and these, together with an uncountable number of Bushmen, amounted to about half the natives in all sparsely populated South West Africa, a territory larger than France. The Ovambas were the spear-and-knife-fighting natives whom even the Germans, with all their machine-guns and bestiality, had been unable to conquer. The Germans reduced the superb Hererro tribe from 90,000 of one of the finest aristocratic cattle-owning tribes in all Africa to 30,000 dispersed and dazed wanderers between the years 1904 and 1907. At about the same time (1905–6) they slaughtered 120,000 highly developed natives of what is now Tanganyika in the so-called Magi Magi 'rebellion', when the natives revolted against the seizing of their lands by the traders and military. But the Germans never got north of Etosha Pan against the Ovambas. The last German outpost lay just across the pan from us: that immense, unbelievable fortress of Namutoni, its high towers and crenellated, loop-holed white walls glowing flamingo-pink in the rising sun. A little tribe of Bushmen was hunting some wildebeest on the mud-flats between us with their poisoned arrows—people back in the Stone Age.

The other man with me that morning, lying flat on his back with his home-made veld shoes pointing skyward, was the famous Jan Vannell. He had been Botha's Bastaard Scout: half-Hottentot, half-Boer. Born in this country, it was he who had shown Botha's striking columns the lay of the land in this unmapped country above Etosha Pan. His beloved Mauser lay beside him, for this was 'the land of the bedside rifle'. A tuft of white hair showed beneath the old Boer hat he had canted over his nose to keep off the moon. It was his goatee. When he sat up he would look, with his neatly trimmed moustache, a bronze dead-ringer for General Smuts; and of this he was well aware. Old Jan never had to dress; he went to sleep with his clothes on, usually with his lighted pipe in his mouth. But he would have felt naked without that rifle. These two men had been together, up here in Ovambaland, for twenty-three years, sitting before the same camp-fires, sharing everything equally—including a few dangerous moments.

Etosha Pan is a vast triangle of mud, eighty miles long, pointing east. Unknown poisons in its soil prevent any plant growth. In the rainy season it becomes a vast shallow lake, like a saucer of lukewarm tea and about that colour: but turquoise at certain angles of the sun, or silvered. It is dotted with rafts of all the ducks found in that part of Africa, and rimmed with wading waterfowl. I counted six species of plover around the pan. It was a wonderful sight to watch the red-shanked plover rising and falling in the wind; to see the secretary bird, his quills erect, striding across the plain like, as the natives of the Sudan call him, 'the British officer'. There, once again, I listened to that lonely space-haunting cry of the curlew. Sun, sky and plain, I felt that I could go on this way for ever. . . .

South of the pan, in the swamps and thorn and mopani forests, was the elephant terrain. Giraffe, too—they need cover: bush, trees, or high grass. But up here, on these flats, it was the wonderful antelope country. It made me think of what the American plains must have been like in the days of the old North-West. With the buck standing around, the scene was like some of the paintings of George Catlin or Charles Bodmer: this landscape was what they looked at when the Sioux and the buffalo still held the plains. This thought was brought to mind by the astounding herds of bison-like wildebeest (gnu) standing like black islands under the sweep of sky—thousands of them. These flats are unbelievable: a vast plain, unbroken by a single tree, shrub, or even stone, stretching away from you as far as you can see—a scene that fills you with the immensity of space and the endlessness of time, and makes you want to go on for ever, to find what lies beyond that skyline. The marshes around the pan teem with birds. With three-foot brown hawks—wheeling, whirling, dropping, as they hunt half-inch frogs. With rafts, rafts, rafts of ducks:

black duck, whistlers, spoon-bills; knob-billed muscovies, which came down like heavy bombers. With waterside murals of flamingos, feeding with their heads upside down—they use their upper bill as a scoop—and standing like clusters of pink lilies in the shallow pan. With cranes and storks plodding thoughtfully about their business. With everything from the tiny cinnamon teal to the big spur-wing goose—he has a seven-foot wingspread and a spur on each elbow like a fighting cock's. And with, over it all, the old *aasvoel,* hideous vulture, circling high in the sky, often materialising from nothing, and peering down for his spot of blood. This, you knew with grati-tude, was Africa the way it was meant to be before the Europeans came to defile it. "Benefit of the European Example"—my God!

Old Jan Vannell sat up. In this world he could find his way about with his eyes closed. He said he had heard a lion cough during the night. "The lion, he coughs, Master, sometimes to wet his nose. He smells better." He sat there on his heels, starting a small fire. We had come down there to get a lion, but it would not depress any of us if we didn't. Jan and Hahn had killed plenty of lions in the course of their work, and I had begun to reach that point when, if I came on a corner of the world where I saw the animals enjoying their daily lives, the grass growing and the trees standing, I wanted to leave it alone. I think raising cats, watching all the fun they get out of life as they play with their kittens, had helped to cure me of my early passion for killing things. I have watched lions and their cubs playing just like that; watched with a Westley-Richards in my hand. And when I did shoot a lion, my first and only one, over in Kenya, and when I looked down at that magnificent beast stretched out on the ground—that magnificent life I had just ended, *and for what?* —all I could say to Sidney Downey was: "I'm sorry. I wish to Christ I hadn't done it." I had expected triumph; all I felt was dismay. I am not being sentimental. I walked that lion up on foot and shot him in broad daylight with his eyes facing me, and that is the blue ribbon of all shooting. But I have just come to the conclusion that there is something damned silly about this business of killing animals.

We were shooting for the pot on that trip, sleeping with just our bedrolls spread out in the short grass and only the stars for cover. Hahn had his .400 along, in case we did come on a lion. I was shoot-ing with my shotgun and a .303 Lee-Enfield service rifle, which was all that one needs. Old Jan Vannell's .303 Mauser had killed lions, plenty of elephants, whatever came his way. It was the same rifle that the old Boer ivory-hunters used. "If we meet a lion today," said old Vannell, as we investigated some bits of higher grass, "you say to that lion, Master: 'You and I have had a quarrel a long, long time ago—and today I'm going to settle it.' Never take your eyes off him." Very sound advice. Better, I think, than that given me by an old Boer elephant-hunter I had been with, who had been hunting ivory up in Portuguese West Africa for the last forty years: "Shoot him at the third wrinkle down the nose," he said, "if the elephant is coming at you." "If the elephant is coming *at* me," I replied, "I'll be in no mood to count wrinkles." Actually, I have never fired at an elephant. I have never wanted to. I think that to kill those wise old beasts, for sport, is quite unnecessary. But once I did 100 yards in 9 seconds flat when one of them put his barn-door ears out and came at me. I can hear that tiny squeal yet. . . .

It was grand country. Here you felt all the poetry of the veld. There were no paths and very few animal trails in this short grass. The lions like to lie in the depressions: any ridge, or scrub knee-high, is sufficient for their cover. Working the glasses hard, we saw some vultures circling, and found a lion's kill. It was a wildebeest, killed the previous night: legs broken off and crunched through; deep dark sockets where the eyes had been—those empty eye-sockets in the bone-white skulls that haunt you all over the plains of Africa; white leg-bones that the powerful jaws of the hyenas had crunched into splinters; hoofs bitten to shreds; the interior shining red, black with matted blood—hollow. . . . Another kill, possibly three days old—what remained of half a body—had been dragged several yards from where the kill had been made. There, the ground was covered, as always, by a big greenish ring of the digested grass manure inside the wildebeest's stomach, scratched by the lions as they kick with their hind legs and tear at the meat; and by black hairs from the animal's fly-swotter tail. Its yellow teeth were glistening in the sun from a soft edible nose that had been chewed off. There was no trace whatever of the meat, bones, or hide of the other half of him. Meanwhile a huge herd of wildebeest grazed so close that I was able to take some photos of them. An occasional bull stared and stamped, huffed, and pawed the ground. The lions had killed, and moved on. . . .

The springbok is the life of the plain. It would seem dead without him. You see them first in great shining herds; they go in waves, leaping in the sun, and they look like running water. They sparkle. Then you notice that one is standing right in front of you—a Y-shaped head and pair of ears are staring at you from the grass. They are the most difficult little buck to hit in all Africa. Something in the colouring of this lovely 70-lb gazelle—bright fawn along the back, with its dark lateral band: face, belly and chest white—makes it almost impossible to get the range. The old Boers used to train their sons on them. They would not let the boy gauge the springbok's range by any intermediate object, by estimating it, for instance, in relation to a nearby rock or bush: they took them out on the open veld, where the buck, in the blaze of sun, might look as big as a horse, and asked "How far?" And nearly always the boy shot short. "Give them the full bead," said Hahn, "and you will seldom go wrong."

When I sighted on the first springbok the bead of my Lee-Enfield seemed to cover the entire little animal. My first shot skipped up the dust well this side of him. My second went straight between his legs—sent the buck up into the air in a shower of dust. He bounced off a few paces, and stood there undecidedly. I took up all slack, gave a careful rifle-range squeeze, and—there was no buck. "That's it!" said Hahn.

We paced the distance as we walked up to him: 360 yards. He was lying in the short grass. Just as the springbok dies, the white erectile hairs down the centre of his back, three or four inches long, rise; and he gives off a smell like thyme. They rise, too, in the passion of mating, and probably when he is moved by any strong emotion: and that may be why he always raises them when dying. Sad thought. He was lovely in shining death. I hate to look at a dead buck's eyes: there is something so reproachful in his last stare. But springbok chops are the tastiest venison I have ever eaten, and we were shooting for the pot. "Now," said Hahn, when we had walked back and got the truck and thrown the little 70-lb gazelle into it, "let's take that big wildebeest."

This was an old bull, obviously an exile from his herd, that had been racing our truck that morning. Racing you at night, especially on a rainy one, with their wild manes flying as they try to cross the car in front of you, they look as if you were pacing something straight out of hell. But now this old fellow stood there challenging us: huffing occasionally, and pawing the ground. He was about 400 yards. I got out, sat down on the ground, rested my elbows on my knees, and took a slow squeeze. The old bull gave a lurch. Then he set off in a wild gallop, swinging his head from side to side, shying as if at imaginary objects, and swinging his tail like a propeller—as a wildebeest does when it's been hit. I felt that if I didn't stop him he would go over the horizon. But God was on my side that day, not the wildebeest's; as I was standing there, staring at him hopelessly, he turned and crossed us. I took a chance shot, leading him like a duck—and he went down in a cloud of dust.

He was a most repulsive object when we got up to him—a Blue Wildebeest, rare except in that part of Africa; and this one was as big as a horse. We ripped him up. Vast, stinking insides. Disgusting. Our Ovamba boys went crazy at the prospect of so much fresh meat. First, they cut off the testicles, the choicest bit; then, as the steaming insides came out, they took the lining from the stomach and any amount of odds and ends from the intestines. Even when they had paunched it, it took Hahn, myself, and the four boys to heft this heavy carcass into the truck.

It is the springbok, leaping in the sunrise, that I shall always think of when I think of South Africa. No wonder they have made it their national emblem. And that joyous little animal stood me in good stead when I got down to Capetown. I had been having a desperate half-hour with General Smuts in his Prime Minister's office, trying to get a straight answer from him. He was the most difficult man to pin down that I had ever interviewed. I wanted him to tell me whether the South Africans would take up arms to retain their Mandate over South West Africa. There were 9,600 Germans in the Mandate, many with two passports—German and South African— and I had come out on the boat with 200 of them who had just had their two years' training in the German army and in the labour corps. I said they had been trained to make trouble. This angered Smuts. Finally, the great man permitted himself to say: "I know more about Africa than you do. How long were you up in South West Africa?"

Stung to retort, I told him how I had been on the expedition looking for new land on which to settle some Angola Boers in the unmapped country above Utjo; how I had seen the Doctor Dance of
the Bushmen in the Kalahari Desert, a thing not many white men
have witnessed; how I had trekked with Hahn out into the unoccu-
pied country along the Okavango River; and then, without thinking
about it at all, I just said "And I have seen the springbok *pronking*
in the sunrise".

That had the most astounding effect. Instantly I saw a change in
those blue eyes. Smuts let his swivel-chair come slowly forward. . . .
"So," he said softly, "you have seen *that*." He stared at me reflectively,
then said: "Isn't it beautiful?" And from then on the interview was
his. He did the talking. It was not Smuts, the Prime Minister; it was
Smuts of the veld, the old Commando leader. He talked about South
Africa as I have never heard it talked about since. And I saw the
truth of what Hahn had told me: "Smuts loves South Africa more
than any South African ever loved it. That's the key to his character." After one of the most exhilarating talks I have ever had with a
world figure, I put the question again; and this time Smuts answered
straightly. "Yes. You may say I said we would even go to war to
retain our Mandate over South West Africa. Our position is inde-
feasible." And he took my arm as he walked with me to the door.

I did not talk about springboks with Dr. Malan. It was the last
thing I should have thought of, or that would have interested him.
After one of the most distasteful interviews I have ever had in my
life as a journalist, I came away sizzling with resentments. Yet when
I sat down to write it I could think of no alternative to what he had
said. It was the *way* he said it: he was so pious about his lack of mercy
—so sure he was right. The South Africans, if they can't solve their
colour problem, have nowhere to go. But neither has the black man.
It is a tragic problem for both. But Dr. Malan was not the least
interested in the tragedy of all this: he was just bulling ahead on
the assumption that the black man is a human being who can be
trodden upon with impunity, and—"We will have a Republic within
our time." I knew that Smuts was equally determined to maintain
White Supremacy—but with this difference: Malan, that pious bigot,
regarded the blacks as *Untermenschen,* an under-breed destined for
ever to serve the *Herrenvolk;* Smuts held out the prospect that *one*

day the black man might fit into the white man's world—*one day* there might even be a black man in the Cabinet. And of course every African was entitled to feel that he might be that man. Under Smuts there was hope: under Malan there was none.

Hahn was a South African, and one of the most understanding friends of the black man I have ever met. But he was an outsize man. Strange as it may seem, this troubled continent, which produces some of the most unpleasant white men you will meet anywhere on earth, also occasionally turns out a man of a calibre far bigger than the general run of mankind. And South Africa seems to be the country that can produce the absolute limit in both those extremes.

The old Boers of the back-veld tell you they can name the specific day when life in South Africa began to go wrong: the day gold was discovered on the Rand. From that day on some of the cleverest and most corrupt men this world has ever been cursed with began to pile into South Africa and build Johannesburg: the City of Fear, as it is so rightly called today. Gold, greed and those colossal crooks killed the South Africa that might have been. Yet odd as it may seem, even when you are on the spot, it is the directors of the large Anglo-American mining interests who would give the native his best chance in the industrialised Africa in which he must find his future. These directors are far-sighted men. The most brutally stupid backers of *apartheid* are men of the veld, singing their song of resurgent Afrikanerdom—"The farms we were born on we love above all else" —before the statue of Paul Kruger in Pretoria. They have inherited, or think they have, the space-hungry spirit of the old trek-Boer, who felt stifled if he as much as saw the smoke of another man's fire on the horizon: men unable to express themselves, who had read only one book, the Bible, and whose Predikants of the Dutch Reformed Church are to this day still citing Scripture in support of white supremacy—for the divine right to enslave the Sons of Ham.

But Hahn and his Ovambas were living in a temporary paradise. First, South West Africa was then a Mandate under the League of Nations, and this at a time when world opinion really did count for something, even with the South Africans: next, Ovambaland was a "closed territory"—no white man was allowed to settle there, and it required a Government permit to get in: finally, the Ovambas' cattle were suffering from lung-fever and could not be exported, so Ovambaland had no money economy, and therefore no traders.

"And if God gives me strength," Hahn smiled to me, "I'll keep it this way."

We had two objectives on that trip. One was to pin a witch-doctor murder on the oldest, richest and craftiest of the Ovamba chiefs, who lived up near the Kuenene River on the border of Portuguese West Africa. The other was to obtain some more specimens of a plant that Hahn had found on a previous trip up into the Kaokoveld, then the last bit of unexplored land left in Africa. It was believed that there were natives in the Kaokoveld who had never seen a white man. A letter from Kew had reached Hahn just before we set out, brought the last 175 miles by motor-truck, saying that this specimen of plant he had sent them was entirely unknown to botany: it might be a hangover from the Coal Age. (It was.) Like most men who live their lives in lonely places, Hahn had filled his days by studying everything around him. He knew the native name for every tree, bush or root. He told me he had personal knowledge that some of their medicines worked: "They are frightfully purgative!" "Lovely plant, isn't it?" he said, getting out of the truck to show me one, about shoulder-high, that had horn-shaped flowers, purple-and-white like a morning glory, and leaves like holly. "Well, *above* ground, this plant is quite friendly. But just let an Ovamba put some of the ground-up *roots* of it in your coffee, and you'll be shaking hands with St. Peter that afternoon." He added, not without pride: "These Ovambas are among the best poisoners in Africa. The one we are going to see has sent out word that he will poison anyone who gives evidence against him. They're scared stiff."

"It may seem a queer thing to have dropped in your lap in the twentieth century," he said as we were having our coffee, "this witch-doctor murder. And I'm not sure that I want to find old Muala guilty. If I do, I shall fine him fifty of his best cattle—that will damn' near kill the old miser. Hanging old Muala won't do him any good—he's too stubborn!" He leaned forward and poked the embers. "Besides, what if he were right? What if his witch-doctor did 'smell out' the woman who put the Evil Eye on his child? What do you think, Jan?"

The Hottentot-half of old Jan Vannell smiled. He knew that people could be "wished" to death: he had seen it done. But he was

not going to talk about these dangerous truths before a stranger. It
had not been so long ago that his father's people had hunted his
mother's people like wild animals. And then, I think, he just did not
like to talk about the difference between black and white. Any idea
that we weren't all cast in the same mould upset him. He was unwilling to disturb the peace of mind he had won through years of
association with Hahn. These two men were bound by a mutual respect for each other—simply as men. Old Jan would probably not
have known where to look for London on the map; but trek once
with him through a bit of new country and you could rely on his
carrying a map of it ever after in his head. He could take you back,
pick up the same game trails, point to where they crossed; and, with
an instinct born of sensing a lay of land, tell you the best place to
look for water. He was a natural for existence in *his* world. It did
not matter to him whether a man was an Englishman or a German;
it was the sort of *man* he was that counted. It was almost certain
that I was the first American he had ever seen, so he had little to go
on there.

Hahn was the first native commissioner that I was out with in
the field. And the further they are away from the Secretariat or Government House the better they are. Hahn's final court of judgement
was Geneva. He told me that I was the first journalist who had been
allowed north of Fort Namutoni, and that I was going to be the last.
A bit grey about the ears by the time I met him, he had the right to
wear the Springbok on his cap: for he had been a rugger International and had played for South Africa against England. His reputation was that he could out-run, out-think, out-fight any Ovamba, and
that they knew it. He had tackled and beaten up a couple of the
local bullies who were striding around the scenery when he took
over. But when I asked him how he worked the miracle of governing
117,000 of these notoriously unchastened people without any soldiers
or police, he smiled: "Oh, I don't *govern*. That's the wrong way to
put it. I am the Voice Behind the Chair." And I saw him at it.

He talked Ovamba, of course, probably as well as any of them.
But he would never hold an official talk with chief or headman except in the presence of his official interpreter. "They're very artful
dodgers, these chaps. I don't want any of them to be able to deny
afterwards that they had understood what we had agreed upon in

conference." So, being party to the talks, I had the fun of watching
Hahn go through the equivalent of trying to catch darting trout in a
pool with his bare hands. Until . . . I would see a smile come over
those wise old faces . . . then came a helpless chuckle, then open
laughter . . . he had them. For if you can make the African laugh,
he's yours; and he won't laugh if he thinks you are trying to put something over on him—the African can size up a white man long, long
before the average white man knows it. But he won't show it;
years of being under alien rule have taught him all the arts of dis-
simulation.

Alien rule. No one who knows Africa can deny that the average
African lives in a constant state of terror because of his belief in
witchcraft. Yet I believe that few but religious zealots or business interests exploiting Africa and its cheap labour (before Mau Mau the
average wage of a farm labourer in Kenya was 6d. a day; plus *posho*,
ground-up maize) could honestly deny that—provided such a thing
had been possible in this predatory world—the African would have
been better off if left alone. True, the British did put down the slave
trade; but they followed it by a policy which cut off native life at the
roots. The white man has destroyed one way of native life after another, however suitable for the environment, while failing to put anything equally suitable in their place. And more black men have been
killed in the white man's wars than they ever killed among themselves. More Africans were lost in East Africa, mostly as porters, in
Smuts' futile campaign against von Lettow, than Chaka, contempo-
rary of Napoleon, killed or lost in subduing an area of Africa greater
than all Europe. As I have said: it all depends upon who does the
talking.

In order to persuade the black man of the white man's good intentions, the white man must have them. The thing most lacking
over all Africa today is *heart*. Hahn's job, as he saw it, was to show
the Ovambas the compromises they would soon have to make with
modern times. There were eleven Finnish Missions in Ovambaland
—good and godly men and women, doing a splendid job of work
with their hospital by way of relieving the African of some of his
bodily afflictions; yet so stern were these people in their sterile faith
that, if they could only have had their way, they would have drained
native life of its earthly happiness. They were always petitioning

Capetown (and I believe Geneva) to make Hahn prohibit polyg-
amy. Hahn would not do it. "I'm not going to stop what I know is
right for native economy," he said to me. We were talking outside a
'Christian', one-wife kraal: where with only one woman to plant the
maize, and too few children to look after his cattle, the dreary
Ovamba we had talked with spoke as if he had found life just not
worth living. Whereas I never saw Africans who had it so good as
Nehemiah and his thirteen wives (this appointed headman had
once been a government clerk in Windhoek): they were all fat as
butter, dancing and laughing their heads off. The missionaries
wanted Hahn to stop the dancing. Hahn would not: "It's a crime to
try to kill all native enthusiasms. That's not Christianity." We talked,
also, about a truism, namely that the white man was trying to force
on the black man the very thing that was making his own life so purposeless—the money-urge: was giving him "wants" he did not want
at all, in order to make him work for the white man or buy things
made by the white man. (The poll-tax is what forces him to work
for the white man.) I don't know whether Hahn was a religious man
or not. We never got on to that subject. But his grandfather Hahn,
the old missionary, had been one of the first white men up into
Ovambaland; and there are some grand illustrations, in the old books
on what is now S.W. Africa, of that stubborn old man and his party,
firing from behind their laager of ox-wagons and trying to fight their
way out.

Like most men who have been placed in charge of Africans, Hahn
had become fond of them; and few tribes in Africa have been lucky
enough to have the same commissioner with them for twenty-three
years. It is this being put in charge of primitive people, who come to
trust them, that makes these Provincial and District Commissioners
the exceptionally fine men they usually are: just as, conversely, trying to keep the black man in perpetual subjugation has debased
most white men in Africa. Something always happens to the white
man when he lords it over the black man: it takes him away from all
realities, gives him an undue sense of his own importance in the general scheme of things. It is the District Commissioner in the bush who
has given British colonialism, so far as Africa is concerned, its high
moral reputation. And, of course, Hahn had no settlers or traders to
contend with. He knew that this paradise could not last, but mean-

while he was enjoying it as much as any Ovamba. "I don't know what I will do with myself when I am forced to retire. I don't know where I can fit in."

Briefly, the story of old Muala and the witch-doctor murder was that, years before, a Portuguese Ovamba princess, pestered by the attentions of some Portuguese Don Juans, had fled across the Kuenene River and sought refuge in old Muala's kraal. Muala, a randy old boy, soon had her in the family way. The Portuguese Ovamba princess (and she did look royal—standing there glaring at us in nothing but a short skirt of cow-belly, her slender body painted red) had brought her own servants with her. One of these, who had been made nurse to Muala's 'October' baby, had been 'smelt out' by Muala's witch-doctor, when the child fell ill, as having put the Evil Eye on it. Muala had had her knobkerried to death.

Now the Portuguese had found this out, and, always trying to make trouble for Hahn and his Ovambas across the border, had demanded that old Muala should be executed for murdering a Portuguese subject. Muala first tried to deny that he had ordered the murder. But Hahn had him there. On our way up to his kraal, as we were trying to get the car and truck through the mopani trees— there were no roads, of course, up here—the two men who had killed the woman came out of the forest, got down on their knees, and (like the German generals at Nuremberg) made the substantial plea that if they had refused to obey his orders the Chief would have killed them. It was the official interpreter who suffered most during this investigation. Old Muala used the interpreter's fingers as tally-sticks: taking them one by one and pushing them hard into the sand —and making them stay there—as he answered each point. "All right," he said finally, when the interpreter was on his hands and knees, "I did have her killed." The last finger was jabbed excruciatingly into sand. "And baby get well!" He had presented us with an incontestable fact. He rested his case on that.

"He's a wonder!" Hahn laughed under his breath as we left the kraal. "He knows damned well that I know that he thought he was doing nothing wrong. And what are you going to do about that?" Old Muala did not swing. "If we left," said Hahn, "people like my-

self and the missionaries, the witch-doctors would be dancing over
all Africa within a week."

Hahn and I went up along the high-rushed bank of the Kuenene,
taking a rifle along in case we stumbled on the odd crocodile. Walking ahead with a shotgun, in the hope we might put up some ducks,
I suddenly stepped into a hollow where the high grass had been
pressed flat, and it smelled as if I had my nose pressed against the
flank of a very hot horse. . . . "There he is!" said Hahn. "Look at
him." It was a hippo. He came past us, coasting down the stream,
less than twenty feet off: then he submerged, came up again, and
gave an ecstatic puff . . . he wiggled his little cat's ears . . . he went
on down, and then he waded out on the opposite bank just before
he came to the falls, plodded back up through the rushes, and waded
into the river again. Again he came past us—*Paaaah!* he puffed as
he came up for air. "By God," I laughed. "He's playing a game!"
"Of course," muttered Hahn. "He's enjoying his life. It's great, isn't
it?"

We went up on the bank and I sat there smoking. Of all the sights
I have seen in Africa that was the one that has probably pleased
me most. There was something so right about the immense enjoyment
of that monstrous animal. "Now if you were a Boer," said Hahn,
"you'd shoot it. Even if you knew you couldn't get across river to
pick it up. . . ."

Hahn is dead now. South West Africa has been made a Fifth
Province of the Union, in fact if not in name. The Ovamba paradise
is ended. When we camped outside their staked kraals they were
celebrating a good harvest; their corn was in, their cattle were mul-
tiplying (never mind sick or sound, it was numbers that counted);
their drums were throbbing, and they were dancing until far into
the nights as the flames in their kraals waved up to the stars—boom-
ing like happy bullfrogs. It takes a lot to kill the African. Maybe they
are dancing yet, though I doubt it. Minerals have been discovered
in their territory. New wealth has been found in Africa—but not for
them.

As my train left South West Africa for the Cape through those miles
of dusty hell above Deelfontein, a stunned Englishman in my compartment said to me: "In this miserable country, it is no wonder that

people have such unpleasant minds! I could not believe that anything could be so awful as this." He had yet to see the lovely vine and orchard country in Cape Province and the green rolling hills of Natal. But these red wastes were, anyhow, more the result of what man had done to the land than of what the land had done to man. I sometimes felt I was waking from a dream when I closed a book such as Stuart Cloete's beautiful *Turning Wheels,* or *Jock of the Bushveld,* where you could read of a time when there was always more land to be had for the taking, always more of unknown Africa to lure you on beyond the blue horizon: and when the veld was green and flowered.

The Englishman and I stared dumbly at the hot ironstone rocks, glistening as if wet in the eye-searing sun: disintegrating black table-tops, with slopes of broken rubble. . . . A dust storm swirled across the landscape. . . . "Mummy! Mummy! Look!" cried a child in the corridor. "Look at the perfectly beyoot-iful river!" Upington! The train pulled slowly across the Orange River on a bridge three thousand feet long, over a broad, swift flow of liquid mud. It rolled on. The Englishman closed his eyes. . . .

Then he was talking again. "You take a nap," he groaned. "You wake up—and you feel it can't be true! This awful aridness! These same stupid hills staring at you! . . . I think I am beginning to understand the South Africans. If you do have to look at scenes like this—all day long—all your life—then, by God, you *need* the Bible! You have to believe there is a future life—otherwise, this one would be hopeless. . . ."

HEART OF

DARKNESS

I can well understand how Schweitzer found his Reverence for Life. On a steamer slowly creeping up the Ogówé River, they passed through a herd of hippos in the sunset—and suddenly, after years of searching, "there flashed into my mind, unseen and unsought, the phrase 'Reverence for Life'. The iron door had yielded: the path in the thicket had become visible. Now I had found my way to the idea in which affirmation of the world and ethics are contained side by side!" I can well understand how, in the colours of that peaceful sunset—seeing those immense beasts so happily at play, and thinking how right it was that they should be able to enjoy *their* life— Schweitzer found the key. After struggling for years with *Wir Epigonen* ("We Inheritors of a Past"), and talking with some of the best minds in Europe, Schweitzer saw the relationship of the ideals of civilisation with life in an African river. "I am life which wills to live, in the midst of life which wills to live."

You will find that note in many an old book on Africa, usually written without its author being aware of what he was saying. It was just the call of Africa to him. *Jock of the Bushveld* has this philosophy lying in the darkness just beyond the glow of every one of its camp-fires (and Sir Percy Fitzpatrick was far from being a starry-eyed sentimentalist when it came to grabbing *his* share in the scramble for Africa). You will hear it talked around campfires by some of the toughest, roughest men you will ever come up against. In that best hour of the day in Africa, when you are enjoying the luxury of be-ing absolutely dead beat but contented, and are having your sundowner by the fire, you will often hear an old-timer say: "Seems a damn' shame to break a peace like this, doesn't it? And I've known times when I just wouldn't—wouldn't pull the trigger. I've lain there, watching them enjoy their lives in the sunset. Then I've sneaked quietly off and come back to camp." That feeling is common. And any man who has not felt that sympathy for the animal he was about to shoot, and that hesitancy to shatter the scene, has never known Africa.

But there is another side to all this. There is something dark in the heart of Africa. I have been in some parts of it where I am absolutely certain God never intended any man to live, black or white. They destroy him. The white man, oddly enough, seems to stand up better than the black man in these malignant spots; but that is his medicines. His is an interior rot, a spiritual collapse—not that so many of them have had so far to fall anyhow. But the black man is deformed both physically and mentally. He loses his shape. He looks hardly human. And, in some parts of Africa, he scarcely is. The hostility of his habitat has become part of his mind; it functions in his subconsciousness long after you have placed him in shorts and Mother Hubbards. Richard Wright, the American Negro writer, who went to the Gold Coast thinking he would be able to get to the back of the black man's mind because he was of the same colour, was warned in the Prime Minister's own office: "Don't you be funny about *juju!* There's something in it." This from Kwame Nkrumah's secretary. The B.A. from Balliol comes back to Nigeria, and puts the stylish safety-pin back in his ear-lobe. An African Assistant District Officer in Nyanza (one of the six at that time in all Kenya), a graduate of Makerere, asked me whether I didn't think he would be justified in begging for a Government grant to replace the two teeth his parents had knocked out, so that he could spit better—or look pretty. He had a copy of Aldous Huxley's *Perennial Philosophy* coyly placed on his desk in the Commissioner's *boma,* where he hoped it would be noticed. Kakamega, January, 1948.

Africa is the most brutal of all the continents. How difficult it is to live in some parts of it no one can imagine who has never tried to push his way through the thorn-scrub, with its interlocking three-inch spikes—so choking that you think hardly a snake could breathe there: or to wade through its malarial swamps or penetrate a rain forest: or to cross some of the waterless spaces of its advancing deserts. Over large parts of Africa there has never been even an approach towards that dubious thing we call civilisation. Instead, square mile after square mile, African existence has always been an abject thing of unbroken misery. Here is where the witch-doctor thrives. This is the land of the sorcerers.

Having travelled through the country of these hideous distortions, chronically suppurating sores, rotting limbs; having seen, over immense areas, people who were racked by fevers, eaten by worms and parasites, wasted by ever-present semi-starvation, I say, and it would be hard to deny, that if the European, with his superior knowledge and skills, can bring release to such misery, then he could be pardoned for almost any act of exploitation. The fact is that the European in Africa today is suffering more from his goodness than from his badness: every hospital he puts up, every clinic, every veterinary station, adds to the pressure of man and animal on the land—makes too small a living space for Africans. So they clamour to drive the white man out. The population problem hangs over all Africa like a black cliff. And now each man needs the other, black and white, if Nature is ever to be held off from solving this problem in her old way: by starvation. The white man has the know-how. (And it is going to be no advance for the African if he replaces the witch-doctor by the communist.)

These gruesome disfigurements you see in some parts of Africa speak of agonies that man was never meant to bear. And in these scenes the thought comes that people mutilate their own bodies—carve their faces into waffles with cicatrices, etc., or cut off one testicle, although that has now gone out of fashion—as if in unconscious derision of such human suffering. It is the masochism of despair. In some parts of Africa I have felt that Horror was ever-present in the atmosphere; that Horror was its strongest characteristic. The carved masks of Africa show that terror in the black man's mind. Over most of Negro Africa, Horror is still made a *practice*. It is so deeply rooted in the African's subconsciousness that, one comes to believe, even a European university education will not drive it out; not until the second or third generation of the same African family. Even the African clerk, sitting in the District Commissioner's office, and very likely a graduate of Makerere or Achimoto, lives in two worlds—and the Spirits of the Departed, who inhabit that Other World, are infinitely more real to him, and more to be feared (witness the terrifying power of the Mau Mau oath), than any human being walking about in this world. Invoke the Evil Spirits against him and he thinks he is finished. This does not apply to only the skin-clad native.

Furthermore, anyone who has had long to do with the Africans, such as the District Commissioners and *Administrateurs,* will tell you that these fetishes and taboos and death from the Evil Eye do have a lot in them—if only the overwhelming power of suggestion. From what I have seen with my own eyes on both coasts, and in central Africa, I know that these superstitions work. I know it from intelligent old Muala's absolute faith that his witch-doctor had smelt-out the woman who was wishing his child to death, and from the simplicity with which he said "And baby get well." You could have argued until you were black in the face and not have shaken his fixed conviction. And I know it from the way a Masai *laibon* at Arusha, Tanganyika, when I was there in 1939, was dying in hospital —with nothing wrong with him whatsoever, so far as the European doctors could make out (and this was confirmed by the post-mortem), except that he was unshakably convinced that he had been bewitched by another Masai *laibon.* All of which shows that these powerful medicine-men, who terrify the warrior Masai (and it is about the only thing that does frighten them), absolutely believe their own stuff. It is a known fact that all the Masai *laibons* have died young, and all from "heart failure": except old Lenena, who was one of the two top *laibons* when the British came to settle in East Africa, and died at a ripe old age as late as 1911. But then, the Masai hasten to tell you, he was the most powerful *laibon* of all.

I remember what happened on the Loita Plateau, where the Kenya Government had quarantined the entire Engidongi Clan at 8,000 feet, forcing them all to live within sight of a police post which had been established there. This tribe, from one hill, used to supply all the *laibons* for the Masai of both Kenya and Tanganyika. And a more sinister set I have seldom looked at. I was up there with Eric Sweatman, Officer-in-Charge of Masai, who had been in Africa for twenty-six years, and is still in charge of the Masai. And as he held court, and the charges were read out against twenty-one of these 'bad hats', even the Tribal Police turned their heads away—afraid to meet their eye. In that Country of the Magicians, lost in the clouds, with the lovely impala staring at us from the poison bushes, the spotted cattle grazing peacefully on the plains, and thousands of guinea-fowl scattering before us like mechanical mice, we were none of us at all certain, as we walked back to our camp, that we had not been listening to black wizards who knew a lot of things which the white man didn't or had forgotten. It was disturbing. Three of these *laibons* had been quarantined there because their own clans had asked to have them taken away from them. And at a forced cattle sale at Narok I saw the beautiful fierce Masai senior warriors turn their heads, and get up and walk off, when a *laibon* with that black head-piece they wear strolled on the scene. At a sale just such as this, in the same spot, a young Masai warrior had killed the District Commissioner Major Hugh Grant in 1946, throwing his 7-foot steel spear clean through him. What had made it absolutely obligatory to hang him was that it was shown he had *greased* his spear, as the Masai do when they intend to kill someone—or a lion. That men like this can be frightened to look at another man, just because he has that strange black cloth wrapped round his evil head, is pretty good evidence that a Masai *laibon* does have something. I can only speak from what I have seen: I am convinced he has.

When I was in the Belgian Congo the Governor at Stanleyville told me that he had six Leopard Men in prison there, and was waiting Brussels' permission to shoot them. At lunch he showed me a personal letter he had written to a friend of his in the Belgian Government:

"In 1938, 400 native women were killed around Wamba. One Leopard Man, caught, took the white police to 38 dead bodies—all with their breasts cut off and their hearts cut out. The Leopard Men had eaten them. Who knows what goes on in it [the forest]; it is full of dead bodies!"

"I need all the influence I can get," he smiled, "because it is hard to believe such things—in Brussels." He told me how the Leopard Men tear out a child's eyes and put them in a bowl of oil with the little knives they fasten to each of their own fingers. This is so that the 'Knives may have Vision!' The knives are worn on the inside of the fingers: they make marks like a leopard's claws. The Leopard

Men are probably the most powerful secret society in Equatorial Africa.

"I want the other natives here to *see the blood run out* of these Leopard Men—that is why I do not want to hang them in prison—I want these poor dark-minded natives to watch a Leopard Man die—right before their eyes—so that they will know they are not supernatural. I have little hope, and it is not very pleasant to shoot a man full of holes so that an audience may watch the blood run out of him—but it just might start some of them thinking that the Leopard Men they now live in abject terror of are, after all, only mortals, just like you and me. This is no question of fighting horror with an even greater horror. The natives who will watch this disgusting sight will be completely unmoved, and so will the Leopard Men. I just want to start them *thinking*." And he shrugged his shoulders.

I had come this way on my 120-day drive across Africa from the Indian Ocean to the Atlantic—it was before the military roads were built during the last war—because I wanted to see something of the river. And below Stanleyville, where I went ashore at a landing on the left bank, I saw some of the most horrible human types I have seen anywhere in the world. It was not that they had been debased; it was just that they had not even begun to move along the road of evolution. Or so it seemed. The figures even of the women were hardly human, still less feminine. These tribesmen, who had come to the river from the deep, interior jungle, probably from the great swamps that lie south of that part of the Congo, were thin to the point of emaciation; the women had no hips; their breasts, leathery straps, were the only parts of their bodies that distinguished them from the scrawny men. They were a ghastly example of that chronic undernourishment which afflicts most natives all their lives in Equatorial Africa. And the chief objects of envy in their barter-market on the bank were some smoked rats. Some of these rodents were the size of a cat. They were cut into sections. The Congo here may be ten miles wide; but all you see are two walls of jungle, sometimes less than a hundred yards apart, with little red and white buoys bobbing between them. At one of these channels the captain swung his tug around, up-current, and anchored: "I'm not going down that stretch of water with the sun in my eyes." He would not chance it.

It was this stretch of river that Conrad saw, with such a lasting effect upon him, on his voyage up the Congo as first mate of the *Roi des Belges,* his only fresh-water voyage; and he returned from it with malaria, dysentery, a disgust with white traders and exploiters, and—*Heart of Darkness.* In that haunting tale he pictures the moral desolation of the white man, debased by Africa. He also gives a bitter picture of the white man's mission, as interpreted by Leopold II's International Association for the Civilisation of Central Africa, remnants of which remain to this day in the interior Congo. If Conrad saw Africans labouring with chains around their necks at Matadi in 1890, I saw them in other parts of the Congo with chains around their necks in 1939. Though not in the main towns. And going up on the new road to cross the Ubangi River to Bongassau in French Equatorial Africa, I saw, in one remote convict camp in the bush, the flogging posts. This camp was being run by a Belgian pervert, whose sole amusement seemed to be some night-club dolls he had brought from Europe to keep him company—toy dolls, with pierrot hats. I have met few things more revolting than those limp, painted dolls lying on his sofa in the jungle, where he could look out and watch the natives being whipped.

In Ubangi-Shari, which I think was the most desperate region I passed through in Africa, though that may have been my malaria (it is the only place I have ever been where I saw the entire French community tiddly at ten in the morning—and it was where I fell off the wagon, after eighteen months), André Gide found white men so debased, so vicious—working the Africans as slaves in the great forests—that he put his indignation into *Voyage au Congo:* an indictment that shattered the big French *concessionaires,* if only for a time. I know of no book that is so full of pity for the blacks—or the whites, for that matter. He dedicated that book *To the Memory of Joseph Conrad.* I read it in the Belgian and French Congo; and when I met Gide later at Ascona in Switzerland I had the satisfaction of repeating one of his sentences to him, a sentence that had given me such pleasure when I read it, for I had found it true over all Africa: *"The less intelligent the white man the more stupid he thinks the black."*

Gide had a body-feeling for the man of colour, as he revealed in *The Immoralist*—with all the insights, into virtues as well as vice, which that terrible understanding brought with it. Schweitzer would have been revolted by such knowledge. Schweitzer, one feels, is always conscious of being white, which is not necessarily to say superior—though it has always seemed to me that the good Dr. Schweitzer is a little too sure of himself in his paternal handling of the African, and in his feeling that the black man is still a child, and that "Father knows best". He has said: *"Ein Wilder ist ein Wilder! A savage is always a savage."* He has done a noble amount of good just by being alive; but his influence has been far greater in the United States and Europe than it has been in Africa. And that is the way I think he intended it to be. Schweitzer wants the white man to have a change of heart. In Africa, his personal example, his influence and his ability to do good are limited strictly to the sick Africans around Lamberéné.

Schweitzer is not interested in African nationalisms. In Washington, D.C., in 1954 a discontented Nigerian intellectual complained to me: "Dr. Schweitzer is not interested in the things we want him to be interested in. He is not interested in our political ambitions." Wise Dr. Schweitzer. If the Africans had studied Dr. Schweitzer more intently, they would have seen that he has little admiration for the civilisation of Europe, and would therefore have no reason to back their entering it. Perhaps he sees beyond politics and knows that self-rule will fail to bring them the happiness that they accept as automatically coming from it. Perhaps he knows that they are unready for it, or it for them. And he has made it plain that he has little use for African intellectuals who feel themselves so superior to their own people, and won't work with their hands. Schweitzer's own fulfilled life, in self-isolation, is sufficient proof of what he thinks of modern times.

Conrad, plainly, hated Africa, and all there was in it. He shows merely a passing compassion for the starved and dying Africans he saw on the river bank at Matadi. But Africa fused his genius. "Before the Congo," he said, "I was just an animal." Conrad, Gide, Schweitzer: the three different Africas they saw lay within themselves. Schweitzer saw in the walls of jungle, as he went up the Ogówé River in that peaceful sunset, not Africa—"silent, inscrutable, implacable"—but a symphony. "I am life in a life that wills to live." Gide saw an equal fellow-man. All three Africas are there.

APATHY AND AFRICA

A thinking man cannot be long in Africa without beginning to resent the phrase "Leave it to the man on the spot". The African is also a man on the spot, and with a much longer residence. If the white man thinks he has an African problem, we also are the African's. It would be well not to forget that. The "man on the spot" misjudged the situation over Mau Mau—and the Kikuyu—as disastrously as could be. The Kenya settlers' continual charge was that the Kikuyu were a worthless and cowardly race, etc., etc., etc. "Oh, I wouldn't have a Kuke on the place! Not if I could get anyone else. They're a cowardly, slinking lot. And they're not *grateful!*" You heard that everywhere. "Black baboonery, my boy. Black baboonery." This last was the stock reply of Colonel E. S. Grogan, the most senior of all Kenya elder statesmen: that fine gentleman (as he most certainly is), who as a young Cambridge undergraduate walked from Cape to Cairo during the years 1897 and 1900; who, as senior member of the Kenya Legislative Council, advised that body, on November 21st 1952, to "catch a hundred of these rascals . . . charge them with treason . . . hang twenty-five per cent of them in front of the remainder . . . who should be sent back to the Reserves to break the joyful news to the others. . . ." "Black baboonery, my boy," seemed his only answer when you asked him what he thought should be done about such and such a Kikuyu complaint, as you came on him sitting in his usual noon-time place at the table in the café-lounge of Torr's Hotel (which he owned), surrounded by his ring of admirers—of whom I am one. It has always puzzled me how a man I was so fond of could talk like the Gestapo. And be so blind! They have hanged over 1000. Less than 300 of these were charged with murder.

It was estimated in 1952 that there were 7,000 Mau Mau in the forest—and they have kept an equal number of British troops, with aeroplanes, engaged for over three years. Furthermore, the suicidal bravery of the loyal Kikuyu chiefs who have stood up against Mau Mau has excited worldwide wonder and admiration.

On the other hand, the same thinking man cannot be long in London without beginning to know that the white man who has made his home in East and Central Africa has a tragic amount of right on his side. The ignorance and apathy about Africa in England is appalling. This does not matter very much so far as the general public is concerned, but when it is allowed to exist in official quarters it becomes colonial suicide. That is *the* reason why the desperate Kenya settlers today have been taking the law into their own hands, and getting away with it. Before this last war shook Britain out of her complacent colonial dream, only one day a year was allowed in the House of Commons for the Colonial Debate—with never more than a handful of Members present. Sir Richard Acland, probably speaking without thinking—which is the way truth so often does get into print—said: "We [the M.P.s] always regarded it as an occasion for a day off."

When I returned to Africa in 1947 (at the request of the Kenya Government, to study and write a book on that Crown Colony), the August two-day debate on Colonial Affairs never had more than 46 Members in the House, and no more than 30 for most of that apathetic session; and during some of this speech-making—when Smuts had just warned England that "Africa is the last continent"—only 12 Members were in their seats. The speeches, all told, covered a mere six hours. "In short," said F. S. Joelson, in his *East Africa and Rhodesia,* "a House of 640 Members could hardly have demonstrated more forcibly its indifference to Colonial Affairs." In 1954, the two-hour debate on Colonial Affairs, mostly about Kenya, before the House of Commons rose for its Christmas recess, "was to an almost empty Chamber, which halfway through the discussion contained no more than 14 Members. . . ." "Thus again [warned that good man, F. S. Joelson] did members show their scant courtesy and lack of interest in matters which are of the highest importance to the

United Kingdom." And yet they still talk of guardianship! What kind of concern is that, for either black or white man in Africa?

This Parliamentary apathy, and lack of public interest, has resulted in my opinion, at any rate, in the chief thing wrong with colonialism: the fact that it has never been applied. Lack of interest led to lack of development in the colonies: of people as well as of resources. The office of Secretary of State for the Colonies was allowed to be a second-rate political plum, usually handed to some faithful party hack, and not infrequently to a pompous ass. The planters and settlers, left on their own as it were, carried on with their amateur development, literally shut off from modern times. There were riots in Trinidad, British Guiana, Honduras, Jamaica; and the British public was surprised. Planters and settlers, isolated for so long, become maniacal egotists; remember the bedlam that broke into print when Lord Corvedale, the son of Stanley Baldwin, stepped ashore as the newly appointed Governor of Antigua. Thousands and thousands of Jamaicans leave the island and make their way to England, seeking work—and England begins to get an active colour bar. Put any name to it that you like: these are the results of the fact that the concept of colonialism has not been carried out. London has not been interested.

It was for this reason that when I was on some of the big farms in East Africa I found myself agreeing heart and soul with the settlers. It was, in fact, the way I got the title for my first book on Africa. I had been listening to a group of settlers in southern Tanganyika explaining that "the worst obstacle that we are up against is this lack of interest back home": they had just received the *Sunday Express* of March 12th 1939, whose leading editorial ran as follows:

"These ex-German colonies cannot be incorporated into our Imperial System. They stand in the way of the United Empire. For twenty years the Sunday Express *has been saying: 'Get rid of them. They mean trouble for us. We are bound to let them go in the end. And the sooner we release ourselves from these danger spots the better.'"*

"There you are!" challenged the red-faced leader of these settlers. "Press lord shouting that Tanganyika should be handed back to the Germans—so that they can buy peace in Europe! That's how the Mother Country loves *us!*" I tried, politely, to say that Tanganyika belonged to nobody at the moment: it was a Mandate—a "nation under tutelage", as the preamble had it. "Not that anyone believes that sophistry," I added. "No, no, no," laughed an old elephant-hunter in that angry party: *"that's* not the point at all. Point is—and it's got nothin' to do with right or wrong, or whether anybody loves us—which they don't—nobody just gives a damn what happens to us poor bastards down here behind God's back." *Behind God's Back.* This was the title, right then and there, for my book about the incredible moves on this chequerboard of black-and-white, so soon to be smeared with blood—smeared so that the rights and wrongs of any move cannot be seen clearly any more.

It is useless to speculate about the impossible, so I shall not discuss love between white man and black, though it has existed. I was on farms in Kenya, as late as 1948, where the relations were touching. It made you happy, as you looked out over the golden wheat to the blue Escarpment, and saw the African workers living with their wives and children on the farm—which is the way it should be—, to feel that here was a life on the land that was good for both black and white. Most white settlers hate having African families on their land: they say that "squatters" ruin a farm. They say nothing about how much they grudge giving any African any land to live on in the White Highlands—that earthly paradise, which they are trying to label FOR EUROPEANS ONLY! I have my own opinion why Mau Mau was allowed to come about. I think it was because of that type of settler who was afraid to concede anything for fear he would lose everything. They were very plentiful in Kenya Colony. They were the most vocal of the settlers, the most stupid: and they held the safety-valve down too long. I don't see how any white leadership, or laws, can now cool off the hatreds which were allowed to boil over, bringing to the surface that hereditary addiction to horror, with its attendant evils, which seems, as I have said, to lurk in the sub-consciousness of every African. Only the years, and they must be years of comparative peace, can wean the African from that dark past of his. Thousands of Kikuyu (the latest number given from Nairobi is 12,000) will have to be held in custody in Kenya for some years to come, call that form of preventative detention by any name you like. And as to how all this will end, only one thing is certain: "in order to persuade the black man of the white man's good intentions —the white man must have them."

As it is, settlers who misinform London about situations as serious as this, who say that land and low wages and miserable housing conditions have nothing to do with African discontent, only prevent London from *acting*. London does not move until it is too late. It seems impossible to make such settlers see that they are only harming themselves and Kenya by such misrepresentations of a crisis. It was Sir Philip Mitchell himself, as able and honest a Governor as Kenya ever had, with a genuine love for the black man, who, shortly before he retired, asked for a Royal Commission to be sent out to study Kenya's serious land and social problems. This letter of Sir Philip's (which lay on the Colonial Office desk for eighteen months) warned London that "we [in Kenya] are confronted with an agrarian, economic and social revolution", and suggested that a Royal Commission be sent out quickly to study this revolution "*in a modern way*" (my italics) in order that East Africa might not suffer as other parts of the world have done "by allowing the revolution to run its course unregulated and undirected".

Sir Philip Mitchell used the word *revolution*. But the sense of urgency was not so overwhelming in London as it was in Sir Philip Mitchell. For the three most dangerous months of its short and troubled history no new Governor was sent out to Kenya after he retired. By the time the Royal Commission did arrive, Mau Mau had broken out.

In some parts of the South Marigoli District of the teeming Kavirondo Reserve the population is over 900 natives to the square mile. This is in the comparatively rich grain-growing province of Nyanza, which produced immense supplies of maize during the last war—and where the natives are always hungry. I have stood on one plot in that territory where four families, all agriculturalists, were trying to make a living (to keep alive would be the right way to put it) on 2¼ acres. As I know this statement will be challenged by the incredulous, and I do not blame them, I give the exact location: it is among a maze of grey boulders in which the Kavirondo were huddled like rabbits (before myxomatosis), on a 47-degree slope, at a place called Lotego, near Majengo, in South Marigoli—four families in four huts; twenty-five people on 2¼ acres, planted in cassava, sor-

ghum and early maize. I don't say this is typical of the Kavirondo
Reserve—far from it. But I do say that the inability to redress such
a shocking example of destitution at once does show the alarming
conditions which must exist in the remainder of that overcrowded
and worked-out reserve. It may require some hard thinking to put
yourself in the place of a native cooped up in one of these human
zoos, but it would be worth it. For the situation is becoming increas-
ingly dangerous for the white man. The white man has to think of
something better than this obsolete system of the reserves. As one
Agricultural Officer who heard I had been at this place exclaimed
bitterly:

"We can sit on the safety-valve for so long. But that is all we are
doing. Something *big* has got to be done, *and not in the reserves*.
And we'd better be damned quick about it!"

The only answer, he said, was the alienation of big blocks of land
for big schemes, using machinery. It is idle to tell Europe that the
native way of agriculture is insufficient unless you give Africans the
land they can cultivate in European fashion. At the present moment, if all the land in the Kavirondo Reserve were cultivated by
the natives in the very best type of small-holdings, that would just
barely give a living to the present population, to say nothing of the
future.

With Europeans numbering less than 1 per cent of the total population, and some 70,000 Africans in prison or behind the barbed
wire—approximately double the number of the entire European
population—one set of the Kenya settlers asserts that it is now a
multi-racial colony. The other set—and there are always two sets, at
least, among the chronically quarrelling Kenya settlers—is angrily
declaring that the new constitutional proposals for Kenya, which the
first set accepted, were jammed by Mr. Oliver Lyttelton, then Secretary of State for the Colonies, down the Kenya settlers' throats. Now
which side is "seeing things as they are"?

A few days ago, I took the notes of the last three years I had been
keeping on Kenya, and put them in the garage: they are a Kenya
of the past—though among them was the curious letter about Mau
Mau written by Sir Alfred Vincent, Kenya elder statesman and then
Kenya member of the East African Central Legislative Assembly,

which appeared in the *Daily Telegraph* of November 21st 1952; and in which he said:

"We all know this present trouble has nothing to do with land hunger or lack of housing, but is part of a greater subversive activity emanating from without, which first raised its ugly head in its distinctive form in 1948. The Government was warned at that time in no uncertain terms."

What a staggering statement! And what was this sinister outside activity of which the Kenya Government had been warned in no uncertain terms: why not name it? Sir Alfred Vincent is of South African origin, and he made the speech at a dinner in Nairobi given by the South African Society of East Africa to Dr. Albertus Geyer, retiring South African High Commissioner in London, who was visiting Kenya on his way back to the Union. During that speech, General Sir George Erskine, Commander-in-Chief, East Africa, got up from his chair and walked out. Sir Alfred Vincent blamed Britain's "weak and unrealistic colonial policies" for "East Africa's deplorable state" and said that British colonial affairs were "becoming more and more at the mercy of British party politics and queer societies in London". General Erskine doubtless left the dinner because he could not tolerate such drivel.

The chances are that if Sir Alfred Vincent was obliged to define what he meant by the ominous implication in his letter, it would come down to the charge that the communists were behind Mau Mau. For the communist is the nigger in every African wood-pile these days. He is the whipping-boy, a handy explanation given Europe for bad management and outbreaks of native discontent; but he may be there in the flesh if some native wrongs, and genuine unhappiness, are not righted.

The Kikuyu have been agitating for land ever since 1928, when, as Jomo Kenyatta said at his trial, they first became aware of the 1915 Crown Lands Ordinance,* which defined as Crown Lands (i.e. as belonging to the Government) "all lands previously occupied by native people". From 1922 onwards one Commission after another visited Kenya to hear evidence on this dispute: the most important

*Amended in 1939.

being the Kenya Land Commission, under the chairmanship of Sir Morris Carter, which published its report (some essential recommendations of which are still unimplemented) in 1934. When in 1948 I was in the Kiambu District of the Kikuyu Reserve, its richest district—and the one in which the Mau Mau trouble broke out—I was so impressed with what the leading Kikuyu told me there, and with how it wildly contradicted what I had been told in Nairobi, that I got the official report of Mr. Colin Maher on that district, and found that it placed the *landless* Africans at Kiambu at as high as 40 per cent. He stated:

"On the assumption that 40 per cent of the population is already landless and that 10 per cent of that figure are engaged in non-agricultural work, on the present density in Kiambu some 90,000 persons might become without means of support within a short space of time: something which cannot be viewed with equanimity."

How anyone can say that land-hunger had nothing to do with the outbreak of Mau Mau is beyond comprehension. Apart from all the other evidence, I would trust that grand old man Chief Waruhiu, whom I met at Kiambu, and who was about the only man I did meet in Africa in whom I felt that the teaching of Christianity had completely fulfilled its mission. (The Africans take it so literally.) It was the strength of that grand old man's character alone that was keeping his people at Kiambu happy and away from the savage discontent that was already apparent in that district. That is why, in my opinion, Waruhiu was the first big African chief that Mau Mau murdered: they had to get him off the scene. And it was his son, David Waruhiu, whom I had to stay with me here in my house in North Devon. David is now M.R.A., working at the rehabilitation camp on the Athi river to "change" some of the Mau Mau and their sympathisers there and help them "up the ladder to freedom", as it is being called. They could not have a better man.

I asked him to write down, in his own words, what he thought the Africans *needed* most; which, of course, was not necessarily what they wanted most. His answers placed first things first. I give them, copied out of my notebook where he wrote them:

"1. *Education.* Compulsory Education—for all school-going ages of all races. Local Government (the Local Native Council) to be responsible for Elementary Education, and Central Government for Higher Education. Meals should be provided to school-going children. More schools are needed in order that long distances walked by children are reduced.

"2. *Technical Education* [he underlined that!]. Technical schools must be established whereby children, irrespective of race, can be *trained to use their hands,* etc. (My italics.)

"Agricultural Schools.
Veterinary Schools.

"3. This is the only way we can ensure that Africans are being equipped for the posts which in the long run they must fill in the Railway and Telegraphs Depts., printing works, etc. Africans should be taken as artisans [I think he means as apprentices] so that they will eventually become qualified to take up the responsible positions.

"In any field of Education, Religion must be included in the curriculum, for any education without moral education is a very poor form of education."

Most thinking District Commissioners in British Africa will tell you that the reason why so many Government plans fail is because the minds of the African peoples have not been prepared for those plans. They place education as the foremost need—if only, they say, to help them handle their major problem, the psychological problem: to get the African to believe in the white man and his good intentions, and to teach him that he must co-operate in plans for his own salvation. Education is still not compulsory for the African in Kenya, and it will be a long time before it can be made compulsory. This is the African's greatest deprivation. But that is not the white man's deliberate intention: he has no wish to keep the black man in ignorance (it is only in South Africa that they are now trying to do that by means of the Bantu Education Act). The Kenya Government claims, with truth, that even if the colony could shoulder the enormous expense of putting up schools to educate its 5½ million Africans (and Kenya is a poor colony, with none of the mineral wealth of the Rhodesias and the Belgian Congo) it could not possibly find enough teachers to conduct them. That is absolutely true. They can't in England! So it is nonsense, all this talk that is so popular today about having jumped the African from the Stone Age into the Atomic Age. What has really happened, I say again (for it is worth repeating), is that the European has destroyed the old African way of life, and the restraining power of the tribal elders, without putting a new African civilisation in its place. He has left the African between two worlds.

"Just out of the tree!" as some of the settlers (though their number is sharply decreasing) still try to tell you in Kenya. There is nothing atomic in Kenya—except the white man's growing apprehension about his own position in the world. This sense of insecurity inclines him to violence when crossed. One of the most obvious things I noted when I was last in Kenya was that the white man seemed to have lost a lot of his self-confidence—*and that the natives saw it*. It was contagious. And when the native sees that the white man is no longer quite sure of himself, he is no longer sure about the white man. That, make no mistake, is one of the reasons for his running amok, as it is called. The majority of these Africans have been stuffed in Reserves; the rest have been brought shockingly little forward; the black man, for the most part, is still regarded as a cypher, a cheap labourer that can be used at will. And now they are beginning to revolt against it all.

One grows tired of those after-dinner reminiscences of Colonial Governors: "Why, when I came out to East Africa, forty years ago, these chaps here didn't even know the use of the wheel!" They haven't got so many wheels today: a few bicycles, perhaps.

The philanthropic excuse for colonisation is that it brings backward people forward. Now it stands to reason that if the 40,000 Europeans in Kenya cannot possibly raise the money to educate 5½ million Africans, the 11,000 Europeans in Tanganyika are even less able to educate the 7½ million Africans in that so-called Trusteeship. What can be done about it? The desire of the African for education is touching. What he gets is even more pathetic. When I was in Kenya in 1948 I went into the records. The statistics, for what they are worth, showed that there were over 2,000,000 children of school age in Kenya. Out of these not more than 200,000 were at school at any one time. But there was no continuous education even for these. One half of them left school within the first two years, never to return.

Only about 10,000 ever finished their primary school. Only 6,000 of these ever went on to secondary, and of how many completed that course I could find no record. Only about seventy students a year went on to enter Makerere College over in Uganda, the peak of African education in East Africa. The British had been in Kenya fifty years—and had not yet appointed a single African to a major post in its civil service.

As for the Benefit of the European Example in agriculture, I have yet to see a farm where the individual African has been given enough land to use a tractor. Though this must be emphasised too—it is largely the African's fault that he has not got that tractor. I was on the big Makueni scheme where 250,000 acres were being cleared of bush and tsetse-fly in the Wakamba Reserve (they had to shoot 1,000 rhinos, sad to say, to make the bush safe) and found that the Africans, who had been given a plot, all found, were trying to prevent the communal manure-cart from crossing their land. They are suspicious not only of the European but of their own fellow-tribesmen. But the latest news of that settlement scheme in the Machakos District is that it has now got under way: once the African does "see the light" he is a very hard worker. And that brings us back to the appalling need for more immediate African education.

It is not generally realised how much the Africans pay for their own education, and how readily, under the right policy, they would be willing to pay more. The 180 Independence Schools in the Kikuyu Reserve (closed because of the influence of Jomo Kenyatta on them) were all maintained by the natives themselves, with an attendance of 34,000 pupils. In 1946–47 the Local Native Council at Kiambu gave a capital grant of £5,000 for building schools—*mostly mission schools*—and this is what David Waruhiu most likely had in mind when he said that Elementary Education should be the responsibility of the Local Government: he was Secretary of the Local Native Council at Kiambu when I met him. I spent two mornings with Jomo Kenyatta at his Teachers' College in the Kiambu District. It had the best *esprit de corps* among its 900 happy African children that I met in any school in Africa. Yet I wrote at the time: "The first book I picked up on entering one of these mud-and-wattle classrooms was *Race Conflicts in Africa;* and I am sure that when, or if, his young pupils ever graduate—and they come from all parts of Kenya, from nearly all the tribes—they will teach the young Africans more of what is in that book than about what the Iron Duke did to Napoleon at Waterloo." And have they not!

As it is, elementary education in Kenya has been left to the Missions, and so it has in Africa as a whole. The cost is smaller, for nearly all the support comes from outside. These are excellent institutions, and the people are admirable: one Catholic Mission in the Kikuyu Reserve gives an education up to the grade of matriculation for Oxford or Cambridge. I have never met an African who had been to a Mission school who did not speak of it with love and tenderness. But these Missions place too great an importance upon the part God is supposed to play in the white man's world. Even while he is at the Mission school the average African begins to suspect that we do not live by the precepts we tell him so much about. Later he is sure of this. How could he help it? Eventually comes the alarming conviction that we do not, ourselves, believe in the God we are trying to make *him* believe in: that we are cheating him even there. Thereafter the African may still believe in God, but not in *us*—and he refuses to go to God via the white man's interpretation. Hence one of the reasons for the secret religious cults that are now poisoning the blood-stream of Africa. These are the real source of Mau Mau. Some of these secret religious cults even preach that Christ was a European (a white man), and so had the typical settler's attitude toward Africans. If we had placed less stress upon the teachings of Christ in the African's early, impressionable years we should have let him in for less disillusionment and suspicion of the white man. He sees we don't practice what we preach; and we are only deluding ourselves if we try to make ourselves think he doesn't see us as we are. The African intelligentsia, moreover, is clearly affected by the psychological insecurity so prevalent in the western world as a whole.

In Kenya, overloaded with woe as it is, every effort has been made for years to get Africans to learn skilled trades: the exact opposite to what you see in South Africa, where the African is barred by law from engaging in any of them. The big railway shops in Nairobi are a splendid example of this white man's attempt to bring the black man on. Nothing but praise can be given Kenya in that connection. But, unlike those of the West Coast, the natives of East Africa are heart-breakingly slow in learning skilled trades, or most of them; and in Kenya the education the African has been given—it is too academic —makes him feel that to work with his hands is beneath him. He might never have heard of the dignity of labour. . . . When a Negro leaves Alliance High School in Nairobi and goes to Makerere College in Uganda (and only a handful do) he graduates from that excellent Negro university further away from his own people than are most of the Europeans—especially the Provincial and District Commissioners, who are often maddened by such Negro snobbishness. Also, the white man sets the black man a bad example in East Africa. The Negroes see very few white men working with their hands. It is hard to get a white man to remain even at foreman level in East Africa: the snobbishness of British colonial life makes their lot too unpleasant. The *club* is the reward of the day's work in any British colony, and not to be able to go there for tennis and the cool sundowners as darkness falls is hell. It is even worse for a man's wife and children. The *Kenya and Uganda Railway* members have their own club, golf course, tennis courts, etc., etc.: and it could be said that, as a direct result, they are a very useful set of white men. They provide the model for similar clubs as Africa becomes industrialised. As it is now, the Indians do practically all the skilled manual work in Kenya: they are the skilled mechanics, the housebuilders, shoe-makers, tailors, artisans, stationmasters, etc., etc.: and if many a Kenya settler could be granted his deepest secret wish—to ship the Indians back to India—Kenya Colony would come to a full stop in a week. In East Africa the Indian holds every job or post that the emerging African might fill.

This brings me to an interesting question: it may be better, from the Negroes' viewpoint, that they should have an élite, even a discontented one, than that all of them should be trained merely as hewers of wood and drawers of water. They might get their full civil rights quicker that way—such as they already have on the Gold Coast and are rapidly getting in Nigeria. Self-rule is neither taken nor won, and certainly not held, by hewers of wood and drawers of water. It would be better if more Negroes went to the London School of Economics, or to the colleges in the United States, as Kwami Nkrumah did. When I first went through Africa I was tremendously impressed by that statement "You can't force the pace of Africa"—it sounded so sage. Then I began to suspect it was too often being used by people who were unwilling to give the black man the privileges he was entitled to, and could both earn and hold. Finally, I threw it into the discards along with that other embarrassing phrase: "The benefit of the European example."

Today, in East and Central Africa, every effort is being made to bring in Europeans to increase the numbers of the white populations against the overwhelming numbers of the blacks: Poles, for instance, whose tragic history makes them more adaptable in foreign countries than almost any other European (they are so used to exile); Germans, who know how to work hard at almost everything, and do work hard, even in the tropics; Italians, excellent skilled mechanics, who, in the few short years they occupied Abyssinia, built more miles of good road than the British have built in East and Central Africa since they first came there; and thousands of the displaced and jobless people from unhappy Europe. But it's a hopeless effort, if the main intention is to counter-balance black by white. To bring the 40,000 Europeans in Kenya up to within striking distance of the 5,500,000 natives is a task beyond the possibilities of immigration or human cohabitation. And it is just as futile if these newcomers are to be considered as candidates for farms in the White Highlands when some of the immense grazing estates are broken up: as they will have to be if they are not farmed more efficiently, or worked as co-operatives. What is actually happening with this stream of immigrants, hastily imported into East and Central Africa, is that thousands of Europeans are arriving who have a wide range of "know how"; and—who will work with their hands. And this, in a very valuable way, will be an education by example: an education in *practical* things—probably far more useful than book-learning.

These emigrants from Europe, either jobless or displaced, will have neither money nor background to fit into the old type of farming in feudal Africa. But they are almost certainly forerunners of the Africa to come.

In Tanganyika racial feelings are more friendly than anywhere else in East or Central Africa. This is largely due to the impeccable honesty with which the British administered their Mandate over that territory, former German East Africa, between the two wars. The

British were so fair in their administration of this trust that they leaned over backward, even to the point of penalising their own countrymen: there were more German settlers in Tanganyika than there were British when this last war broke out. And they were very good settlers—as long as they remained settlers. But that is precisely, it seems, what the Germans cannot do: if it isn't Hitler, it's just Germanism. No African natives ever had a more fair, honest, kindly, or even understanding set of men over them than the British at Dar-es-Salaam. In those days (before the Labour Government's gruesome groundnut scheme) the principle really was observed in Tanganyika that "native interests are paramount". Today, Tanganyika is reaping the benefit of British honesty.

And then, Tanganyika has been miraculously lucky in having Sir Edward Twining as Governor during these last six dangerous years. The history of the African colonies can nearly always be read in the personality and character of their Governors. Unfortunately, there was only one Lord Lugard. He went across the African scene like Halley's comet—and the Africans are still watching the heavens for another appearance. . . . There have been splendid scholar-administrators—no, there has been only one—Sir Harry Johnston, in Uganda, who wrote *The Opening Up of Africa* and *The Gay Dombeys*. Fascinating man. Then, not always to the benefit of British colonialism, there have been men who have been given Governorships simply because they were the sons of someone else. A Governor is not worth his salt if he is afraid of the settlers. Sir Edward Twining, against a howl from the settlers in Northern Tanganyika such as had been seldom heard in Africa, forced a new constitution on that territory, giving the first racial-parity Legislative Council in East Africa: ten Africans, ten Asians, ten Europeans. True, the Government still holds the control with 31 votes on the official side. But parity in the Legislative Council does mean fair sides in any debate; and at its first session, in May 1955, all three races petitioned London to have Sir Edward Twining's term of office extended.

But the problem in Tanganyika is not white against black, or vice versa; it is how the African can progress in spite of the Indians—or, as it will probably work out, how he will progress with them. For although it may never be called that in name, we see in Tanganyika the embryo of an Afro-Indian state. This is because some of the In-

dians in Tanganyika are among the most distinguished, cultured men
in all Africa, Europeans not excepted. They will play a major and
proper part in shaping both the intellectual and the material development of the colony. At the moment the big Indian merchants
are, after the Government itself, by far the biggest importers into
Tanganyika; one Parsee company even maintains its own buying offices in Japan. And individual Indians hold every post, job, or shop
in the native locations that an able young African might hope to fill:
they are devilishly clever and co-operative in backing the interests
of their own kind. But they are also very wise, and have read the
lesson of the times: the rising tide of colour. And the Indians will
go with it—floating on the top. At last count there were 7,408,000
Africans in Tanganyika, 46,000 Indians and Goans, 11,000 Arabs and
11,000 Europeans. So one thing can be seen at least: Tanganyika
will never be a White Man's Country. Dar-es-Salaam, that lovely
landlocked harbour with its whispering casuarina trees—its Arabic
name is Haven of Peace—still has the old German Church, and the
protesting clock still strikes *"Nein! Nein! Nein!"* Only time—and perhaps the Aga Khan—can tell what its future will be.

The Aga Khan is one of the greatest statesmen that Africa has
ever known. Both in East Africa and in London (where he plays
an impressive role behind the political scene as a wise counsellor,
never emerging) his advice has often been decisive. No other single
individual has such widespread influence in East Africa, where he
is the champion of racial co-operation. The Aga Khan backs no nationalisms. He is always telling the Indians in East Africa: "You must
remember that you are *Africans* now." He means that brown, black,
or white, all men in Kenya and Tanganyika, should consider themselves Tanganyikans and Kenyans—and not Indians and English living in an alien country. He said it at a time when, classed as an
Indian, he could not have stayed at either of Nairobi's two best hotels
—though the Savoy or the Dorchester would welcome him as their
most distinguished guest, and he receives bigger cheers than almost
anyone when he leads in the winner at Ascot. But the Aga Khan understands. He knows that there are hundreds of Europeans in Africa
who are doing everything in their power to abolish the colour bar.
For this reason some think it strange that he resolutely refuses to
join Colonel David Sterling's Capricorn Africa Society, the main ob-

jective of which is to remove that "emotional explosive" of colour. Perhaps the Aga Khan, a super-sophisticated realist, believes that this very Society is founded upon emotions, though good ones; and that this is not the right way to go about it. Changes in the colour bar can never come from concessions. They will come from events. But it may be that he never bothers to think along these lines at all: he knows that in the *real* life of East Africa the Indian position is as strong as the Rock of Gibraltar.

When I was back in East Africa in 1948, I heard that the Aga Khan was investing heavily in Uganda—buying up bus routes, etc. To me it was good news, though the Baganda may think otherwise. They want Uganda to be "a purely African country". Up till the 1955 agreement with the British, which they signed so as to secure the return of their deposed Kabaka, they even refused to have an Indian in the "Council of Ministers": the Indians, they said, "are an alien people whose way of life we do not wish to follow". And they know that the Aga Khan, even though he is the champion of harmonious racial relationships in Africa, will back the Indian's right to have a political and economic share in the development of Uganda.

Then, though it is incomprehensible to most Europeans, there are many Baganda who do not want their country to be industrialised. They know (and who doesn't?) that the machine can never provide the satisfactions necessary to happiness. And many a European who loves Africa will hate to see the native crafts and customs, and their happy laughter, disappear into a race of machine-tenders. The Baganda fear, moreover, and with reason, that the Indians will own the machines before they do. They have nearly revolted at times against the Indian monopoly of the cotton-ginneries. But the Owen Falls Dam has been built: it says "USE ME!" And Uganda has already entered the machine-age, whether the Baganda like it or not.

The Kabaka is back—not without memory of the way he was deposed and of his two years' exile in London. His reception was hysterical: his subjects prostrated themselves as his Rolls Royce convertible rolled slowly along the twenty miles between Entebbe and Kampala—a strangely symbolic stretch of road, for it marked the progress from the old British-administered Africa to Kampala, the commercial city, centre of the modern Uganda.

This young Kabaka—a monarch whose lineage goes further back

than that of the Kings of England—brought a British officer back with him as his A.D.C., and also Oliver Messell. The sight of these two Europeans, personal friends of the Kabaka, did a lot to damp down the anti-white feeling that had begun to appear during his two years' exile. But the present situation is far from easy, despite the good face that some London newspapers tried to put upon the ovation that this cool young Kabaka received when he returned to his own people, and, as one of the more realistic London papers said, upon "the cool contempt with which he treated the Governor". The future of wonderful Uganda depends on the good sense of this young African ruler; on the moderation of London, I mean its willingness to give the natives of a territory their proper share of its increased wealth; and on what the British learn to think about their future in Africa—it cannot be the old colonialism. They did not gain much— except knowledge—by exiling the Kabaka. It was a tactical mistake. But they have at last seen the impossibility of pushing the Baganda too far. London knows now that it will never be able to fulfil that dream of the City and the Kenya settlers—the dream of forcing the comparatively free natives of Uganda into a Union with Kenya and Tanganyika. As the father of Mutesa II said in 1926, when the British first tried it: "I will not be made a horse in the Kenya stables!"

Writers looking for evidence to prove that the Africans are unfitted for self-government will prove nothing if they cite the trouble Kwame Nkrumah is having, and will continue to have, with the Ashanti. The British had a first-class war with the Kingdom of Ashanti as late as 1900—largely touched off because an opaque-minded Governor, when visiting Kumasi, demanded to know why he wasn't given the Ashanti sacred Golden Stool to sit on. There is no such geographical, political, ethnic, or even ethical unity as Gold Coast. Its boundary, as has often been said, was an idiotic line drawn without consideration of local peoples in the scramble of the European Powers for the division of Africa, when, unable to seize the whole piece, they were driven by greed to split both Togoland and the Cameroons. And it would be a superhuman African statesman who could impose Negro rule from Lagos on the Hausa and the Fulani of north and eastern Nigeria—their real links are with the fanatic Moslems of the Sudan and Egypt. No statesmen in Europe ever faced problems more stubborn than those which the Negro will have to meet in West Africa. They can well say, when Europeans criticise them: "We are the inheritors of the past—*your* past."

Dr. Kwame Nkrumah (the black hope of some 180 million Africans, as well as uncountable millions of resentful Negroes in the U.S.A. and West Indies) was born in the Gold Coast in 1909; he studied eight years at Lincoln University, a Negro institution in Pennsylvania, U.S.A., winning several degrees; took a post-graduate course at the University of Pennsylvania; and then went on to study law at London University. Today, owing to his own personal worth —and a chain of circumstances—he is the first black Prime Minister in British Africa.

Those who apparently feel hurt at the sight of him in this high post have described him as "a black leopard" (Stuart Cloete in *African Giant*); "an angler of genius" whose "part is that of the saviour of his people from foreign oppression", who "had to invent the oppression", and who "appealed to the young, the impatient, the semi-educated, the under-privileged, the half-baked" (Elspeth Huxley in *Four Guineas*). Considering that Dr. Nkrumah's party, the CPP, won 90 per cent of the votes in the first general election to be held in the Gold Coast (1951), it strikes me that the above harsh list of categories—the semi-educated, the half-baked, etc., which seem to include nine-tenths of the population of the Gold Coast—is a very sad indictment indeed for any colony enjoying British rule.

Such a superficial explanation is too much like describing the configurations and colours of an iceberg only one-ninth of which shows above the surface, and ignoring that eight-ninths below the surface and the deep currents that can drive it against the wind. The deep currents, I mean, of native resentments. I believe that the chain of events which led to Dr. Kwame Nkrumah becoming Prime Minister —in what even some well-wishers of the African think may be too premature a handing over of self-rule—can be traced link by link. Cocoa is one of them.

When I was in that hell-hole, Ubangi-Shari, I got a wire from the *Daily Mail* asking me, after I had finished my drive from coast to coast across Africa and had reached the Atlantic, to fly to Accra on the Gold Coast and investigate a certain situation there. I flew out of the Cameroons over Nigeria, looking down on the high trees growing along the Oil Rivers and thinking what a shock it must have been to Mungo Park when, searching for the source of the Niger, he came on it where it was flowing *East*. I touched down in stifling French Dahomey, and was enjoying a half-bottle of champagne on the sweltering veranda of the Sea View Hotel at Accra when its hairy-armed proprietor appeared, his eyes popping, and announced: "The *Governor* is on the telephone!" "The—*who?*" "This is Arnold Hodson speaking," said a quiet voice. "Why don't you come out here and stay with me? At the Castle." "Well, sir—I——" "Oh, I know why you're here," came the next words, clipped. "The *Daily Mail* has asked you to come here to write about 'colonial maladministration'." I said: "That's right." He said: "Now that you know that I know why you are here, there is no reason why you should feel embarrassed about accepting my hospitality." "Not in the least," I said. "Good. I'll send a car for you."

I knew a lot about Governor Sir Arnold Wienholt Hodson before I met him. He has a string of Consulates and Governorships after his name in *Who's Who;* he was with the Abyssinian army in its expedition against the Tigre; his book *Seven Years in Southern Abyssinia* is regarded as first-rate by those who know and love Africa; and his *Where Lions Reign* is perhaps the best book on lions ever written. He was a noted hunter and naturalist. "But he's an odd chap," one of his best friends told me in London. "He's absolutely dotty about the Africans. Loves them." To me, I could think of no better qualification for a Governorship in Africa.

There were no A.D.C.s between us. He despised this official nimbus. He met me at the foot of the steps of old white-washed Christianborg Castle: that haunted Danish fortress that had been there since the earliest slave-trading days, when the Gold Coast was the White Man's Grave. "There's another man," he smiled as he shook hands with me, "*Daily Express*. Also racing here to write about 'colonial maladministration'. First come, first served. I'll show you to your room." I got into my white dinner jacket and black cummerbund, and felt that I had overdone it when I came back to him, sitting there in a crumpled black alpaca suit and pair of high mosquito boots. He offered me a drink. "No thanks, sir. Not tonight." He laughed (the only time he did) and sat there in silence for a time, staring at me steadily. "Right. We'll go in to dinner. You can ask me any questions you like." When he saw the slight smile I thought I had repressed, he said, snappily, "And I will answer them."

But there was no dinner for me that night. I saw the walls of Christianborg Castle begin to swim before my eyes; I ran for my room, crawled out on the 10-foot stone-wall window-sill, vomited on to some old brass cannon I saw lying in the heavy surf below me, crawled back, was lying in a long Calcutta cane chair—and saw Sir Arnold Hodson sitting on my bed. "You have malaria. Didn't you know that?" he said. I shook my head. "Well, you're going to hospital tomorrow morning." I lay stretched out, smoking. "I knew you had it when you got out of that car," he said. "How was X, when you left him?" This was the friend who had told me about him in London, and, as it happened, was an old friend of mine. "Did he give me a good reputation?" I laughed weakly. . . . Sir Arnold Hodson was what is known as a sour-puss. The Colony was infuriated with him because he would only serve beer at the official functions, having said openly: "That's good enough for them." He was not a *raconteur* who liked to talk about "when I first came to Africa". In fact, he would have made many a clam look talkative. "You are going to stay in bed," he announced, as he took my dinner jacket and hung out the wet rag it had now become to dry. "We have a first-class hospital and a first-class doctor. I'll come over there and talk with you. We'll have plenty of time: you're sick. In the meantime, read this." He left on my bed table the Commission's report of the cocoa-strike on the Gold Coast, which the natives had won hands-down.

The Gold Coast, at that time, was exporting 47 per cent of all the world's cocoa. Cocoa was the backbone of its economy, providing some £2,500,000 out of the entire £3,700,000 income of the colony. And every single solitary bean was grown by the natives. The Europeans had nothing whatever to do with it—except buy it. In November 1937 fourteen huge European business concerns, mostly British, entered into a secret "buying agreement"—to abolish their own ruinous inter-company competition—and, it was believed, into a secret "selling agreement" too; and this produced the disastrous eight months' strike of the native cocoa-growers, as well as a total and successful boycott of European—mostly British—goods imported by these companies. The Gold Coast chiefs even invoked *Juju* to enforce the ban. Of this I wrote:

"Every Briton who is in any way interested in Britain's colonial administration or overseas development should read the report of the Government commission sent out to the Gold Coast to suggest the settlement and the future relations of the native growers with London business interests.

"The report is an African drama more thrilling than a magazine exposé article, and costs 3s. 6d. at H.M. Stationery Office. (If you can get it.)

"In the report you will read how the Secretary of State for the Colonies in London, without even reading the agreement which the buyers reached in secret, and without consulting the Gold Coast Government or the native cocoa-growers, accepted the verbal explanations of two of the most important representatives of a London combine and wired the Gold Coast Governor that he should advise the natives to accept the buying agreement as it was 'in their best interests'; how the Governor of the Gold Coast replied hurriedly that the one thing the Africans dreaded was a European 'pool' combining to fix a buying price, and that the agreement would certainly arouse determined native opposition throughout the colony; how even when the native chiefs demanded to see the agreement they were refused.

"I believe that the Governor of the Gold Coast has not seen a full copy of this agreement to this day . . . an agreement which affects vitally the sole commodity on which almost the entire life of the colony, social and economic as well as political, rests.

"If there is one thing the report shows incontestably it is that if alleged slackness in colonial administration is to be investigated the investigations should begin in Whitehall—and at the top.

"How is it possible that the Secretary of State can advise the Gold Coast Governor that he should sponsor an agreement when he has not even read it himself? [Hodson told me of some of the unbelievable cables that had passed between them.] How is it possible that he is so ignorant of the psychology, as well as the economic position, of the natives of whom he is supposed to be the ultimate administrator, that he disregards the local Governor's protests that the attempt to enforce

the agreement can lead only to a whole-hearted native strike and boy-cott?

"*The story is not perhaps so sensational as the Trinidad, Jamaica and British Guiana commotions, but it is along the same line of the official Whitehall economic complacency, of which Africa reeks.*"

I sent that cable off before I showed a copy to the Governor. But he already knew what was in it. Perhaps a leak in the Gold Coast cable office? Perhaps stiff comments wired back from London? It did not matter. I thought the *Daily Mail* might feel it a bit awkward to attack such big advertisers as the chocolate and cocoa interests. But not they. They printed every word, just as, three years later, they were to print my dispatches from Russia. That was one of the pleasures I had in working for that paper.

"One of those important big men from London came out here to address these 'natives'," smiled a man in the Secretariat I was staying with, after the earthquake that hit the Gold Coast at that time had made the hospital temporarily uninhabitable. "I don't know what it was he thought Africans *were*—bush pagans, perhaps, or babies—but I had to sit there on the platform and listen to him talking to these wise old chiefs as if they were children. . . . Finally, one of them stood up, a grand-looking chap, and said: 'We know that you would never do anything behind our back to harm us. No, we could never be made to think *that!* But if this agreement—which you have reached in London between yourselves—is so *good* for us, why can't you tell us what it is? We will sit here and listen to you.' And I have never felt more sorry for a man in all my life," said my friend. "He just did-not-have-one-word-coming. . . . It was awful! Some of the old chiefs just sat there and laughed . . . but there was no fun in that laughter."

Sir Arnold Hodson said to me: "That secret agreement between the Europeans to 'fix the price' did more to kill what lingering faith the black man might have in the white man than anything that could have been invented. And, of course, the evil that it has done will last for years."

That, in my considered opinion, is one link in the chain of events that made Dr. Kwame Nkrumah Prime Minister of the Gold Coast. What, for instance, led up to the boycott in February 1948 of European goods in the territory? To the riot when the natives at Accra, marching on the Governor's residence at Christianborg Castle, were fired on by the Gold Coast Regiment? To the Coussey Report? At the time of the riots the Governor, Sir Gerald Creasy, gave out that the disturbance was either instigated or inspired by communists— a thing that made us smile in Kenya, where I then was. But a Report of the *Commission of Inquiry into Disturbances in the Gold Coast,* sent out from London, did not substantiate this charge at all: its findings attributed the unrest to "economic conditions". Yes, it was "economic conditions" that moved young Dr. Kwame Nkrumah into his present position. These, plus the fact that there are no British settlers in the Gold Coast, and that—the British were honest about meaning to hand over self-government.

Despite the way in which the merger of the Rhodesias with Nyasaland was jammed through a flaccid House of Commons against the unanimous opposition of the natives, on the specious promise of "partnership" between white and black man in Africa, most observers believe that here lies the last chance if there is eventually to be a successful multi-racial state in Africa. If I were a white man in Africa I should put my blue chips on it. This merger's main aim was to form a big enough political bloc to take its control out of the hands of London. The men who have to face the problems are now the men who will be able to make plans to cope with them. Self-governing Southern Rhodesia has been free for years from any interference from Britain about its native policies; the riches of the Copperbelt in Northern Rhodesia will now underwrite the finances of the new combination; and the only real sufferers in this case (but it is not at all certain whether they will suffer more or less because of Federation) are the two and a half million natives of Nyasaland. They are merged now in a big political unit that will never give self-rule to the Africans. Their hopes and protests were ignored. But they were going to lose anyway. This world will not permit a native paradise. Their idyll is over.

Now that "Gold-Coastism" has been successfully prevented from being imposed, as Big Business would call it, on the territories of this Federation, capital can be safely invested. It is certain that an immense amount of American money will pour in for the development of mining resources; and the future of its Africans will be far more dependent upon the Anglo-American Rhodesian Development Corporation, and liberal-minded financiers like Sir Ernest Oppenheimer and his son Mr. Harry Oppenheimer, than upon the politicians. More will turn upon what agreements can be reached, giving greater scope for the Africans, between such big companies as the Roan Antelope mine and the Northern Rhodesian European Mineworkers' Union, than upon votes. That will be a *real* advance and not a matter of mere paper promises. But to call this "partnership" still seems an abuse of the King's English. (Semantics are violated at every turn of the road in British Africa.) And apart from any feelings they may have about the rights and wrongs of colonialism —not always so altruistic when their money is endangered—the American partners in these big mining interests had better back everything that may lead to a contented native population, if they want to get their money's worth. Here is a lesson that New York is going to learn, and in a big way: you can't scoop profits out of British Africa and at the same time criticise the responsible British for the way they are handling those territories—you are equally to blame or praise. And why should it not be praise? If ever there is to be a road out of the racial nightmare in southern Africa, this one—the Federation one—looks the most promising. There is every reason why the world should keep an open and fair mind, and hope for the success of Federation in Central Africa.

Lying on the beach at Malindi, the Melind of *Paradise Lost,* I knew that this would be my last time in Africa. There was a full moon. The surf was breaking white on Barracuda Reef, a mile off shore. The wind was sighing in the casuarina trees. And I had a bottle of gin. . . . Once again I felt I had all I wanted. I wanted to be nowhere else in the world than where I was. I needed no more than what I had with me, which included my wife. Nor could we have wished for better company. Archie Ritchie was there, French Foreign Legion and Grenadier Guards; he had been senior game warden of Kenya for twenty-five years, just one half of that beautiful but troublesome colony's short and hectic life, and loved every tree, bird, or four-footed animal in Kenya. And Jack Bonham, Warden of the Coast, was there also; he had shot over 800 elephants in the course of his work in game control, and had enjoyed (yes, that was the way he would regard it) being shot at with poisoned arrows by ivory-poachers on the Tana River. One of his attackers he had caught and tamed; he was Jack's cook at that Malindi camp. We had come there to dive in the coral of Barracuda Reef, down to that painted world of the painted fishes. Now we were gabbing. We spoke of many things. . . . But as neither of these gentlemen enjoys having people write about him, I shall say my last words: "Here's to you, Archie Ritchie and Jack Bonham."

It was ten years since I had first stepped ashore at Walvis Bay. And Africa still had me. I had begun at the beginning. There were some Bushmen shell-mounds below Walvis unpicked-over by any museum expedition, lying at the end of some dead salt lagoons. We went down to them. The mounds were lonely humps slowly rising to about ten feet high, glittering with mussel-shells bleached white by centuries of blazing suns, with the winds of yesterday uncovering the relics of the men who had eaten those mussels. I found an ivory needle, glistening in the sun; six inches long, oval in cross-section, as sharp and polished as the day it had been made, say some five hundred years ago. And we found a bone knife, rotted with time; some ribs of whale and jackals, and, to judge from one tooth still left in it, the jaw-bone of a lion; and hundreds and hundreds of tiny whitish beads, about half an inch in diameter, neatly bored, and made from ostrich shell. Thousands of disturbed flamingoes passed in pink clouds along the space over the lagoon: there was no sky. Three herons stood like a Japanese print upon a mud-bar. We sat there, an Afrikaner, an Englishman, a German, and myself; we talked about the life that must have been lived on this spot, made moody by one of the most mournful landscapes I have ever seen— though the memories it evoked may have had something to do with our feelings. "What gets me," said the Port Captain of Walvis, the Afrikaner of our party, "is these dinky little beads! They make the same kind for their kids today, you know. Fancy the little blighters . . . playing about on the seashore, five hundred years ago! And then —*we* came." He did not need to go further. . . .

Drinking that bottle of gin on Malindi beach, with the stars of the tropics swinging over me, I wondered what I should say in London or New York when I was asked how I justified the settlers hanging on to their farms in Kenya. I knew what my answer would be: "Because they love them." It may be difficult for anyone who has never looked down into the Great Rift, with the bronze volcanoes forty miles away against the pastel blues of the Escarpment, to understand the love, the almost holy affection that the Kenya farmer feels for the land he has 'settled' on. But he does feel it; and it explains, though it may not excuse, almost everything.

RUSSIA
REVISITED

Africa and Russia are the two great problems of the modern world; and Russia, like Africa, has been a *leitmotif* in my music. Even on Vancouver Island, long before my African experiences, I could not forget Russia. Sometimes I would rest from my wood-splitting, and, lighting a cigarette, would sit on a log and stare at the fresh lake—until I was back in Petrograd. Nearly always I went to the Maryinsky Theatre. . . .

There it was: the first four rows stiff with generals, in their glittering gold shoulder-boards; the Grand Dukes in their boxes; and their ladies—what wonderful creatures those women of old Russia were—tauntingly displaying some of the loveliest bosoms that man ever kissed. . . . For me the most magic moment of the Ballet was when the orchestra tuned up (how many violins was it?). And when the lights died and Albert Coates raised his baton, I had the feeling that I was about to enter a dream-world. . . . The ballerinas danced to that audience: to the Grand Dukes in their boxes, to the generals. That dream-world died with Imperial Russia—the world of Vronsky and Anna, of Natasha, of playing cards until two in the morning at the New English Club. I knew that it was gone like blood run into the sands. I knew that not all Tchaikovsky, Borodin or Rimsky-Korsakoff could recall one day of it.

There must be many whose life has been spoiled for all the rest of the world by having known Romanoff Russia. It made you feel that everything else you met would never come up to it; and it seldom has. Yet I think a certain comradeship was established among people who had known that Russia, a comradeship that gave them a peculiar attitude toward life. We have an uncommon denominator. We have passed through one of the greatest experiences that life could offer a man. And many a time I have hoped that I would take adversity as well as some Russians I have known.

In 1928, I went back.

The winter of 1928–29 was the peak of the pass between the October Revolution and what they have now, which is not what Lenin intended—though no one can be certain of that, for Lenin died without tackling the peasant problem. I met many young Russians then, men and women, whose lives I envied. There could be no doubt of their genuine happiness, of the exhilaration they felt at being allowed to do responsible work for the betterment of the lives of less fortunate Russians. They were lucky. And at that time, the *winter* of 1928–29, I think that some of the top men in the Kremlin still had the same pure fervour. I have no way of proving this: it was just 'in the air'. And I can easily understand how so many generous British and Americans visiting Russia at that time became fellow-travellers. If I had left Russia before the spring of 1929 I might have been a fellow-traveller myself. Never since has the dream of 1917, of the Old Bolsheviki, looked so near to being realised.

That detestable organisation, the secret police, was still devoting its attention to the comparatively few, rather than to the millions they began to kill or send to slave labour-camps in the forced collectivisation of the farms that began in the spring. It was not until I went down on the Don steppes in September 1929, with Paul Scheffer of the *Berliner Tageblatt,* and we wrote the first eyewitness accounts of the brutal uprooting of the peasants, that my faith in the October Revolution began to die. It was a slow death, at that—chiefly because our Western world was so lacking in any cause calculated to enlist one's enthusiasms: it was not until the purges of 1936 that I began to hate Moscow.

In the winter of 1928–29 Red Moscow was the most exciting capital I had ever been in. The Russian theatre was in full blossom: its petals had not yet begun to drop in the ideological frost. We saw those three stirring plays of the Revolution and the Red and White wars: *The Armoured Train, Roar China!,* and *The Days of the Turbins.* They made you hold your breath! The ballet, for me, did the opposite: *Red Poppy* I thought footling. We saw the exciting "modernistic" theatre of Meyerhold, who was allowed, or so it seemed, to do anything he liked with a stage—even to playing in a fourth dimension. And the experimental stage of Vachtangov! The incomparable little Art Theatre still had Stanislavsky: and at its 30th Anniversary (a night that brought tears to the eyes of many Russians in the audience as well as to mine) we saw Moskvin and Knipper-Chekova (Chekov's wife) play their original parts in *The Cherry Orchard*. We saw Kachalov's "green" *Hamlet* (unquestionably the gloomiest Dane who ever trod the boards); and we saw *Boris Godunov* given as a straight play by the Art Theatre. Realism was pushed to such an extreme that costumes were actually borrowed from Moscow's Historical Museum.

I got a cable of rebuke from my paper for over-filing on my story of Stanislavsky and the Art Theatre's anniversary. They wired me the next day asking me whether I had gone crazy. I think I had. The Russian theatre is the most powerful medium of propaganda I have ever encountered. You see acting more real than life itself, in scenes that place whatever interpretation upon history the playwright, or his boss rather, would have you believe. The Russians know this. They sent travelling troupes to China; and the Chinese sent travelling troupes of their own to Nehru's India, to woo the populace. There is nothing new in all that. There was the Passion Play at Oberammergau; and Holy Week in Seville—before a materialist and mistaken Spanish tourist-bureau turned it into a Cecil B. De Mille production—was staggering. (For the real thing today, go to Toledo; look down into the darkness of the Plaza de Zocodover; and see what you feel as the hooded monks slowly stride in, carrying only one candle.) This is all theatre. And today Moral Rearmament teams are invited to put on their shows anywhere in the world, even in Negro Africa. A play to the senses? Why not? If you object, you will have to throw out books, music, painting. But it is certain that as a school for historical misinterpretation the Russian theatre has left the rest of the world back in the kindergarten.

Stanislavsky, that very aristocratic director, was delighted, after his first apprehensions, by the spontaneity and keenness of the proletarian audience. Life was wonderfully free and easy in that Moscow of 1929. My wife and I became friendly with Danchenko; he took us one day to have tea with Stanislavsky—just the four of us. This led to our being given seats directly behind Danchenko for the first night of the play that, I think, ended the life of the Art Theatre as such. The Kremlin knew that the enthusiasms of seeing the Red and White wars played over again and again on its incomparable little stage could not last for ever; and now was the time for a play that would glorify the Five Year Plan, just started. This was a dreadful affair called *Blockade*—its last scene, in a printing works, with the glorified machine going flap-flap-flap as it turned out the Revolutionary news-papers for the proletariat, symbolised the triumph of the Red Worker over the Red Soldier. My wife and I had the two courtesy seats on the right of the aisle, third row, one of which bore the brass plate with *Stanislavsky* on it. When the play was over Danchenko stood up, stared at us with a dead expression, and gave just the slightest perceptible shrug of the shoulders. "We *had* to put this on," he said in a low voice as he passed us. "This is the end."

The theatre was the communist show-room. The farms were real-ity. The most interesting thing about the forced collectivisation of the farms—and it certainly must be interesting to Comrade Khrush-chev—is the fact that it has failed to work. The Russians have less cattle and livestock on the land today than they had in 1928; and that means less food. The men in the Kremlin have been unable either to convince or to conquer the peasant, who is still in revolt against Moscow. And if communism fails in Soviet Russia, which is not at all beyond the realm of possibility, even probability, it will be because of just one thing those bloody and bloodless doctrinaires in the Kremlin left out of their calculations: the soul of man—in this case, the Russian peasant's love for the land. With the proletariat that obstacle could have been easily overcome: when you can't con-vince, you kill. But you can't go on murdering the men who feed you. That is the Kremlin's present headache.

When Paul Scheffer and I slipped away from our journalistic comrades in Moscow, which was easy, we just went to the railway station and bought a ticket. That seems unbelievable now. But you could travel freely anywhere in European Russia in 1929, only the Turk-Sib being barred, and the forbidden cities of Bokhara, Tash-kent and Samarkand. And how they tortured us, just the beauty of their names. We went to Nizhniy-Novgorod and took a boat to

Tsaritsyn on the Volga, now Stalingrad. There the head Collectiviser picked us up (that is the way to put it) and we went out on the Don steppes. We were there for about a week, visiting farm after farm, and saw scenes we could hardly credit. For some reason, and you could never know with the Russians, the authorities in Moscow had decided to let Scheffer and me have a free look at anything we wanted. Therefore nothing was done (while we were there) to the suicidally brave peasants who seized us by the coat lapels, right before the collectivisers, and shouted: *"Baren! Baren!* They don't want us to live!"

That is all dusty history now. But, for me, one scene is as alive today as at the moment I saw it. I remember it because of its humour, its tragedy and its prophecy. Somewhere or other we sat by the side of a dusty track across the steppe, and watched a Red Caravan, a long line of tracks and tractors, taking a collective's grain to the railroad station. Also sitting by the road, and looking very lugubrious about it all, was an ancient, bearded Russian *moujik:* an old-style peasant. He kept muttering: "The ox is better than the tractor! The ox is better than the tractor!"

Scheffer's girl secretary, who was with us, a member of the Tolstoy family, was amused (and secretly very interested) in what the old man was trying to tell us foreigners. So we pressed him for an explanation: "Why," she asked him, "do you keep on growling that the ox is better than the tractor?"

"Well, I'll tell you. In time of hunger, you can eat the ox. You can't eat a tractor."

When Scheffer and I finally got back to Moscow, after having our sleeping-car derailed during the night (we were the only ones in it, and it was quite a ride lurching and swaying along the ties: I was in the upper bunk and Scheffer always declared, only half-jokingly, that this was a Bolshie effort to bump us off) we found exactly what he had said we should find. Both *Pravda* and *Izvestia* were carrying headline two-page stories on the wonderful success of collectivisation: the intention being, of course, to bury our eyewitness accounts of the thing itself under the mass of cables our colleagues would send. Anything adverse we might have to say, and we had a lot of things, would be buried in the shuffle. But they need not have worried; it took the world a long time to wake up to the fact that a revolution just as shocking and just as important as the October Revolution had happened in Soviet Russia: the peasants, who thought they had been given their land by the 1917 Revolution, were now going to have it taken away from them. Paul Scheffer, I think by far the best of the foreign correspondents in Russia, included some of his dispatches from this trip in his *Seven Years in Soviet Russia:* a book well worth reading now, considering how events have borne out his forecasts.

In a nutshell: the peasants of Russia were getting on their feet after World War I, the Red and White civil wars, and the two terrible famines; and there was the beginning of what promised to be a successful and intelligent peasant farming on the land, with the farmer a free man still. But this was the one thing that Lenin had feared. He had always preached that the success of the peasant bourgeoisie would mean the end of communism. He was a hundred per cent right there. And this was the system, this good and growing life on the land, that Stalin smashed, killing five or six million people or so in the process. That did not matter: like the Chinese, the Russians have millions of men to waste. With his army of the deported Stalin got the forced labour for his First Five Year Plan, which also began in 1928. These two things went together; and not enough importance has ever been given to the way Stalin got his labour supply. Remember, the Kulaks were the most intelligent of the peasants: men who would work for the sake of working, and be ashamed not to do a good job, even if they were slaves in some concentration project, unless their hearts had been altogether broken. Many a Kulak probably died as a slave-foreman on the Stalin Canal. But was all this good for Russia? George Lansbury, that dear old man, had a bust of Lenin on his bookshelf in Bow Road. Beatrice and Sidney Webb spoke of Stalin and the Politburo as if they were Jesus Christ and the Twelve Apostles. Everyone is welcome to his own opinion. Mine is that up until now both Lenin and Stalin have been stupidly overrated. Stalin has already been demoted in the U.S.S.R., and before long will be hated. And Lenin is due for a reappraisal. The West has been lazy in accepting him at the value that the communists place upon him.

(I saw the beginning of the *Ten Days That Shook the World.* I stood with the workers, the soldiers, and the sailors from Cronstadt before the little white 'palace' of Kshesinskaia, former Prima Ballerina of Russia and mistress of Nicholas II when he was young; and listened to a short, dumpy man, with rather a Tartar caste of countenance, speaking mostly with his hands in his pockets—an almost impossible thing in that era of arm-waving, hysterical Russia—asking the crowd: "What do *you* get from war? Death. Wounds. Corruption . . ."

It was said there were over half a million people in that procession; that human river which had poured down the Nevsky with its red banners floating like foam on top. I wedged my way out of the crowd, and crossed the Troitsky Bridge to the red building of the British Embassy which was directly opposite; and met a friend of mine coming out. He asked: "What's going on over there?"

"Oh, nothing. Just another agitator. He's advocating immediate peace. Calling the soldiers home from the front, things like that . . . A man called Lenin."

Silly ass! "A man called Lenin!" Think of that. That was July 17th. The next day Lenin went into hiding. The next time I saw him was September 1928. He was lying, flat on his back, under the flag of the Paris Commune. One hand lay above the coverlet, and its thumb-nail was black, as if he had caught it in a door-jamb. There were a few red bristles on his high-cheeked Tartar-like face; and, I fancied, a smile. He also seemed to be sweating slightly. The two scientists who had originally embalmed him, prodded his neck after the glass case had been taken off, to show that he was not made of rubber; then explained—"Our task was not so much to preserve the flesh as to preserve the likeness." They explained the 'sweat' as leaking of the embalming fluid; how the room had to be kept always at exactly the same temperature—that was why only a certain number of people were allowed in it at any one time—and then they told, for our interest, how hair grows on the body for several days after death: how they had had to shave the dead Lenin.

I went out; and there, on the thin strip of green sward that was then allowed to grow below the pink, crenellated walls of the Kremlin, stood the black granite plinth marking the grave of my friend John Reed. That was why, in September 1928, the first thing I did on my return to Moscow was go direct to that spot. In 1941 I did the same: Lenin was not there, he had been removed to a place beyond German reach: and John was gone: he had been labeled a Trotskyite—and had, therefore, been erased from Russian history. And in the Censor's office, the nicest of them said to me; a young man who had been in their Embassy in Japan: "Mr. Farson, I have read your *Transgressor*. If I were you, I would not mention my friendship with John Reed.")

The saddest thing about some of these collectives was not their bad side, but their good: I mean the hopes they aroused. It is worth recalling, I think, what I wrote on the Don Steppe at that time:

In those civil and sanguinary wars that ravaged Russia after the Oc-tober revolution a group of hard-riding Cossacks attached themselves to the Red general, Budenny, and helped drive out the armies of the Poles and Denikin. Then, their vocation as professional killers abol-ished by the Soviets, these old janissaries of Czarist days looked about for a New Life. They found it on the barren steppes they had ranged so freely as children. Grouped about the personality of one of their sergeants, a thinker as well as a fighter, they set up a communal farm. They secured a credit from the Government and started a herd of cat-tle, which got foot-and-mouth disease and promptly died. Some of the Cossacks went off after that and settled down as individual farmers; but fifty-seven of them—the reddest of the outfit—went off with the sergeant and started all over again. They obtained from the Soviet a grant of land that had not been worked for over ninety years: bare, desolate sun-baked steppe by the flanks of a muddy little river. They lived in tents at first; then built a log-and-mud cabin. They hoisted a flag and called this the "Red Lighthouse".

There it stands today, looking out on the unbroken sea-like horizon of the mighty steppe. It has other buildings around it now, a white-washed communal dining-room, cattle-pens and tractor sheds. I sat in the communal dining-room and ate cherry jam from their orchard, and I swam with them in their lazy little stream, boys, girls, and women, inhabitants of the Red Lighthouse, so gloriously free in their loneliness of the steppe that they had long ago given up the convention of bath-ing-suits. And one of them, as we dried ourselves in the sun, told me another Cossack commune had been started next to them—and that was called "Paradise".

I wondered. Anything less idyllic than those wood-and-mud build-

ings above us, baking, fly-buzzing under the pitiless sun, would be hard to imagine. Treeless, with no shade. I ate the jam—but I never did see the cherry orchard. It was probably down in some richer land along the river. The clothes that the swimmers were putting on were patched and tattered. The lips of the girls were taut and their eyes had a grim look in them. Yet they grinned sheepishly when I asked them whether they liked their New Life; lowered their heads, and said, "Of course we do"; and one of the men—the original sergeant—said:

"It may be wrong to say it, but it makes us feel happy when we all sit down together in our dining-room. You see," he added, "we were all very poor."

That was the genesis of this "commune"—a collective battle against poverty. A commune is quite different from those other two collectives: the "Tovarishy" company and artel. In those the peasants pool land they already own and work it in common, but retain for themselves some of their dairy animals, poultry, and, of course, their homes. In a "commune" everything is held in common—it is 100 per cent communal. And usually the commune starts with a combination of landless people—they are very poor. Therefore, with tractors working over their growing acres, nice fat cattle in the communal farmyard, a cheery dining-room where they could chat and hold meetings together —and the communal swimming hole—no wonder those other poor peasants had called their place Paradise.

These communes, of course, have to make their own rules of life. The splendid isolation of the steppe gives them an excellent opportunity to do this. Some of the wildest theories of communism are put into practice. The Red Lighthouse, for example, believing that everything they had belonged to each and all of them, made it a rule that any member could go to their communal storehouse and take out shoes, food, cloth, according to his or her needs. But this apparently did not work out. . . .

"Bog znat! God knows!" sighed the old Cossack sergeant. "Some people seemed to need so much!"

With that reflection on human weakness and aspirations we can leave the collective farms. 1929 was the year of the last wild freedoms. Three factors combined to close the gates on so many human hopes—the collectives; the five year plans; and the end of Lenin's temporary retreat (N.E.P., the right to private trading). The day after N.E.P. ended I went to the little shop in the Hunter's Market where I had been in the habit of getting my Caucasian wine and caviare: it had become a State store—and, believe it or not (I am not being funny), the sturgeon eggs were smaller. What had happened was that, the corruptive power of a private purchaser being removed, the large grey Molosol caviare had gone to the table of the Commissar. But life under the Soviets was still free enough to allow Alexander Wicksteed, the old Shakespeare and Dante scholar, and me to make a horseback ride across the western Caucasus that spring.

The only time we met the G.P.U. was when they helped us: at Kislovodsk, where they looked after our kit while we combed the town to find a cart to take us over the first ridge of mountains to the Karachaite valley of Khassaut, where we hired our first pair of horses—one for me to ride, as my foot was still in a surgical boot from an operation in Sweden, and one for a pack-horse: Wicker, that marvellous old codger, walked the whole distance. Communism had not got above 5,000 feet in the Caucasus at that time, in the remote part we were going to. And as most of our journey was at altitudes of between 7,000 and 8,000 feet, where the streams from melting snow and glaciers were still quite small, and we could wade them, we did not meet any Comrades. This was about the only place in Russia where one could dodge them. It was lovely.

There are twelve peaks in the Caucasus that are higher than Mt. Blanc; over 900 glaciers, several of which are exceeded in length only by the Aletsch; and 125 miles of eternal snow and ice between Mt. Kazbek and Mt. Elbruz, to which Zeus chained Prometheus— and on whose flank I spent the night in the snows of the Klukhor Pass, 9,000 feet up, without cover, on June 27th 1929. This was the end of one of the most fantastic adventures conceivable. Owing to the character of old Alexander Wicksteed, it was pure mid-Victorian.

We were taking a last look at a lost world; for every man that we talked with or even saw on that ride through the Karachaite country is now dead, or deported to Siberia. The entire tribe of Karachaites was deported to Siberia in 1945; together with the Inguish, the Balkars, and the most wonderful of all people in the Caucasian melting-pot, the Tchetchens, against whom Tolstoy fought as a young officer on the Terek. He also wrote *The Cossacks*—that beautiful love story, his own—about this same people. I carried *The Cossacks* with me on that ride through the Caucasus and read it beside mountain camp-fires, and also Lermontov's *A Hero of Our Times*. And I saw the Caucasus as those two great Russians had seen them, their snows fading in the blues of evening and turning to gold with the rising sun. I felt their spell. There is something about the Caucasus that fills you with tenderness: you want to protect them. And once you have seen them you will never forget them.

In the headwaters of the Kuban I caught thirty-five trout one afternoon—the largest number of fish I have ever caught in one day in all my life, or ever wanted to. I would not have taken half of those had it not been for a Don Cossack at Utsch-Kalan, the capital of Karachay, who sneered at my fly-rod, recommending worms. He was an Instructor in communism. Utsch-Kalan was the only place where we encountered Comrades. There were twelve Young Communists, down from Moscow, helping the man from the Don to civilise the Karachaites. But they were a cheery lot, subdued by the majesty of the Caucasus, and sincerely believed they were carrying Moscow's burden. And we liked them. That is, until the sunset, when I staggered back to the school-house, just built, with the thirty-five trout, and the Cossack Instructor insisted on being allowed to show the pretty young schoolmistress how to cook them while Wicksteed and I were hanging on to a rock in the river to get ourselves in proper shape to take on such a banquet. "I have been a poor man all my life," said Wicker. "I have never had enough trout to eat." That blistering Don Cossack had placed all our trout in a bowl of cold sunflower-seed oil. . . . He had the last laugh.

Wicksteed was typical of the changing Russia of those days, though neither he nor I could know it. He was an Englishman, a whimsical expatriate, who had been trying to live like a Russian for five years in Red Moscow. Nothing could persuade old bearded, shaven-headed Alexander Wicksteed—then allowed to teach English in Moscow University—to shed his Russian *rubashka* or stinking knee boots: in Moscow, that would have been treachery! And just because he loved the Russians with every fibre of his eccentric body, they had no use for him.

It is strange that no one has ever written a treatise on this parvenu aspect of the communist so-called civilisation—I mean the way they throw their newly-acquired culture in your face. I was irritated at never being allowed even to tell people that you liked this, that or the other thing they were doing, or trying to do: they told you point blank, to your face, that there never had been any people like them —until you wanted to say "Thank God". When I asked Lunacharsky "Why, when the Russians are now so completely free and you have thrown off all the shackles of the old bourgeois mentality, have the Soviets not produced one writer of first importance—one painter?" that old bull-frog opened his mouth, drew a deep breath, and talked for forty minutes. But he did not answer my question. Secretly the Russians were not at all sure of themselves in those days. They hesitated with a foreigner, never accepting him until they saw what value his own countrymen placed on him. And as we loved Wicker, but thought he was a bit smelly, and that his love for the Russians made his information too sentimental to be trustworthy—and as he could not be induced to put on a necktie for any of the diplomatic corps dinners, etcetera—the Russians just did not 'get' him.

This was his last trip to his beloved Caucasus. The Russians never allowed him there again.

He lived in one dingy room in a crowded, disgusting tenement in Moscow's old factory quarter. He made all his own furniture; you could not cross the room in a straight line in any direction; and it was as much as your manhood was worth to risk sitting down in one of his collapsible 'easy' chairs. I always sat on his bed; and it was thus that we planned this heavenly trip in the winter of 1928-29. Our intention—his, I think, as well as mine—had been to take horses over the main range and, eventually, get down to the Black Sea. But after we had left the Kuban and struck up the valley of the Teberda, I noticed something peculiar in his walking. Up to then he had taken the same pace, up or down—and I may say that that grey-bearded man could walk the legs off any Karachaite—but as we neared the little mountain settlement of Teberda he broke into a trot. Entering its dusty street, he made straight for a little house with an orchard in its yard: for one particular tree: and sat down. There he pulled out his filthy pipe, stuffed it with vile *mahorka*, lighted up, and, after a few meditative puffs, pulled his beloved Sonnets from his pocket, saying to me calmly: "I have reached my objective. Here I shall spend the summer. Under this tree."

A family of mountaineers had rushed out, and now stood around him. They raised their hands in joy. The greatest man they had ever known in their lives had come back to them: the Professor from Moscow! I left him sitting there. He eventually wrote a book about the Russians: *Ten Years in Soviet Russia*. It is charming: if you wanted to buy a pound of butter in Moscow, said Wicker, you just went to a shop and bought a pound of butter: not mentioning that there would be no butter. He died in that little room in the factory quarter. It was two days before he was found. He was the most whimsical, witty, dirty, unpredictable man I ever travelled with.

1929 marked the beginning of a time (it lasted about six years) when the correspondents in Moscow could get favourable reports of Soviet Russia printed in their newspapers—though there were even greater differences of opinion among us, based on first-hand knowledge, than there were among our readers. You could put eight of us in a room, and you would have nine opinions. Included among us were such first-class brains as William Henry Chamberlain, Louis Fischer, Charleton the Cambridge don, professionally (and Germanically) derisive Paul Scheffer, and charming Walter Duranty, the Haroun el Raschid of Moscow. Some of our deep thinkers were dismayingly profound. I do not place in the above coterie those 'liberal' young American correspondents, just out of college, who thought that all left-wing ideology was a sign of advanced thinking. As Buckle so rightly said of the United States, there was no other country where education was so widespread or so thin. Myself, having seen too much of politicians, economists and sociologists ever to accept their versions of what was going on inside their own countries, I wandered far and wide that year, writing life-and-blood Russia. The Russian people are the most story-productive material I have ever studied. I wrote of people in their flats and factories, in their schools, bread-lines, pastry shops and villages. I knew enough Russian myself, carried over from the three years I had been there under the Czars, to be able to talk to a peasant: I had almost as many words in my Russian vocabulary as he had. And I could get along with the Intelligentsia, until they cut into the mumbo-jumbo of ideology—but there I would have got away from them even in English. As I have said, I have always hated the doctrinaires; and the real Russia was far from their picture of it. In a year I wrote over a hundred articles; most of these appeared in the United States while I was still in Russia. Some were favourable, some not. Some I sent by ordinary mail; some by friends who were "going out"—queer, isn't it, how we always spoke of "going out" when we left Russia?—and one or two, when I was particularly anxious to hit the editorial desk, by an Embassy pouch: not the American, for we had no diplomatic relations with Russia in those comparatively happy and carefree days. I was sometimes amazed, when some of these pieces came back to me with their sensational headlines, that the authorities did not immediately haul me up before the Foreign Office and have it out with me. But they never bothered me once. (With my political cables, of course, every word had to pass the stiffest censorship.) I was even able to get a piece through about the Underdogs:

The proletarian revolution had been going on for eleven years when I walked into the tenement buildings of the First Russian Textile Printing Mill and found twelve people living in one small room. There were six single beds stretched around the bare walls. Five of them were each inhabited by a husband and wife. None of these families was related to the others. Their beds stood around the walls with no curtains between them. And if you can imagine five men and five women dressing and undressing before each other, in sickness and in health, month after month, year after year, you will feel grateful for the weakness of the one electric bulb which kept that kennel in semi-darkness.

I do not say that that room is typical of the living conditions of Russian workers. I know that the authorities are building dwellings as fast as they can. I have been in some of these "ideal workers' homes" in Kiev; too perfect, as are many things in the Soviets, in plan, and too few in quantity. I know that the workers in Moscow are agitating to have all former houseowners driven out of their homes—nepmen, priests, former bourgeoisie, members of the so-called leisure class. The workers claim that something like 200,000 more "living spaces" will be acquired by the proletariat this way. But none of these things have any bearing on the sordidness of the rooms I saw in this textile tenement.

It was not that these workers were among the most poorly paid hands. Each one was getting more than the average wage. Four men were making $37.50 a month, and the other man was making up to $50. The average wage of a textile worker is about $30. But none of them was a communist.

It is hard to say whether that was a case of cause or effect; whether they were getting the worst end of the living conditions because they were not communists, or whether they were not communists because they did not think they were living well enough.

"The communists," declared one of these men, a lopsided man with a nose that pointed across his face, "they're the ones who get all that's good."

"Then why aren't you a communist?" I asked him.

"Because we don't believe in them!" roared a man from the circle that hemmed me in. "We have waited eleven years for our lives to improve, and nothing has happened."

"Yes," cried another, "I don't say that we want Nicholas back, but we want to live decent. You come into my room."

He led me into another slit of a room where five people lived, the average in this tenement being five or six to a cell. As we entered it a woman lying in a dirty box-bed pulled the ragged curtains apart to see what this trampling of boots meant, and at sight of me hurriedly shut them again. Another woman, sitting beside a dirty bed in the far corner, just sat there and stared at us stupidly.

"Now look at that light!" demanded the disgruntled worker. "Look here!" He walked back to the door and sat down on the stool by his own bed. There was a bedstand on which stood a tin cup and kettle; and he went through the motions of pouring out his tea. "I can't tell when my glass is full," he cried. "It's too dark. Now how do you expect us to live in darkness like this? Many times we have begged for another light, but what do they tell us—another bulb would use up too much energy. Pfui! Damn them, I tell you!"

"But why do you say that the old times were better?" I asked. "In the time of Nicholas you also lived four or five in a room—I saw you."

"Know it, know it—that's true. Listen, I'll tell you what's worse. In the time of Nicholas, when we wanted to leave a mill we went to the

baren"—*he snatched off his hat and bowed*—"*and we said we wanted to go, and he said goodbye, and we went and got a job in another mill. Now if we leave this mill we can't get no job. Leave one and you've left all of 'em. And there are 240,000 unemployed people on the Moscow labour bourse.*"

"*Yes, yes, we've got to stay here,*" *said the lopsided man.*

We went back to the original room. When I had first entered, a man sitting by his bed was making a fishing net, and he was using a wooden net-needle exactly like those the fishermen use on the New Jersey coast. I smiled as I told him this, but he did not smile; he was tying knots swiftly and grimly, and he looked up, saying, "I'm making this for when I go back to my village."

The tenement had four decks, each housing a hundred people. And on each deck there was a dark kitchen with a big black communal stove. People passed up and down the halls carrying bowls of steaming milk, buckwheat, soup. One man had a tin pail covered with a cloth. Whether it was food or washing I could not tell.

In the first room sat a workwoman dressed like a peasant—white kerchief tied around her chin and head, belted blouse, its tail sticking out around her rough dress, heavy felt boots on her squat feet. She sat on a stool by her draped box-bed, her hands folded in her lap, sunk in lethargic stupidity and resignation. Her bedstand held a frying-pan with a slab of grease and meat, waiting to be cooked on the communal stove. Having told me that their child slept with her, her husband led me out into the narrowing "hall" of the room and showed me his own bed. It was a contraption of boxes and crates, with all his worldly goods stowed away underneath.

In the room with the five people there was an ikon and a dim guttering candle. A damp spot stood out on the bare greenish plastered walls. Surveying this grim cell, I did not wonder that the matron of the dispensary had said "tuberculosis" when I asked her what illness was the most prevalent. My only wonder was that people could exist in such a murk. There were children running up and down the dark corridors, mothers gossiping in groups, their babies in their arms. After a while there was a meeting of the Fabkom, the factory committee, talking about "defending the rights of labour". And that made me wonder the most of all.

The authorities knew I was in that human kennel, of course, even before I got out of it. But they said nothing. Perhaps they were experimenting? Perhaps what I wrote amused them? I could never know. But I became an habitué of the First Russian Textile Printing Mill, so that the sight of my face didn't disturb, I hoped, anybody. And one day I walked up to a young man I had noticed several times as I passed him working at his machine. He was a big, broadshouldered, clean-faced man, with curly chestnut hair: a Jack London or John Reed type. He had a fine face. He had an initial fright when he saw that I wanted to make friends with him; he excused himself, and went across to the foreman of his department. Both of them walked me along to the factory club. I wrote over a dozen articles about Lev Yakovitch. About his home, his wife and two children; our outings in the Park of Culture and Rest; and how, in its shooting gallery, I shot the monocle out of Joseph Chamberlain's eye (thus fulfilling an ancient urge). Of course the G.P.U. had given him permission to become friendly with me. I knew that. And he knew that I knew it. Nevertheless, this did not prevent something very close to a genuine friendship being formed between us, and many a night I sat with him in his little room, with his wife keeping our glasses filled with tea, and his two children sleeping peacefully, while we argued about 'kultur'.

"Moscow is so interesting!" he told me, producing a photograph of a glider the factory aviation club had made, in which he had stayed off the ground seventeen minutes. "What do you want to be?" I asked him. "*Be?*" The question puzzled him; he looked around at his wife. "Why—I am a worker."

Perhaps he asked too many questions of me—and was foolish enough to repeat my replies exactly as I gave them to him. For he knew more about the textile strikes in Passaic, New Jersey, than I did; far more, as I told him—"for now you are going off into a United States that you communists have invented to increase your own opinion of yourselves. Those strikes happened, but——" And I tried to make him believe me when I gave him illustrations of why, despite some of the bad things, the American workers should be the happiest in the world. Perhaps he did believe me. Anyway, while I was waiting for him in his factory club one afternoon a man I had never seen before walked straight in and up to me, and informed me that

Lev Yakovitch had had an accident; his hand had been torn off. When I asked what hospital he had been taken to, the man gave me a dead-pan stare (very G.P.U.), and walked off without answering. At Lev's apartment a girl with frightened eyes, whom I had laughed with before, told me that the Lev Yakovitchs had left Moscow. Either or both of these things could have happened. So far as I was concerned, it had been made plain, this man no longer existed.

He was twenty-eight, born in the Chernigov government, where he had passed through a sort of grammar-grade law school. At fourteen he had gone into a metal works that had been put on a war basis. From 1919 to 1922 he had been in the Red Army. He had seen some pretty grisly things when fighting against Denikin, the shooting of prisoners and so on; but he did not like to talk about that nightmare. After 1922, when the wars of Allied intervention stopped, he had returned to his village, and had been making as much as $75 a month as a thread-waxer, whatever that is. But the Red Army had shown him Moscow. Returning, he had got a job in this textile mill, where he had met and married Valya; and now, although he was making only half as much as he had made in his village, he would leave neither the mill nor Moscow—unless, as I feared, he had left both for ever.

He was a communist and so was she, though neither were of that callow, know-it-all type that puts your back up the minute you begin to talk with them. To the best of my knowledge, I should say that here burned the pure flame. I envied them. I wrote as much: "To begin with let me say that Lev Yakovitch is a communist, and that this makes up for a great deal of what he would otherwise miss in Soviet Russia. In the first place, it gives him a goal, an ideal, a faith; and while it is permissible to doubt that faith can move mountains or even make the factory wheels of the Soviet Union go round any faster, it nevertheless does compensate a large proportion for the present rough road they are travelling. For the life of a Russian today is that of a man who is living in a house at the time he is building it. Moreover, he is tearing down the old structure as he erects the new; he had no even, clean ground to begin with. With this ideal and this faith in the future (even though he may never live to see it fully realised) Lev Yakovitch can put up with hardships that would seem intolerable to any Westerner. He sleeps four people in one room, lives mostly on black bread and tea, has only one decent suit of clothes, cooks warm meals twice weekly on a primus.

"There are a million other communists in Soviet Russia who are in much the same boat. Their maximum monthly salary is limited to $112. Lev Yakovitch is getting $35, the average salary of a Russian workman; but he has the consolation of knowing that Maxim Litvinov can get only $112. By withdrawing from the communist party and becoming a hotel porter he could easily earn double Maxim's salary. But if it is power he is after, a position of importance in his country, then he must abandon the quest for gross, material things. And that is a good, healthy race which many a man in London, Paris, or New York would be glad to get into."

(How naïve this seems now! It needed the communists to show us that the lust for power—the ability to shoot your ex-friends or stuff them into concentration camps—is somewhat more evil than the capitalist money-urge.)

No parents in our "decadent society" ever doted more on their offspring than Lev and Valya Yakovitch. Valya was a thin girl, twenty-four, with that pallor and strained lines of the face that the mill stamps on all of them. Her blonde hair was cut in a very good Eton crop. At home she wore a white cotton shirtwaist, very stiffly starched, and a short blue skirt, probably the only ones she had. When Lev and I came in with four-year-old little Mitka from an outing, Valya took him to the communal bathroom and toilet, gave him a good wash all over, then brought him back for his cup of milk and bed. She took some of his clothes out to a communal cupboard in the hall, as the family had neither chest nor wardrobe of its own. Their little daughter was already asleep, which is why Valya always came home ahead of the rest of us. Mitka went to sleep while we were talking.

I was interested in what Mitka was being taught. While his parents were working in their textile mill, he could spend his afternoons, from three to seven o'clock, in Moscow's Children's Library. He was taken there by his nurse, a peasant girl to whom Lev Yakovitch and his wife paid $7.50 a month to look after Mitka and his baby sister while the parents were helping the Soviet factories to fight the capitalists. There were women and young girls in the Children's Library to watch over Mitka and tons of other kids. He had dozens of friends there; some of them were nine years old.

The library was the former home of a very rich tea merchant, a bourgeois. It had thousands of children's books and of those beautifully coloured pamphlets that Soviet Russia manufactured so enthusiastically for its coming generation. They were all classified by subjects—history, geography, politics, etc.; so that on Lenin's Day, for instance, Mitka could be given an entire file of books and pamphlets, suitable to his age, about the great man's life. On the playroom wall for the youngest children was a picture of Lenin as a curly-headed child—just like Mitka.

As with everything the Russians did for their children, this library was excellent. It was a trifle too pedagogic, for all the books were classified as "positive" or "negative", good or bad for children's temperaments, and the women supervisors stood around with notebooks jotting down various reactions. But Mitka was no doubt oblivious of all that. For him, as a place to play in during the cold winter, it simply could not be beaten.

And as an implement of the communists it could not have been beaten either. If Mitka was going to learn about life, the communists were determined that he should learn about it from their angle. "Give me a child until he is seven," say the Jesuits, "and you can have him for the rest of his life." In the Children's Library the communists had Mitka.

Imagine something like this:

It is five in the afternoon, and one of the young Russian poets, Miss Barto, has come to read her own book, entitled "Brothers!", to the children. It is exquisitely turned out, with vivid illustrations. "Little brothers," begins Miss Barto, holding up her book, "I shall tell you the story of some little brothers of yours who look very different from you and live in different parts of the world." She reads:

"This little black brother has curled hair
Which looks like fur.
He is very, very black and his eyes are too.
He is stamping his feet, saying
'Gilli-Milli-Ga. . . .' "

Comrade Barto holds up the book and shows a little nigger boy jumping up and down outside a Kaffir *kraal*. His mother and brothers are cooking some yams. Reads Miss Barto:

"*This little yellow brother has narrow eyes.*
His hair is stiff as needles.
'Tching-ling-tchen. . . .'"

Mitka yawns. He has seen plenty of Chinese boys in Moscow—all those little knife-jugglers. But he has never seen a black baby. Miss Barto now holds up the book showing a little brown baby lying under a palm:

"*The third little brother is very fair indeed,*
With eyes looking like coal,
And his body chocolate. . . .
. . . Kive. . . . Shva. . . . Shva. . . ."

Mitka sits up. He is intrigued by some draught animals in the background, crosses between water-bulls and yak. They are pulling a strange cart past a temple. And Comrade Barto goes on to another stanza:

"*The white-skinned brother has a sharp and merry voice.*
His eyes are very cheerful,
And his hair is yellow,
He is jumping up and down, saying
'Mama-mama-ma. . . .'"

The children all yell. They have recognised themselves. The picture is complete, the affinity established: little brown, black, yellow and white brothers! Brothers! And now the lady poet turns to the serious half of her book: this is what life is like for the poor little black, yellow and brown brothers. See the little black boy inside his hut, his mother putting him to bed, singing:

"*Father is not yet back*
He left the house with the dawn.
He carries his heavy burdens
Until all his strength has gone.
Oh-la. . . .

"*Grow up quickly, darling;*
You are not alone in this world.

You have many brothers there, and
Much will be had by their sons.
  Oh-la. . . ."

The opposite page is a full-spread in vivid reds, blacks and blues of papa and other Negroes loading bales into a ship, their backs bent, a hard-jawed white overseer looking on. The action now becomes more dramatic: on the next full page a Chinese silk-mill is shown with a suspicious yellow-faced foreman watching a mother and daughter at work. Miss Barto chants:

"Mother sings a song to her little son Iu-Tzing.
'My hands hurt as I have been weaving silk
The whole day long. . . .
The boss paid me nothing for the work I did . . .
    . . . but
You are not alone in the world.
Your brothers are there.
You will be in fire and smoke
With them, and together with them
You shall vanquish. . . .
Sleep, my son. . . .' "

And so on. The Indian mother sings to her son: "Don't waken your father; he came back quite exhausted; to-morrow he will bend his back over the swampy lands he is cultivating, which have killed so many men; the boss will never let him rest." (Full-page spread of Indian papa working in paddy field, with scowling overseer standing by.) And now—why, it might be Mitka's mother singing:

"The time is not far off
When you will become a strong worker who will
Take his place beside his father
Who fought for the mill.
Don't forget your little brothers
There in foreign lands.
Perhaps you will be together with them
In fire and smoke . . .
And together with them you shall
VANQUISH!"*

On the page facing this verse is the closing tableau of the saga: papa and two sons stoking a Soviet steel-mill, with a red fade-out in the upper left corner showing a silhouette of three armed work-men firing on the Czar's cavalry from behind a house. This is the way they won their mill.

"Yaw!" yells Mitka, seizing his neighbour's paint-brush. "I want to draw a cannon!"

Well, there it is—or was—the loves and hates, the absurdities, the cruelty, the great expectations; and the great warm heart of Russia still beating beneath it all. When I returned in December 1941 it was to a State concentration camp.

ON ANOTHER PLANET

Or it was like landing on another planet. The British and Americans lost many fine men and ships getting supplies through to Russia on the Arctic convoys, yet all the inhabitants were hostile, and allies were treated almost as enemies. As we came through the ice-fields of the White Sea on our way in they gave us a slight air cover, little more than a salute: on our way out they gave us none—with the result that we lost a quarter of our convoy in the 100-mile-wide lane of open water between Petsamo and the polar ice. "Those —— bastards!" said our chief engineer, a four-striper, as we watched the ship behind us go down in flames (she was loaded with turpentine). "They'll look after you when you're coming *in*—when you've got something *for* 'em—they don't give a —— for you on the way out. I don't know what's come over the Russians: they don't seem *human!*" And he was more than half right.

If communism fails in Soviet Russia this will probably be more because of its unsatisfying emptiness than of its cruelty. It is an existence that fulfils plans, not men. Yet if anyone should ask that puerile question, whether the communists had bettered the life of the people of Russia, I should answer yes, *yes*, YES!!! Only a fool would try to deny it. Yet here again comes the old question of semantics: the idiocy of arguing about *words*. As far back as the 1930s we were saying that communism had already failed in Russia: that this was State capitalism. Then a few of the wiser among us began to point out that it was neither: it was just Joseph Stalin.

That was the Russia I came back to on Christmas Eve 1941. The

rock-like way in which Stalin was running the war was already becoming manifest. On December 5th the Germans had been within
fifteen miles of the Kremlin, with Stalin sitting there, unbudgeable.
In the *sauve qui peut* exodus from Moscow, some of which he had
ordered—and it was then that rabble anti-Semitism first raised its
ugly head—Stalin stayed. And now we must admit, even though we
may not like it, that Stalin was the one man who got all he wanted
out of the war. Neither Churchill nor Roosevelt achieved their main
objectives: a peaceful Europe and a world free from the four fears.
Stalin continued to make the world unsafe and unpleasant up to the
day of his death.

Western communists and fellow-travellers might argue about dia-
lectical materialism until the cows came home: in Stalin's Russia nobody argued—for long. But that does not imply stupidity in Stalin,
whatever his brutality: any Westerner is uneducated about Russia
until he has read every word of *Problems of Leninism* by Joseph
Stalin—particularly the last chapter, which he read to the Eighteenth
Congress on March 10th 1939. It is the most remarkable, realistic,
and prophetic political document and analysis that was produced
between the two wars. Compared with it, most of our Western
statesmen's contributions were sheer hypocritical drivel. And now,
having gone that far out on the end of the limb, I can say why I am
absolutely convinced that communism cannot work: first, I do not
think that an atheist State can exist: man must have something
higher than himself to believe in, whether it be Christ or Buddha.
The Kremlin is still a long way from having communised Russia: yes,
by many many million Russians. Then, the communist *credo* will always be betrayed by its own people.

Dostoevsky was right when he made the Grand Inquisitor say that
God had placed too great a burden upon man by putting His faith
in us. Man is not fit for Utopia. But a godless civilisation is not fit
for man. With only himself to believe in, in this bloody world, life
would be too lonely. (Perhaps why he has invented gods from the
very beginning.) And life lived to a pattern cut by political doctrinaires is not worth living. When young it is exhilirating to march
behind the banners, shouting slogans. But what about when one
grows up? I kept thinking of that man, the mature man, tired of
being forced to parade behind the banners he no longer believes in,

all during this last time I was in Russia. I kept thinking, too, of what had probably made him tired and unbelieving. It is in the opening paragraph of Tolstoy's *Resurrection:*

"But men, adult men, never ceased to cheat and harass their fellows and themselves. What men considered sacred and important was not the spring morning, not the beauty of God's world given for the enjoyment of all creatures, not the beauty which inclines the heart to peace and love and concord. What men considered sacred and important were their own devices for wielding power over their fellow men."

I also knew the credo of the Kremlin:

"From the point of view of communist morality anything is ethical and moral that promises the building of a communist society. Everything hindering this is unethical and amoral."

This was reasserted on Moscow Radio on July 7th 1955—long after Stalin was dead. The credo has not changed, even if the Soviet face has put on a New Look.

Is this New Look a mask? I don't think so: I think the Russians want to be friendly (though at the moment of writing, just after Khrushchev's visit to India, it doesn't look like it). But if the going gets tough; if, say, there is an *active* revolt among the peasants, for the Kremlin has not yet solved that problem; if an Opposition rises from the proletariat, however unthinkably at the moment—the men in the Kremlin may try to restore the direst form of Police State, with all its bloody purges. Another crisis will have come where situations make the man rather than man the situations. In the meantime Western liberals should be grateful for Russian communism: it has provided the much-needed catalytic agent. It has forced us to make the changes, the compromises, even the reforms (and, God knows, we needed some of them) which we would not have made otherwise. At least, not without serious social troubles inside our own countries. And now if Moscow dares open its doors we shall see the effect of the catalytic agent of the West (I won't call it capitalism) upon communism. That would be an ideal co-existence: these two catalysts working against each other in an otherwise peaceful world.

The result would be more reforms on both sides. There is still plenty of room for them.

There are a few scenes in a man's life that he cannot forget. I shall never need my notebook to recall how our convoy, caught in the pack-ice of the White Sea, was slowly forced aground. It was night. As we were sitting ducks for the Germans, anyway, if they wanted to bomb us, all ships had on their running lights: red and green. There were 19 ships in the convoy—caught at all angles, immovable. This ice is an everlasting field of white, jagged with sharp ridges where the surface has been broken and forced up. The eastern shore of the White Sea is very shallow. Our Irish skipper said that if the ice-breaker *J. Stalin* didn't soon come to break us out, we were going to enjoy the unique experience of being forced aground without being able to turn a propeller. Then she came. She is the biggest ice-breaker in the world: a gigantic cross between a flat-iron and a shoe—the shoe is her slipper-bow which slides up in the ice and breaks it. But all that is beside the point: the point was her light! It was of a peculiar blue—crystalline; and when she shot it across the ice-field it caught each tiny point and projecting ice ridge, until the whole vast expanse in face of the beam blazed like the finest sapphire. I cannot recall seeing anything more startlingly beautiful. She came out like a sheep dog, collecting every one of us. As the ice closed immediately behind each ship—no lane could remain open in that pressure of drift—she had to collect each ship separately. And so, with the fire of dawn blazing along the long low shallow coast, we arrived at the new port on the White Sea—Molotovsk, built by convicts. This was our introduction to the New Life: this, and some of the surliest port officials I have ever encountered. Hostility began even before we left the ship. I had plenty of time to make a note of it: it was night (which begins about 4 p.m. in that latitude in December) before we were allowed ashore.

It is said that you cannot change human nature. I don't know whether that is a good thing or not, considering the story of *homo sapiens*. But the communists seemed to have come pretty close to it. It must be admitted that they did have some reason for being angry and suspicious of the Western world and its good intentions. As Churchill himself said, "One could hardly believe what the states-

men were doing during those years"—the years which led up to the
war; and there is no getting away from the fact that those high up
in Russia, who dictated this hostile attitude towards all Westerners,
could never forget that during the period of Neville Chamberlain's
appeasement the secret wish of British foreign policy was to have
Hitler expand eastwards at the expense of Russia. No amount of
diplomatic eyewash can cover over that fact, for fact it is: despite
the memoirs of British statesmen who were in office at that time,
and now have so much to explain, or explain away. Reading the
autobiographies of Lord Simon and Lord Templewood (the Sir Sam-
uel Hoare of those wasted years) is as good as watching a cat cover
holes in the ground. The Russians had as yet been unable to forget
all that: if, indeed, they aren't subconsciously suspicious, because of
it, still.

They were also in a bad mood because of their own colossal blun-
der in statesmanship: their fool faith in the Molotov-Ribbentrop
Pact. And Hitler had a right to be annoyed with Ambassador Rib-
bentrop for assuring him that the British would not fight. All in all,
the diplomats and statesmen of Europe, any part of Europe, did not
shine during that pre-war period.

As I was the only foreign correspondent to come in on that convoy, I got the full blast of animosity from all these Russians about
the evil intentions of the West: and in reply I could only harp on
the Molotov-Ribbentrop Pact—which did not add to our friendship.
When the young R.A.F. liaison officer turned up in the morning,
smart as paint in his Russian sheepskin hat, I asked him about
Major Baratin, a public-relations man who had been excessively rude
to me on my arrival the previous evening. "Oh—Baratin! Well, he's
the biggest fly in our ointment. He's supposed to be the contact man.
His conception of the job is to lie awake nights thinking up every
obstruction he can put in our path. If we get anything done up here,
it's in *spite* of that sod." A Yorkshireman, who was trying to get
some order into the handling of incoming cargo from British ships,
laughed bitterly when I expressed my amazement at the gigantic
shipyard at Molotovsk, which had been nothing but a swamp four
years back: "Yes. Some of those sheds are bigger than Zeppelin
hangars—but they haven't put cranes on the quays yet. Ships have
got to put the stuff ashore with their own cargo booms . . . and that

ain't so good when you're handling tanks." He spoke of the convict-labour at Molotovsk—of how he had seen one starved wretch jump down on the ice to eat the slop which the steward of a ship had just flung overside: "And the soldier on guard just took a bead and shot him. I tried to tell the N.K.V.D. at Molotovsk that it wasn't good propaganda to have our young R.A.F. boys and the men on the ships see Russians doing things like that—I told them they'd do better to take the poor convicts out of sight before they shot them: and do you know what?—they just *laughed!*" He growled that he would do his job. "But I just couldn't care less what happens to some of these bloody Russians that I have to work with."

Five days later I was in Moscow, a ghost city. The British Mission had remained during the stampede from Mecca to Medina, the rush to Kuibyshev, and so had the American Embassy. They gave a party on New Year's Eve. A magnificent gipsy sang of the steppes, with Cossacks and all the smoke of camp-fires in her husky voice: she broke our hearts. And the next day I left for Kuibyshev, to join my colleagues. I had the fun before I left of finding Ambassador X at the station, squealing like a stuck pig. He had just made the discovery that all his kit, the heavy baggage he had had sent by train from Archangel (which, he informed me, included twenty suits and four cases of brandy) had vanished. I said goodbye to him happily—left him at the Wailing Wall.

It was some Russians who fed me on the five days it took to go the 500 miles to Kuibyshev. I had taken food for only two days. These were young flying officers. "*What?*" they cried when I asked them where they thought I might eat, perhaps at some railway station along the line: "No food?" And they at once produced some *sigi*—that lovely little golden smoked fish with a wooden plug in its mouth—and in this case I could make the proper reply. The most valuable things I took into Russia that last time were 2,000 Gold Flake cigarettes, in tins of fifty, and I gave these sportsmen one of them. There was something splendid about those young Russians: something big-hearted and manly. I enjoyed those days more than any that followed.

I was reading an Everyman Pushkin on the way—*The Captain's Daughter, Dubrovsky* and *The Queen of Spades:* and when they saw it lying in my compartment we set off on one of the most idiotic, long-distance arguments I have ever tackled, to wit—which was the greatest, Shakespeare or Pushkin? I said they were mad. I argued along the line that one was a sea animal and the other a land animal, and that you couldn't make comparisons between two such widely different creatures. This did not satisfy them—and the queer part of it was, *I* knew more about Pushkin than they did, and they found my knowledge of Shakespeare elementary: and that was how I met my first Political Commissar. He was grey-haired and very high-ranking; and he had been listening to this argument for two days. "*D'vai! D'vai!*" he shouted, rushing out into the corridor. "For God's sake, shut up!" And they shut up like clams.

On the road to Kuibyshev we lay as long as half a day on a siding while train after train went by with entire factories, dismantled, on flat-cars—the factories that the Russians were removing in pieces from Kiev, Kharkov, and the cities of the Ukraine to east of the Urals, to reassemble again beyond reach of the German invaders. It was a colossal effort. The weather was then the coldest I had ever known —it touched 52 degrees below zero for two days: and at 52 you do not breathe fast—if you do, you feel the frost in your lungs. Even the air seemed frozen, full of scintillating little glints. It was an awesome sight to see soldiers standing guard on these flat-cars as they slowly pulled past us. There were always two, with fixed bayonets, at each end of each flat-car. They had to stand guard there all night, and it is a wonder that they were not frozen stiff, as some probably were. A box-car full of Polish prisoners was left for a day on a siding along here, forgotten: and every one of them was frozen stiff as a board. We halted beside a train of Siberian troops going west to the fighting, whose train was on a siding: they were out in the open, stripped to the waist, washing with the snow—"This keeps you young!" they shouted at us. And at Ryazan, where we crossed the frozen Oka, I saw them shunting a train by hand—hundreds of Russians on either side of it. Presumably its locomotive had passed out.

The Political Commissar was a bit grumpy (not liking his job, I thought), but he asked me to share his tea. By a fantastic bit of luck I had brought a 1914 Russian Baedeker in with me this time. Once he saw it I could hardly get it back from him. He was fascinated by its superb maps. He came from the government of Kherson; and taking the map he tried to show me the location of his village, which brought us to the Dnieper—and after that it was *Taras Bulba:* and we were off. . . . We had the *provodnik* at the end of the car making tea for us all night. It was a typical Russian evening! He showed me the awful detour that the trains we had seen had to make to get out of the Ukraine and up to the main line to the Urals—and then on to the 5,400-mile single-track road from Moscow across Siberia to Vladivostok on the Pacific: Russia's only other open sea mouth after Archangel and Murmansk. Shaking his old head gloomily, he said he did not think either the road or the rolling stock would stand it. "That's what really defeated us in the last war—those long necks. They, and"—he grinned, rubbed his thumb against the ball of his two middle fingers: sign all over Russia for official graft and corruption. "But we have stood those people up against the wall." He and the young aviators commandeered a waiting car for me at Kuibyshev to get me and my bags to its Grand Hotel.

My bedroom was comfortable, the food was not bad; but the colleagues I met were all of one or two generations after mine. A few were young enough to be my sons, though I am glad they were not. The only one I met of former Russian days was Cholerton of the London *Daily Telegraph,* and he was thoroughly disenchanted. That ex-Cambridge don, with his fine mind and brittle wit, and his sharp-pointed chestnut beard now getting little flecks of grey in it, lay there flat on his back when I went to see him in the morning, seemingly staring at nothing. And I could not help thinking of Don Quixote after Rozinante had thrown him for the last time. He would break no more lances. . . .

When I went along to the first so-called Press Conference I saw the reason why. A billy-goat Commissar named Lozovsky—chin-whiskered and with just a goat's evil eye—delivered a lecture to a room full of courteous correspondents for an hour: some of the most patent drivel I have been forced to listen to. All questions were parried—as if he was fencing. The result of it was that we knew even less after we had left him than we had known when we came in. "What do you think of it?" asked one of the correspondents as we walked away. "Well, unless it was an exception," I said, "we are up against it." He laughed: "Oh, today he was being *informative!*"

This was war; and most of my notes, apart from a daily analysis of the Soviet press, dealt with the unbelievable unanimity of the total

Russian war effort. It was stupendous, inspiring—terrifying. This was totalitarianism at both its best and its worst. I don't know how many Russians were used up in the war—fifteen millions?—nor can anyone prove how many of them were expended needlessly. But the whole thing was utterly ruthless. As Mao Tse-tung is supposed to have said to the Americans: "You may kill a hundred million Chinese—but I shall still have four hundred million." Just like that. This was one face of the ghastly picture. The other was a driving force, an incredible improvisation, which—and this is one of the strongest things in the Russian character—met immediate needs with immediate answers. All over Russia, man-power was used in lieu of machinery. The energy was frantic. I had just left an England where the most disturbing factor was the (it seemed) daily B.B.C. announcement that "a Committee has been formed": then the names would be given of those public figures who would head the inevitable sub-committees—Lord This and Sir That—until general dismay and despondency ensued. Churchill said of these Committees "We are overrun by them as the Australians are by rabbits". The British engineers were protesting: "This is an engineers' war—and the engineers are not being allowed to fight it!" But—I put this in here, for fear of the reader jumping to conclusions that I do not intend to draw—it was the British-invented radar that the Russians were using in their three concentric rings of anti-aircraft guns around Moscow, and these were making that capital not almost, but entirely, impregnable to air attack.

We had one footling little air raid on Moscow during the time I was there. A German plane got through and dropped a small bomb near the white walls of the Chinese City, which was just behind our hotel: and everyone dived into the basement. When Sophiana, my secretary, came on duty the next morning, she spoke of "the terrible air raid!" I tried to tell her what *ours* had been like—and how the people in my district, men and women, from charlady to countess, had turned out to fight them: taking duty every night on the long and often boring patrols. But she just couldn't believe me. It was not that she wouldn't, she *couldn't*: Sophiana's mind had been trained to think that such a thing was impossible in a capitalist society. Anyway, I did not give a damn what she thought.

Having said that, I am free to say many admiring things about the Russians. This frantic effort to convey all war supplies to where they could be used was both stirring and pathetic. It took four days for my train to get from Archangel to Moscow: 400 miles of birch, and pine forests, and tundra—where there was not a bush higher than a man's head; and then after Vologda, where we changed from the narrow-gauge into the smooth, brown, palatial old ex-Czarist Wagon-Lits, another 400 versts—to a Moscow ghostly and unreal under a frozen midnight moon. It took four days to do that 680 miles because, nothing being allowed to impede total war-effort, and man counting for less than nothing, our passenger train spent well over half that time pulled off on sidings, while long trains of flat-cars, loaded with tanks, cars, trucks and aeroplane crates coming down from Murmansk and Archangel, went trundling past. I saw among them—I had to scrape the milk-white frost from our car's double-window—some of the stencilled crates that had come in on our own ship. Every log station was guarded by civilians, mostly women, in sheepskin *shubas* with a rifle slung over their backs; and every mile of that thin neck of rail feeding the desperate Russian army was patrolled by soldiers on skis. Total. All-in. Complete effort.

As to improvisation—while we Americans and British are hardly considered to be slouches at it, I think the Russians might be even better. They have to be: so much of their stuff breaks down. At Archangel the liaison R.A.F. man with the Murmansk wing told me that a tail-skid had been smashed on one of the planes, and that, as they had used up so many, they had no spare. "There was a Russian on the drome—we'd about given it up when he came along—he was a sort of half-assed mechanic—he scratched his head, walked off with the broken tail-skid we'd dismantled, and came back in the afternoon with his idea of a substitute. And I think it was better than the original!" On our way down from Moscow to Malo-Yaroslavetz, where the Germans had blown up all the railway bridges, we saw the Russians building substitutes out of the adjacent pine forests. No committees, no plans, no blue-prints—just the peasant with his axe and adze. The Russian peasant can clean his teeth with an axe: he can square timber with an adze as accurately as on a planing table in a lumberyard. This was war *sans* Brass Hats.

No British or American correspondent was ever allowed at the Rus-

sian front, so far as I know, though the Russians no longer had any
need to be so secretive after they had achieved the miracle of crossing the Dnieper under fire from the high right bank, to retake Kiev.
(Thereafter every political objective of the Kremlin lay within the
inexorable advance of the Red Army—as they have proved to our
dismay.) The only sound of guns in action we heard while I was in
Russia was the distant rumbling of the German artillery as they
pulled back beyond Borodino (where Napoleon dropped his water-
melon). You could, if you felt like it, dateline your cable "WITH THE
RED ARMY"—because everywhere within twenty miles of the actual
fighting was called the "front", as the Russians officially used that
word; but I don't know of any correspondents who availed themselves of this licence. We were taken only where they wanted us
to go; shown only what they wanted us to see; told only what they
wanted to tell us. What one got we all got. Russia, this last war, was
a paradise for the second-rate foreign correspondent. And the Russians treated us as second-raters. We were led around like a troupe
of trained apes.

The happiest moment I had was when I used those exact words
in a cable to the *Daily Mail*, asking them to recall me. I came into
the Censor's office, which was in our hotel, and found a Chuvash,
a censor I particularly disliked, with a wrinkled brow and an English dictionary in his hand, trying to make sure I had used those
offensive words. "*Mister* Farson!—'ape?'" "Yes," I said, making unmistakable monkey-scratches at my side: "Ape." And he passed the
cable. When my overbearing but frightfully efficient Russian girl-sec-
retary marched into my room one morning and told me that the
ape-troupe had been ordered, peremptorily, to leave that day, as a
troupe, for Kuibyshev, which meant being moved another 500 miles
away from everything—we had only recently come *from* Kuibyshev,
that stink-hole where the Russians, still not house-broken, stood on
the seats of the toilets and where the floor of our one washplace
(there was no running water in our rooms) was covered with human excrement—I refused to go. Whereupon, for twelve days, the
Russians made things very unpleasant for me. But by the end of
that time I had reached Murmansk—and got out.

Not even the heads of the Allied Missions were allowed at the
front. General Mason MacFarlane told me that the first time he was

flown over the so-called front (it was never a line: it was like a sea-coast dotted with offshore islands, bays, peninsulas, etc.—along which the Russians often let the Germans break through, in order to close on them like pincers: very effective) it was at such a height that he could not see what was beneath him: "And the second time, I was zipped across so close to the ground that we almost shaved it!" But he was a doughty admirer of the Russian generals ("The nearer to the front they are the more magnificent they become") who would never let him see anything. Air Vice-Marshal Collier told me in March that he had not yet been allowed on an operational aerodrome. And these were top-rank British observers, mark you, who were doing everything in their power, personally as well as professionally, to talk the Allies out of all the tanks, guns and planes that could be rushed through to the desperately hard-pressed Russians. It took these British officers months to make London wake up to the magnificent show the Russians were putting up. This was because they had to combat the unbelievably powerful propaganda of the Polish Government-in-Exile in London: those charming, persuasive people who have every virtue—courage being the greatest—and who have made every political mistake possible in their tragic history. Reborn Poland might have been the most glorious result of the Versailles Conference: instead, it was one of the chief reasons why Europe could not keep the peace. There is plenty of evidence to show that the British accepted the Polish version of the Soviet Army's quality in the various crises which led up to the war: it was the Poles who convinced the British War and Foreign Offices (as well as the Press) that the Russians would fold up within weeks. I have heard them at it: I have had a long personal experience of the professional Polish emigrés. From the very start of the war, and one can hardly blame them, the Poles wanted to use both the British and the Americans against the Russians (and perhaps we should have been better off if we had stuck by them to the end—had they been dependable enough). This explains much of the vicious Russian treatment of Poland. But Russo-Polish hatred after all is historic —look at the way Dostoevski sneers at *Pan* this and *Pan* that in *The Brothers Karamazoff*. And I have always cherished the secret hope that if one of the satellites is to let the Russians down—is to double-cross Moscow at some dangerous corner—it will be the Poles. They are the only people who have the nerve for it.

In the dining-room allotted to the foreign correspondents in the Hotel Metropole in Moscow, we all ate our luncheons together at the same long table, together with the members of the Press Department of the Foreign Office, men and girls, who sat at the far end; and we never had any conversation with them. They might have been in another world: they were. We correspondents got so fed-up with the sight of each other's faces that we always ate our dinners in our own rooms. One day I was left alone after lunch with a tall, pale man in British battle-dress who always sat by himself if he could manage it, never taking part in any conversation; I had thought of him as a Frenchman, for he was always reading a paper-backed French novel. He obviously wanted to speak to me, so I offered him a cigarette and asked "Tell me, what is your job?" "I am a *Pole*," he said, with a peculiar emphasis on Pole. "Oh, I see," I said awkwardly (the Russians having shipped hundreds of thousands of Poles back into Russian prison-camps after their invasion of Poland). I was not going to ask any more questions as there was every probability that the room was wired for listening, just as every foreign mission felt convinced, in spite of careful searching, that its quarters had been wired—so when people had something *very* secret to say to you they always said it when you were alone in the street: preferably in a big square. My Pole was about thirty, blond, very good-looking, typical of the Polish small nobility; and as everyone knows they are among the most suicidally brave people on earth. *He* was. For he took the cigarette from his mouth, smiled down at it, and said: "I am looking for 8,000 Polish officers." "Where?" I asked. He shrugged his shoulders: "Ask the Russians." He stared at me, then raised his eyes to the walls of the room, as if addressing the listening device: "They say they don't know where they *are*—they say they have 'lost' them! And the Russians, you know, could do things like that." Then he gave me a polite nod, picked up his French novel, and left. Since then I have always thought these were the 8,000 Polish officers later found murdered in Katyn forest.

The best men I met this time in Russia were our Russian girl secretaries. They were unbelievably intelligent—and masterful. (One pretty little thing was a "failed ballerina", and got quite a lot of sad prestige from that fact; like the Indian "failed in Matric., Benares.") They could all translate from Russian into English as fast as an ordinary man could read a newspaper: I still have by me many thousands of words that my masterful Sophiana hurled at me from *Izvestia, Pravda* and the *Red Star*. One of our difficulties was to make certain they translated any article we wanted to read: a correspondent who did not know a word of Russian was, it is obvious, quite hopeless there. Theoretically, these girls, some of them very likeable, told the N.K.V.D. everything we said, even in our sleep. But some of them, we had the feeling, protected us even from ourselves: for we talked very freely about the Y.M.C.A. Boys, as we called the N.K.V.D. I think that in their hearts most of these girls hated the N.K.V.D. and the Kremlin just as heartily as we did—though we never discussed *that:* we had a very good tacit understanding, thus saving embarrassments on both sides. The N.K.V.D., I can't help feeling, counted its chickens too confidently.

But I made an enemy of Sophiana, best secretary of them all. First, she was always annoyed when I refused to concoct a cable out of some article she had found for me: about the wonderful work, for example, that the Kremlin was doing for orphans. . . . And then I made a joke. Sophiana, let me say, was slightly of the percheron build. She had been a political prisoner herself: as secretary for an American company in Moscow that the Kremlin had staged one of those idiotic trials against—"spying for the Fascist beasts"—she had got two years in a concentration camp on the steppes of Middle Asia. Apparently, remarkable girl that she was, she enjoyed the experience. And one day, while we were still on good terms, she started to tell me of her life there: how she had been made camp paymaster, and would ride out every morning to the workers on the State prison-farm. "So I took my little horse——" I smiled. "Did you say a *little* horse, Sophiana?" That did it. From then on she hated me. She did let me buy her a bouquet one day: a fairly comfortable afternoon, when it was not much more than forty below zero, and I accompanied her to an antique shop where she bought a string of ivory elephants, from big to tiny, for a child relation of hers, and then led me to a flower shop—warm and moist as the tropics. That flower shop in wartime Moscow!—less than seven weeks before, the Germans had been only fifteen miles away from it. But after she strode into my room and told me I was going to Kuibyshev, and I told her I wasn't, I never saw her again. So I was deprived, not only of her, but of food, cigarettes—and vodka; for she had my tickets for the special store where the diplomats and the correspondents could buy all they wanted in starving Moscow—and the range was surprising. She had gone with the troupe to Kuibyshev, and I was left to sing the song I had composed in my idle moments, of which I had plenty: *"True Blue to the G.P.U."*

The Russians cannot stand mockery. The censor I particularly detested always kicked off at the start of any trip he was bear-leading us on with: "L-e-t-s go! Let's GO!", thinking he was back in Brooklyn. When I mimicked him one day he had it in for me from then on: haggled even over the date on my cables. And as all the Russians I had ever known in 1928–29 (except three) had disappeared into the grave or the concentration camps—and no one had even heard of them, as if they had never existed—I told Vernon Bartlett, when he came back to England and spoke distressfully of the thirty toasts he had been forced to drink at one of those interminable Kremlin banquets, that he could have stopped them at once by simply rising to his feet and lifting his glass to Uncle Joe Stalin: "Here's to absent friends!"

Yet I still had a soft spot in my heart for the Russians. There is something about those exasperating people that has made me love them ever since I first stepped down, one snowy night in the winter of 1914–15, on to the Finland Station: some bigness, it may be, engendered by the vastness of their steppes; some folk-story wonder in their imagination, coming from their illimitable forests in the winter snows; some placidity and fatalism, born of the inexorable flow of the mighty Volga, always in the background of every Russian's mind; some beauty in their heart, such as you will hear in their songs of the flowered Ukraine. Anyhow, I still love *Russia*.

But, exasperating! Since the October Revolution, some four generations of Russians had been born who had never seen the outside world. They knew nothing about it except what they had been told —by the most skillful set of doctrinaire liars that the world has ever known, who could write history backwards, could eliminate Trotsky from the Revolution, and in matters of art, science, discovery and invention could always show that the Russians had been there first. Undisputably, today's Russians have received the finest course of miseducation ever known. And they were taught, also, that it was just an old-fashioned bourgeois weakness to tell the truth or keep one's word; that it was a sin not to inform on one's comrade or one's father or mother if they disagreed with the policies of the Kremlin; that it was—why, it seemed one could go on for ever listing the *opposites* of what we in the West were taught in infancy as elementary virtues. That list of opposites! It was quite an experience, when you had known the old Russia, to look at the Russians of today with the thought of those deliberately-taught evils in your mind. What did they really believe? Foolish question: they did not know what to think until told. This was the unhappy position the British and American communists found themselves in at dawn on June 22nd, 1941, when Hitler attacked Russia. They had to unthink everything they had been thinking when they went to bed the night before.

It must be very confusing to be a Soviet citizen.

It seemed to me that, though it was impossible to get near what the Soviet people were thinking in this wartime Russia where everything was concentrated on the will to win, there must be a dreadful sameness about life under the Soviets. In this dehumanised world, I thought, and subsequent developments have borne it out, the only people who were finding it the heaven on earth it purported to be were the scientists. Doctrine-proofed against the woes of humanity, globular-minded as if inhabitants of another sphere, they were working in their laboratories with equations that did not concern man; or, where it did involve him, they had plenty of cheap human raw material for their experiments—stuff they could throw away. And on the lid of this man-press with its ooze of blood, squeezing the proletariat into pattern—to reverse a vivid communist poster attacking capitalism—sat the Bolshevik Buddha, Stalin.

There were human touches, of course, but I was always surprised when I met one. For example: my leg wound had been opened by a storm we hit off the coast of Norway. Strange accident: in a maelstrom that sent our little cabin-boy skidding on his tail across the floor of our small dining-saloon, among the broken glasses and crockery, a *trunk* hit me. This was, or had been, perched on top of the luggage belonging to the Military Attaché of an Ambassador, coming to take up his post in Russia, for nothing could persuade him to stow it down below; he wanted to go ashore in his full regalia at Archangel. (For some reason, I don't know why—except that it did seem appropriate—the R.A.F. on the ship called him "Blue Balls".) Trying to prise my way out of the door of the stateroom, in a storm in which the ships were rolling so violently that we could look down the stacks of those on either side of us, I caught that trunk on my shin-bone. And as my leg had to be bandaged and would not heal, I went about frozen Russia for four months in low shoes: the beautiful fleece-lined boots I had bought at Fortnum and Mason might as well have been left in England. When I got down to Kuibyshev the leg was so bad that I had to be X-rayed, as the doctor wanted to know if more bone had been killed (I already had several ancient bits of sequestrae in that old wound); and he put me in bed for a few days. He was a typical, kindly old country practitioner type: almost too human a man to find in the land of the Soviets. And he was a great pipe-smoker. He refused to take any money, or to allow me to pay for the X-rays. Incidentally, they were excellent; and he examined them while still wet. But as he sat in my room one afternoon talking to me, I handed him a tin of that beautiful Sobranie tobacco. He packed his pipe with the gorgeous, golden, aromatic stuff, then took a few puffs and closed his eyes as if off in a dream. . . . *"Bozhi moi!* My God!" he said softly. "I am glad to have met you!"

It was he who told me of the psychological treatment that the Russians were developing to handle the dismaying number of frostbite cases: men with neither fingers nor toes. If enough of the hand was left to be split between thumb-stump and the remnant of forefinger, so that the man could hold a pencil—"Then we can see some hope for him. A life ahead." He would be sent to one of the collective farms and given a job as a clerk. " 'But you must not sympathise with him!' we warn them. 'You must make him one of yourselves—a normal man: he must not be a *case.*' " He smiled: "You will see plenty of them in Moscow, poor chaps. In the Amputation Hospital. And you will notice another thing about the psychology of the ward: no matter how badly off the bundle-cases are, they always feel that *someone* will be brought in who is worse off—and there always is. Strange, isn't it, this comfort one gets from being better

off than someone else—even if it's only in the degree of tragedy?
That is an ineradicable feature of the human race. We cannot change
it. We do not want to be equal."

"But 'misery loves company'," I said.

He nodded. "In some cases. But pity is the most destructive thing
in the world. It is the greatest deterrent we have to fight in 'bringing
a man back'. He *must* not be allowed to feel sorry for himself."

But as for making friends with a Soviet Russian, as one would in
any Western country—this was out of the question. (Both British and
Americans have married Russian wives, but that was love, not friendship. And these relationships were themselves exotic, and only just
permitted by the State.) We had no place to go—we were animals
in a hostile habitat—and a few of us stayed in the hotel so long, for
days on end, that we got what was known as the "Metropole pallor".
One or two of us were so full of vodka most of the time (I know I
was) that we scarcely saw Moscow. By now I had begun to feel that
Father Time was taking his toll: I could no longer summon up the
old enthusiasms, or think it worth while to slide about the icy streets
just to be shown some set-up. It was humiliating to be led around in
a crocodile like schoolchildren. The Russians were either the rotten-
est psychologists that God ever invented, or else were treating us
like this deliberately. I am sure it was the latter. Stalin hated the
foreign journalists—they might dare to ask questions that would com-
promise his omniscience. With his own slave Press he could put out
any version he wanted about anything. Although the Kremlin was
right around the corner, we were further from it in Moscow than
we would have been in London, where they always got the news of
any important event or development, or the Kremlin version of it,
before we did. The Kremlin then used our dispatches, which had
been dictated to us, to back up what had already been sent out to
London or New York. Yet I don't know one correspondent who did
not have a deep respect for Russian skill and courage, and a genuine
affection for such a sorely tried people. This despite the cheap way
Stalin treated us.

To escape from my frustrations, and from drinking myself into the
D.T.s in that terribly empty life of the Metropole—I have never been
so close to them—I stirred myself enough to totter across the square

to the Bolshoi Theatre. It was worth it. With great good sense the Russians had returned to the classical ballet. And in my opinion they had better stick to it, for it has set standards to which they can work. I know nothing about the ballet, except that I love it, and have gone to every ballet I could get to since I first saw Karsavina dance in Petrograd in 1915. The Soviets had even restored the old ballet school, and were training children from the age of eight with the same ruthless discipline that Cecchetti had enforced in his School of Perfection. (These children might have been entering a religious order, such was the solemnity with which they approached their vocation.) The result was unmistakable: the Moscow *corps de ballet* was dancing with a skill and grace, a verve and perfect timing, in the straight Russian Ballet tradition. There is no other quite like it.

The first ballet I watched was that pleasant little piece, *The Vain Precaution*. It was like going to a bull-fight. The tiers and balconies were packed with *aficionados* who knew every movement. The Bolshoi Theatre holds thousands. When you turn from the stage and look back, you see nothing but an ocean of faces, eyes glued to the stage. Suddenly—for what may seem nothing at all to the uninitiated foreigner—the people go into a frenzy. They shout—they cheer! They have seen a movement, a subtle bit of technique perfectly performed, and they are as frenzied with admiration as the Spaniards watching Belmonte kill a bull.

I saw Lepeshinskaya dance the second and third acts of *Swan Lake*. She made one forget the rest of the world. In the third act this lovely little ballerina did fifty *fouettés* across the wide Bolshoi stage. It is vain to make comparisons: memories of the past are always exaggerated. But for me she was perfect, with the most expressive arms and face I had ever seen. Lepeshinskaya was prima ballerina of the Moscow ballet: Ulanova of the Leningrad one. I have spoken of the Grand Dukes in their boxes, the four rows of generals and their gold shoulder-boards, the lovely women of old aristocratic Russia with their jewels and bared breasts: well, here was certainly a different audience. About a third of it was composed of young army officers in uniform—infantry, artillery, air force, tanks, cavalry: they left their seats in their enthusiasm and crowded down the aisles as Lepeshinskaya took her curtain calls. But the five rows of horseshoe balconies, on this particular night, were packed with schoolgirls. They broke into a tornado. Looking up, I felt that at any moment we should have half a dozen of them come tumbling out of the balconies and down into our laps. And here Lepeshinskaya did a very interesting thing—she nodded to them. Then she went back into the wings, after having made her bow in the classical tradition; and the next time she came on—she *ran* out . . . swinging her arms like a hoydon . . . and, looking up to the balconies, laughing, she waved to them. It was terrific. The schoolgirls screamed until we were dizzy. I felt they would have to call out the artillery to silence them. And all the proletarianism in the world did not detract one iota from the classical purity with which she had danced *Swan Lake*.

The aristocracy and the sophisticated Russian audience of Czarist days were gone; but the proletariat and these ex-peasants were quite capable of recognising a stirring play, or superb dancing, when they saw it—especially when it was straightforward—and it is priggish to talk about raising people to the level of Gogol or Chekov. It was Chekov himself who said: "There are theatres enough for the intelligentsia and the middle-class public in Moscow, and if there is a need for an additional theatre it is for a People's Theatre." And he meant not a fraud, but a people's theatre that would be guided by taste and intelligence. If the young girls in the five balconies screamed—because they had been taught some of the beauties and technique of the ballet—what a pity that we Westerners don't have the wits (or the taste) to do something as good ourselves!

There have always been two schools of the Russian ballet, each in its own tradition, but both founded on classical models. Leningrad has always been the purist school. When I was there in the winter of 1928, and that haunted city had not even begun to recover from the Revolution—there were big pits in the wood-blocks of the Nevsky and those pathetic little shops were still selling heart-breaking relics of the old régime, music-boxes, fur stoles, top hats—Semenova was dancing *The Hump-backed Horse*, the first of all Russian ballets, and dancing it as it had been danced in the days of Glinka. My wife and I went behind and talked with her. She was then eighteen years old, had married her bearded ballet master (she left him later and married another), and had just had twins. *The Hump-backed Horse* was put on after Glinka had stopped writing his operas. It is founded upon an old peasant fairy tale, all *moujiks* and birch-bark shoes and samovar . . . and that lugubrious winter's night, stepping from the dismal streets into the Maryinsky Theatre, we were transported into the fairy scene itself; for behind the supreme skill of the Russian dancers and ballerinas was a stage décor without equal anywhere else in the world.

My wife and I had both seen *The Hump-backed Horse,* in this same theatre, back in 1915. When we told them that, the old ballet master's eyes lighted up. He at once asked us about Karsavina. And when we told him that she was loved and admired in England, secure in their affections as one of the greatest ballerinas of all time, the old chap was incautious enough to raise his eyes in despair—before his young wife, then the prima ballerina of Russia—and say: "Ah, there will never be anything like them!" Little Semenova gave him quite a look. We talked of the old ballet, and I was foolhardy enough to say that, in this same Maryinsky Theatre, when reopened after the Kerensky Revolution, I had seen a ghost. There it was—the same ballet, the same ballerinas, the same orchestra—lifeless. We argued whether the Russian ballet would ever return to its perfection of old Imperial days: Semenova thought it would. This let the old ballet master down completely. He went on to talk about that famous quartette that we had frequently seen dancing together, all potential prima ballerinas—Gert and Geltsa are the only two names I can remember of it. "Ah!" he sighed, again with uplifted eyes, "such perfection!" He loved the ballet more than he loved love. No wonder pretty little Semenova divorced that tactless man. In those dark days it seemed that Red Moscow had sucked all the blood out of stricken Leningrad, once the most beautiful city in all the world: or so I had thought it when I saw it at dawn from across the Neva, with its long blocks of buildings, some a fifth of a mile long, of primrose and terracotta reds, and the gold spire of the Admiralty blazing in the rising sun. I feared it might never rise again. But:

"We shall dance *Koniok Gorbunok* (*The Hump-backed Horse*)," said Semenova firmly, as we said goodbye, "as it has always been danced. And with the same perfection!"

Moscow was more robust. Moscow always preferred exciting action and went in for *fouettés* and jumpers. In Leningrad, the swan dies, as in London, Paris, New York and Buenos Aires. But not in Moscow. Moscow ballet was at the cross-roads when I saw it in

1928–29: it was dancing the *Red Poppy,* as I mentioned in a previous chapter. This was a *ballet plastique,* as far removed from the conventional classic ballets as Picasso's present paintings are from his blue period. And, somehow, the Russians do not seem psychologically suited to it. They probably realised that this type of ballet could be developed better outside Russia. Anyway, when I returned to Moscow in 1941 the *Red Poppy* had been dropped: *Coppélia* and *Giselle,* one of the oldest ballets of all, were the top favourites. Moscow had trimmed *The Hump-backed Horse* of some of its acts—the oriental part: it was now only the peasant fairyland of the Russian *moujik*—and watching it I relived all the Russia I had ever known. I came out into the cold dark street with the broken fragments of many memories: some so sharp they hurt. I was plunged into black gloom at what the world had come to: especially Russia.

I was thinking of people—the last thing to be thought of in the communist credo. I had the impression in the Bolshoi Theatre that the dancers I had just seen, and the orchestra that had just enchanted me, were trying to break *through* something—or else were deliberately isolating themselves. What they were trying to break through —or had managed for a time to escape from—can be defined when you understand the effects of communism on the lives of ordinary men: when you understand what it robs them of. Or, to put it in another way, it struck me that all this magnificent playing and dancing was *in spite of something*.

I spent the whole of one February morning in 1942 with Nicholas, the Metropolitan of Moscow. This was the only interview I managed to get entirely for myself alone, and the only one worth its cable tolls. Though perhaps I overdid it: the London *Daily Mail* had always been outstandingly generous with me—and so I reciprocated: I sent them a cable of 1,750 words. Why? God knows (in this case, possibly He did). It was a detailed account of the fall and partial resurrection of the Russian Orthodox Church. The Bogoyavlensky Cathedral is in one of the least modern parts of Moscow. It is an unimposing structure. Its domes might have been golden once, but they were now sooty grey, and the plaster was dropping from its walls. The Metropolitan's little green-painted one-story home made of logs is behind the cathedral. As I turned into its shabby street

a radio loud-speaker suspended over the cross-roads was singing
from *Sadko,* and three silver fighting-planes shot like bullets overhead. An old woman led me into a bare room. Nicholas, formerly the
Metropolitan of Kiev, had arrived from Ulianovsk only two days before. He had a strong, slightly too clever face. He was what the Russians would call a *keetrie* and not an *oumni* man: clever rather than
wise. We should say he was wily, but very intelligent. Dressed in a
black cassock, he had a silver mane clipped square over a short collar;
fleshy hands; and a short, square beard, also silver. His face was the
colour of dough, and sweated slightly. His eyes had the look of a
man who has seen things he would like to forget. I was shocked to
learn, after I had been talking to him for over an hour, that he was
only fifty: two years younger than myself. He had certainly passed
through the fire. . . . And I believed most of what he told me.

"Ah, but of course he was a shrewd politician," said many of my
friends in London when I described this scene to them. Of course he
was. He would not have lasted through the Godless years—in the
high position he held in the Church—unless he had been the sort of
man who could use his wits to keep both himself and the flame of
faith alive. And it was alive.

He began by saying that in Moscow, whose proud boast was once
that there were "forty times forty" churches, there were now only
forty (which I believe was far more than the Kremlin had permitted); but that to this forty anyone who desired might freely come
and worship. He told me that Red soldiers came and prayed in the
Bogoyavlensky Cathedral before they left for the front. I already
knew this. So that I could insure myself as much as possible against
having a Soviet version of the freedom to worship forced on me, for
I realised he would be told what to say and what not to, I took a
tram one early morning—before I asked for the interview—and attended the first service of the cathedral, which was conducted by
the Deacon. I had seen the long queues waiting outside the church;
I had seen the Red soldiers standing there; and I had seen them
in the cathedral with its glittering ikons shining behind the burning
tapers, so tightly packed (this is literal) that I could hardly move my
hands from my waist. But most of the worshippers were old women
with shawled heads, crossing themselves constantly. I had also seen
the ikons, still up, in every peasant home we had been allowed to

enter outside Moscow. I needed no one to tell me that religion was still alive in Russia.

When I told the Metropolitan that I had already been at service in his cathedral, he brightened. He said: "You have known the old Russia. You saw us in the very worst days of the Church, 1928 and 1929. Did you believe what you saw today? Did you believe the long queue you saw waiting outside? Did you see the policeman keeping order so that the people waiting to get in to worship should remain undisturbed by the passing crowd? Do you believe me when I tell you that the people of Russia are absolutely free to worship?"

I replied that I could freely say "Yes" to every one of his questions, except the last. The communists were the Party of Leadership in Soviet Russia. All communists must be atheists. Therefore if a man wished to become a member of the Party of Leadership he could no longer remain a Christian.

He nodded. That was right, he said. That was a restriction, if looked at in that way, upon the absolute freedom of worship. And the Church, as a consequence, was absolutely divorced from the State. Here he was saying—and in the context of our talk it could, at this juncture, have been entirely unintentional—the exact opposite of the truth. Never since the October Revolution in 1917 had the Kremlin more consciously used the Church than in this last war. For to the millions of peasant partisans who fell upon the Germans from the forests, as they had fallen upon the retreating Grand Army of Napoleon, this was a war to save Holy Russia. This peasant war, this holy war, was part of a much bigger thing: Russianism. To exploit this Russianism the Kremlin used every device: and one of them was to call upon the Patriarch of the Russian Orthodox Church to bless the Russian arms. The most difficult problem that faced Stalin after the war was to displace Russianism and replace communism: this was the chief reason why he demoted Marshal Zhukov, so symbolic of the glory of Russian arms. And if the Kremlin did not immediately set in to break the Church, this was because it thought, and obviously still does, that the Church could be used as an instrument of Soviet Russia's foreign policy. Hence this propaganda display of the freedom to worship.

I believed the Metropolitan when he said that although the Government gave not one kopeck support—"for that," he remarked, with a quickly snuffed out smile, "would revive the evil associations of the old régime"—they often went out of their way to see that the Church got essential supplies, such as firewood, etc. For the rest, it was maintained solely by the voluntary contributions of its supporters. But he had to smile as he saw the look in my eyes when he told me about the Patriarch's blessing of the Soviet arms and the Red soldiers—and declared that there had not been the slightest scintilla of expediency in this gesture.

When I asked whether he had noticed a marked increase of worshippers since the war, and especially after the Patriarch's blessing, he answered carefully: "It is a difficult question to answer. But one thing is most noticeable—the faith is stronger. Much stronger. So many people come here to pray for their relatives at the front." And so they did. 1,500,000 Russian soldiers had surrendered in the first few months of the war. The Kremlin knew better than to undermine the morale of more soldiers by letting them know that their relatives could not pray for their safety. Not the most vicious bars of censorship could conceal from the Russian people the ghastly number of dead; perhaps even more awful was the army of men who came back without either hands or feet—for a leg wound which would have been trivial on the Western front meant, if not picked up, that toes and fingers began to go at 40 or 50 below zero in less than an hour. The Moscow Amputation Hospital (so named) was full of "bundle" cases. Frost killed more men than bullets—as the Germans found out to their terror.

I had always felt that the Russian Orthodox Church would be purified by the Revolution and would return, in the ensuing years, to something like its original fervour and sincerity. Nicholas had been a monk, and when I told him of the "black monks" I had seen at the dead Monastery of St. George outside Old Novgorod in 1928 —its domes sit like a pile of golden tangerines atop the pine forest on the shores of Lake Ilman; when I spoke of how I had seen the small remnants of "Black" monks cutting their own firewood and carrying water in yoked pails up the lake, just like any peasants, he remarked earnestly: "That was good for them. We must return to simplicity." He as much as said that the old Orthodox Church, which so badly needed reformation, was passing through fire, and that only the good, strong and pure priests would survive. But he let me know by the way he said it—despite the stare of Sophiana, who as he knew would repeat this interview, word for word, to the N.K.V.D.—that these priests would survive. There was a sort of triumph in his simplicity.

I did not tell him what had really happened to me in the Bogoyavlensky Cathedral. I couldn't. In that church with its wax tapers, its jewelled ikons and its waves of mighty singing, I was back in old Russia again: not the Russia of the Czars—I want to make that distinction—just Russia. And as the majestic voices filled the cathedral with their spell I felt my own soul being lifted above earthly things. In short, I felt like the Russians who were breaking my ribs to get near the ikons. And if its service can do that to a man like me, think what it can mean to a naturally devout and religious man like the Russian peasant. They haven't fallen for the jargon of Marxism. And never will.

It is there that the Orthodox Church in Russia will meet its test. The peasants are still in revolt against the Kremlin. They are naturally godly people. Or are they? How much of this faith was the superstition of the uneducated? The theatre of the Church: its glittering ikons, incense, singing—how do these effect, say, a young man of twenty-two in a peasant farming district? There are the old peasants, still 'of the faith', but they are dying out now. This argument between faith and superstition could last as long as the Thirty Years' War; and, for that matter, is probably still being argued in Russia at the moment, between the communists in the country districts and their religious parents. Perhaps the Kremlin sees that it has reached a point where it can permit free worship in the countryside, neither molesting nor protecting the Church, and leave it to the growing generations to take their choice. One thing they will not permit is for the Church to take any part in politics. If, therefore, the Church cannot be active politically when the peasants are revolting against collectivisation and all its works, will the great mass of peasantry find it still able to give them that 'something else', the emotional satisfaction, which was part of the old life? One thing only is certain about all such conjectures: the outside world will know no more about the position of the priest in country Russia than the Kremlin will permit. Meanwhile we in the West would do well to study our own case, and to ask ourselves whether religion is a living force or not.

TRAIN TO
MURMANSK

I came closer to the Russians in some twenty days of railway trains than during all the rest of the four months I was there on that last trip. I don't know why it is, but it has always been so: get a Russian in a railway carriage going from one place to another, and he casts off all restraints. He will say things, giving you his opinions or confessions, that, you think, will get him shot when the train stops. It seldom does. Even in Stalin's Russia there was a sort of sub-conscious agreement, between passengers and police, that a man could say freely what was on his mind when intoxicated by travel. When on the move, he could be himself. After all, there's a nomad under the skin of every Russian: they all come from the canoe- or horse-people, hereditarily accustomed to opening up new country; and if a man can't open up his heart occasionally when he's got this heady feeling of *space* in him, what the hell . . . ! It was not by accident that Tolstoy, that wily old master craftsman, staged his *Kreutzer Sonata* in a railway train.

I can say cheerfully, now they are over, that it was at a railway station which had no name on it, 1,000 kilometres from Moscow and 1,000 from Murmansk, that I passed the three worst days of my life.

When Sophiana swept out of my bedroom the morning I told her I would not be "ordered" back to Kuibyshev, I knew she would be in the Censor's office before me, to break the glad news. She was. In any other country than Stalin's State concentration camp it would have been funny to watch the effect of my entering that room—the apprehensive indecision of people who did not yet know how to treat me. They were waiting to be told: for I was the first correspondent who had refused to obey Uncle Joe. The girl typists, forgetting themselves for a moment, stopped their work and just stared at me. In their eyes I was as much of a curiosity as that Frenchman who, with a pair of home-made wings, was about to jump off the Eiffel Tower. Indeed, I felt much the same.

Chuvash, my pet hate, was the only male censor on duty, as it would be; and for once he did not know what to say. Unaccustomed to such impotence, he banged his metal stamp on the triplicate cable to the *Daily Mail* informing them that I was LEAVING RUSSIA FORTH-WITH, and shoved it at me across his desk. It was not until I had reached the door that he collected his wits and thought of something harmless enough to say (so as to avoid being accused afterward of deviating from the party line): "*Bon voyage,* Mr. Farson!" He knew I knew what he meant. It was not going to be *bon* at all. He would have been sinister if he had not been such a silly son of a bitch.

When I went down to the Intourist office in the hotel and asked for a ticket to Murmansk, they backed off as if I had just told them I had smallpox. An exit visa is customary in any land, and I knew I should have to have one: but this consternation verged on panic—not a single man there was going to get himself involved, even by merely talking tickets, in the trouble that they saw I might have coming to me.

When I came back to my room I saw that Macloughlin's door was open. His girl secretary was sitting in his deep armchair, having a morning nibble, as was customary. We correspondents, and the diplomats of course, had lashions of food while the rest of hard-pressed Moscow was near starvation: with a full belly, an Ambassador can be safely counted upon not to know what is happening in the street. Or care. And we correspondents always had food in our bedrooms, for we were so browned off with the sight of each other's faces, from having to lunch at the same long table in the Hotel Metropole, that we preferred to eat our dinners alone. Mac was lying on top of his bed, fully dressed, with his Russian knee-boots projecting over the brass foot-rail; and I thought he was still asleep.

This young secretary had a child beyond the Urals which she could never get permission to go out to, and at one time we had been rather friendly as I also wanted to see what was east of the Urals.

At the beginning, when I was still fatuous enough to believe that I might get permission to make such a trip (for which I applied), she asked me to take her along as my secretary. She already knew about my few words with Sophiana: those Russian secretaries had a sorority room somewhere in that vast and haunted hotel. And I don't think she liked Sophiana. "What are you going to do about *food,* Mr. Farson?" And now I knew they *had* been discussing me in the sorority room: for only Sophiana knew that my locker was quite exhausted, and that she had the permit for my new batch of food, drink, and cigarettes. "Why don't you use mine?" muttered Mac. "Wait a minute. Lemme wake up and I'll leave Russia with you."

"You!" laughed his secretary. "How much food do you think *you've* got?" "Don't care. Long as the vodka lasts." Then we heard the ghastly news that Mac had finished it. His secretary said: "I think Mr. Macloughlin should go out with you. He has been here too long." Mac sat up. "All right," he announced, "I *will* go!" We discussed this startling idea for some time, he made up his mind, and I went back to the Censor's Department of the Foreign Office and told them that Macloughlin was also leaving; his secretary would be along in a minute or two to confirm it. M. Pulgranov, head of the department, had now come in. Although we called him the "Goon", I had a half-liking for that man: he was so *encouragingly* intelligent. You could never tell what he was thinking, of course, any more than you could with any Russian of those days (or these either); and in Pulgranov's case this obscurity of thought was barricaded behind ½-inch bifocal lenses (almost a Spaceman's optics) which made his eyes look no bigger than a newt's. And I flatter myself that he had a half-liking for me; at any rate, possibly bored by the juvenality of some of the correspondents, he had frequently asked me to ride in his car when we had been out on our trips. He sighed. . . . "Are you absolutely certain, Mr. Farson? Have you really made up your mind to do this?" I told him I had. He nodded: "Very well. I will make arrangements for both you and Mr. Macloughlin."

My cable to the *Daily Mail* got through all right. But their reply, asking me to try to leave by air via the Caspian if possible, and report events in Persia, did not. The Russians never gave it me: the first I heard of it was when I got back to London. And then it was only by chance: Bob Prew mentioned it at a lunch we were having

with Lord Rothermere and Stanley Bell at the Dorchester—a lunch
at which I told them that I could write better from London what
was going on in Russia than I could from the Hotel Metropole, which
was just off the Red Square and Kremlin. I should be able to use
the knowledge, I said, that four years of Russia had given me. They
agreed, and gave me a handsome retaining fee, and I worked for
that very pleasant paper until near the end of 1944. I was usually
quite pro-Soviet—until near the end. Maisky asked me out to the
Embassy and thanked me. And, interesting point, so did the White
Russians.

There is no need to describe how the Russians made Mac and me
twice miss the train, and how we had our bags down and sat there
in the lobby, waiting for the promised car which never came. But
one thing happened during that waiting which redoubled my anger
at what the Kremlin was arbitrarily doing to us foreign correspondents. On the second night, long after I thought the entire ape-troupe
had gone to Kuibyshev, the secretary of Parker of the London *Times*
knocked at my door; a distinctly good-looking girl, and made even
more attractive at the moment by a big bottle of Vouvray she had
in one hand. In the other were two little Bohemian wine-glasses.
"These are a farewell gift for you," she said.

We sat there, and she eyed me with a strange intensity. "What
do you want from life, Mr. Farson?"

"Peace."

"Oh no! Not that! We must work. We must——" She stopped and
looked at me. "I have a little note here for you. I was going to leave
it, in case you were not in your room: now I will say what I have
written: 'Mr. Farson, when you get to England please do write good
things about our country. Tell them what we are doing. . . .'"

There was not the least question of her sincerity. Of all those girl
secretaries, I would have bet on her a hundred to one as being an
up-to-the-hilt communist believer and worker. And—I want to make
this point strongly—she was a good worker. That strange girl was the
1942 edition of the idealists I had met in 1929. There was no question
about it; and I can look back to that last moment, that almost naïve
appeal, with gratitude. We were just setting in to talk about what
the future of Russia might hold when Parker turned up. He looked

either huffed or worried, or just nervous (he was later, I believe, Moscow correspondent for the *Daily Worker*); and he told her he wanted her to go and fetch the last Tass bulletin as it came out. They left. But why was it that, when all the other correspondents had been ordered back to Kuibyshev, Parker was left in Moscow? This was what sent me to bed in a rage that night: the fact, not that he was allowed to remain, but that there had been no valid reason whatever for sending the rest of us away. It was just pure Kremlin bloody-mindedness: Stalin *liked* to do things like that. At the core of him was the pettiness of all Asiatic despots.

The train we got was a very comfortable Wagon-Lit, hangover from Czarist days. We had a double compartment. And in the other half were two officers of a service I will not even associate with them: for if ever I met a pair of T.G.s, so prevalent in the 1914–18 war, these were prize specimens. We heard them working their little Tommy cooker all day long: lovely bacon and sausages. Whereas Mac and I soon came to the gastronomic problem of how to split evenly the last sardine. They never offered us one bite. Or even a drink, when they were dousing themselves with Johnnie Walker. Cheerio, chaps!

Ahead of our car was a Wagon-Lit full of young Political Commissars—a nice and neat-looking lot, wearing the gold badge of their sinister service on their sleeves—and half a dozen pretty girls in uniform. Also a young Russian civilian, who told me that he was a "trade expert", going out with his wife and baby to become an attaché at the Russian Embassy in London. She was a petulant, bossy young thing with pouting lips, who seemed to be trying to run the whole car, leaving him to hold the baby. These young Political Commissars were a type that we correspondents did not come across in our work, at any rate in such a number; and I found them highly interesting. Judged by either their good looks or their manner, they might have been superior students in any American university. They were friendly at first, in the free atmosphere of a moving train. Not only that, but they both wrote and staged a play about the train, even as they were travelling on it. They invited Mac and me to be the audience.

It was a weird performance, because you couldn't tell, when a girl or young man started to speak to another, whether it was part of the play or not. This was a parlour-car Wagon-Lit, and with the frozen forest as our perpetually moving backdrop the stage setting was unique. "Can you make any sense out of this?" asked puzzled Mac. I said that I could not, but that I was sure it was something clever. Everything would have been fine, had it not been that the little "trade expert's" wife got Mac into an argument. . . . Mac was holding to his point: that Lenin was a greater man than Stalin—and no two names could have been more fatal. This was *sacrilege!* When the performers heard the holy name of Stalin being bandied about their play just folded up. In a macabre silence everyone went back to his seat. The little "trade expert" looked very pale: the next time Mac and I ventured into that car we were met by a row of faces as expressionless as the wax dummies in a hat-shop window.

The days dragged along. We had to give right of way to every munitions train coming down from Murmansk and Archangel; we lay for hours, even half a day, on the sidings. Forest, forest—a clearing—forest, forest—clearing. . . . This was near spring, and the streams were running in some of the sunny spaces. Then the tundra, as we neared the Arctic: limitless space, still snow-covered, with not a bush higher than a man's shoulder, where we watched the sun dip to the horizon, slide along, and then mount up into the sky again. In the forest we had passed two convict camps, one abandoned, the other with guards and machine-guns in its watch-towers; grim stockade, outside which two padded wretches, a bayonet pointed at their backs, were hauling a log over the snow. Presumably their firewood. Then the forest, and oblivion, closed over them. . . .

This was before the days of what the Czechs did to Otis. Still, I was wondering (very frightened) how I should get out of Russia. My apprehensions became active at a point about 1,000 kilometres from Moscow, 1,000 from Murmansk—where we were both taken off the train. There was a station there. We were escorted into its waiting-room. A soldier, with bayonet, was posted at the door. "And this," I said to Mac, "looks like *it*." Whatever that was. "And nobody knows where we are," I added.

This was a junction, a little before where the road splits: one fork goes up to Kandalaksha and the Kola peninsula to Murmansk, the other to Archangel. What it was used for I didn't yet know; but I have never seen so many N.K.V.D. troops in all my life. They had their own office inside the railway station; and, as it was at the other side of a three-ply partition that had only recently been erected in the waiting-room, we heard the N.K.V.D. commandant using our names in a telephone talk he was having with Moscow. Just our names—and then the *Slooshieyu,* 'I hear', which I give in phonetic Russian. They were talking about us! I have experienced various degrees of fright in my life, but this was something I had never known before and have never known since. It made our battering on the convoy, which was continuous from the afternoon after we left Murmansk until we got air-cover off the coast of Iceland, a mere joke by comparison. This was Terror.

I speak for myself. Remember, it was *I* who had refused to go back to Kuibyshev: Mac had just come along. And if there were any doubts about that, they were soon settled: after the long telephone conversation with Moscow, when we were sitting in the waiting-room wondering why they had taken us off at this place, a young N.K.V.D. officer came in and nodded at us. We both stood up, but the man just waved for me. I was taken into the N.K.V.D. office. There was the Commandant: grey-haired, rather good-looking, with not a trace of an emotion on his face. You have to see that sort of human visage to believe it. I was not asked to sit down; the young N.K.V.D. officer just left me standing there. "Yes?" I asked.

In quite good English this man of the police said: "You have been in Russia for only four months, Mr. Farson." And then added, just as a snake forks out its tongue, "What is the trouble?" "Trouble? Why, I—er—I am going out." "Why?" "To get back to my job." (You can see how difficult it was.) "And your job is——?" "I am a foreign correspondent—you have it there on my passport. Second page." I reached out to show it to him but he put his hand on it. "Oh no, Mr. Farson," he smiled. "I know what is in your passport. I have been reading it. . . ." "And so," he concluded, after looking at me for some time, "you will leave Russia?" "Tell me," I countered, for I thought that was best, "when can we expect a train for Murmansk?" "One is going out today," he said, "but there is no room on it. As soon as we can find a place for you we will let you know." "Thank you," I said, staring at him blankly: I might have been talking to Thos. Cook & Co., London; he could not have been more polite. "We will let you know, Mr. Farson."

About the time I was beginning to cook up a philosophy to enable me to endure being lost sight of in Russia—and I know I am one of those men who would crack up in the concentration camps—something even worse happened. I saw a prison train—for Russian political prisoners. I have never seen anything that frightened me so much in all my life. It made me sick with fear, for I thought that, by some incredible act at Moscow, I might soon be on one. Better people than I had been put away. There were about forty long red-painted box-cars. And now I at once understood the reason why so many N.K.V.D. were about. They at once posted themselves at intervals the entire length of that train as it slowly came to a halt at the station. It remained there all day.

Projecting from between the two sliding doors at the centre of each car were what I at first thought were the tails of salmon or some other fish. They were not, of course. Approaching as close as the hostile backs of the N.K.V.D. would permit, I saw that each of these strange contraptions was a long V-trough made of two boards nailed together. They were the latrines for the poor wretches confined inside the dark cars. The remainder of the aperture between the two doors had been blocked up. The only light that could possibly enter that long red box on wheels was through two little apertures high up at either end—18-inch-square windows.

There were faces at these windows. Some of them opened their mouths and poked their fingers in them. This was the way they begged for food. From one or two of these ghastly squares with a sub-human face in it, a little canvas bag tied on a piece of string was hopefully lowered. No one came near them. Nobody looked at them. All day the faces remained at the windows: eyes that looked at passing life with a misery beyond description. And all day the bustling Russians on the platform went about their business just as if that quarter-mile-long trainload of human agony was not there.

Why didn't the Russians look at that terrible prison train? In the old Czarist days the Russian political prisoner, sent to Siberia, was regarded by almost everybody as a hero. He was marched through the streets to the long green train in broad daylight. His relations and friends could, in that way, see him off. He (or she) could hold his head up, show just how bravely he could comport himself as he passed them. There was a moment of glory in all that, brief as it was. The Russian political prisoner in, or from, Siberia was the stock hero of Russian literature.

But today—what happens? The prisoner is never seen. He vanishes from sight as quickly, and in most cases as finally, as a stone thrown overboard in mid-ocean. "Forget him. Forget that he ever lived." That is the Russian official advice to his relatives. They recommend you to exercise the psychology of forgetfulness. And today that dread complacence has spread throughout Europe. It works. It even makes it easier to be a secret policeman: you have less strain on your conscience. So that in Russia and her satellites, in China and the Far East, hundreds of millions of people think life *is* like that: that concentration camps and State murder are quite natural. Not a pleasant thing to remember when you have just heard the N.K.V.D. talking about you over the phone to Moscow. Stalin, who had given the order of execution for so many of his old comrades, and who could have built a pyramid of human skulls from the other millions he had had murdered, probably never once thought about retribution in all his long, evil and very successful life. But I have often wondered if the N.K.V.D.s, the M.V.D.s, and the various secret police of Eastern Europe, haven't looked forward to that day—if it ever does come—when these prison-camps will give up their living dead. Or will the prisoner, too, have forgotten?

We learned another possible reason for the prevalence of N.K.V.D.s. This junction was a secret assembly point. Trains coming from Archangel and Murmansk stopped here to have part of their loads taken off. These, so it looked, were the boxed aeroplanes. I saw men handling crates that in any other country would have been considered immovable except with cranes or derricks. Forty men, fifty, a hundred would topple a crate off a flat-car, holding its weight as it came down; and slowly let it come to rest on a set of sledges. Then another fifty or so would haul it off. Gulliver in all his travels never saw Lilliputians toiling with such frantic energy. Some crates were walked off with human legs and feet below them working like centipedes. And these men were being driven! This was the way they built the Pyramids.

They went down a long road. And without thinking about it, one moonlit night—not wanting to go to that awful iced-up privy—I walked off down the road a pace to pumpship. While I was standing there I saw a figure rushing at me: it was the commandant of the N.K.V.D., the one who had interviewed me. "What are you doing *here*, Mr. Farson?" he asked, as if he had reached the end of his patience. I told him he could see. For just one second I thought that human touch had softened him: but no. He shouted, and the soldier with the rifle came up. "Please, Mr. Farson," said the N.K.V.D. man, polite as ever. "Go back to the station." And that night I heard him using my name, talking to Moscow again. All very frightening. It seemed that someone, somewhere, could not make up his mind. . . .

They had also taken off the little "trade expert" and his wife and baby. She was now red and sniffling: he white and furious. They were quarrelling bitterly. We had nowhere to sleep in that waiting-room: there was only the usual flat station-bench running along its walls. They had settled down in the far corner—as far, it looked, as they could possibly get from Mac and me. We could not have had a more intimate view of Soviet family life. It was the first time I ever watched a man change the baby's nappies. He seemed to be an expert, probably from long practice. His pouting wife had now just gone *woof!* and he never spoke to her except to snap. They were both badly frightened. Whether or not they were put on the convoy I don't know; they might have been on another ship. Mac and I were the only two passengers on ours. But at Murmansk they were met by three tall types who just strode out of the station N.K.V.D. office, with that robot step that characterises the dreaded secret police. And that was the last we saw of them. But anyway, if ever I saw fatherly love, it was in that frightened man for that child.

Then, before we even knew what was happening, the N.K.V.D. stood before Mac and me, shouting "Murmansk! Murmansk!" We needed no urging. We were both travelling light. But it took some doing to get my heavy duffle-bag over the couplings between two freight-cars in the long train that lay between us and the one for Murmansk. Mac was splendid here: all the Australian in him came to life. We hurled our stuff ahead of us. And then, at the Murmansk train, we were made to wait while a family was thrown out. First came the fattest man I ever saw in Russia, so fat that he was sinister. Maybe he was a Rumanian, for he kept jabbering in a tongue which, for some reason, suddenly made me think of gipsies and violins. Wife and daughter followed. The latter, who put up a fight, was literally pitched out into the snow. "Please!" said the N.K.V.D. guard, like the *maître d'hôtel* when he leads you to your table. We were given the end spaces in a car full of ski-troops and young naval officers, all submariners, as we soon discovered. The train began to move. . . .

As on the other train, these young submarine officers also began by being friendly. In one way or another I have seen quite a few naval officers in my time, both American and British; and these young men seemed no different from them. They had that same undefinable *look*. They also had apparently the usual Service wit and sense of fun—though it was alarming to see the way they opened tins of fish with just their penknives. The sight also made me ravenous. One of them caught the envy in my eye; then, frowning, he asked: "When do you eat?" I laughed and said that that was just what had been bothering me; for, apart from a bottle of Bovril (a strange object I found in my book rucksack, relic of London), Mac and I had now reached the bottom of the barrel. "What!—no bread?" "*Neit!*" I replied. He went back into the car, and soon a senior submarine officer came along and stood beside us. "Come!" he said, as the train began to slow up. Mac and I followed him into a railway station. Now, we did not know it then, but there was something very close to starvation along this Russo-Finnish frontier: when the girl in the station shook her head and said they had no bread she was probably near the truth. To cut it short: he would not take no— which produced a triangle of black bread for Mac and me, large and heavy enough to have ballasted a small yacht. The girl also brought two plates of fresh fish, cold, which looked like baby pike and probably were, as there were plenty of lakes in that region. We wolfed those down on the spot. Then we ran for the train again: the senior submariner gave us a salute and dropped into his seat as we passed it. He did not come forward to talk with us.

But another man did, as weird a wanderer as I have ever come across. A Pole, obviously, and a very suspicious one; he had, apparently, been fighting ever since the birth of Christ. I have seldom seen a man so criss-crossed with odd nicks and bullet holes. He was obviously a bit touched. He began to tell us about the fighting he had seen in Outer Mongolia—and then, as I was always interested in this semi-secret war, I, for the first time on this train, reached in my pocket and took out my notebook. It was as if I had produced a revolver. . . . One of the young officers sitting directly across the aisle jumped to his feet and went forward. An N.K.V.D. man followed him back, and gave a jerk of his head to call off our talkative friend, who got up and left instantly. And from then on the young submariners all turned into clams. Only the senior officer, when I looked back, shook his head at me. Sorrowfully.

The line was electrified across the Kola peninsula, and we went at top speed. The Germans had been flying over and blowing up bits of track. We carried a flat-car with spare rails behind our own engine. We weren't bothered. And so, ten days from Moscow, we reached Murmansk. And there a miracle happened—I met a Russian I had known before! "Well, for God's sake, what are *you* doing here, Mr. Farson?" "What are *you?*" "Me? I'm the manager of this god-damn dump (the Intourist Hotel)—have a snifter?" I almost fell on his neck. I introduced Mac, who said he would wait in the lobby and look after our bags; then I got this man, who had been one of the under-managers of the Grand Hotel, Moscow, when I lived there in 1929, to take me to his office. "I want two things," I said as I sank into the chair before his desk. "First—get on the phone right away to the British Mission. Next, as soon as they answer, give me the two biggest bottles of vodka you've got in the north of Russia—*and* about a thousand smoked salmon sandwiches. What's the number of my room?" He grinned at all this, grabbed the phone, pressed a button, and handed me a key. "Mac," I said at the door; "here's our room. Coming up! You just wait there a few minutes!"

"Well! Where on earth have you two been?" came a voice from the British. "Come to dinner tonight. Tell us then."

My Russian friend, who knew "good old Chicago" a lot better than I did, asked me to bring him up to date on all the correspondents he had known while I had been in Moscow. Meanwhile, from a vodka bottle of his own in the desk, we snifted. "What are those men, lying out there all over the floor?" I asked him. "Yanks. What's left of a convoy that got it a week or two back. Some of 'em got their feet and hands frozen. Open boats. . . ." "Have to sleep out there on the floor?" I asked. He looked embarrassed. "Uh-huh," he said, nervously. "You see, we gotta keep a few rooms free in this place. Can't tell what the next train might bring." "I see," I said. And he just nodded: he knew what I was thinking. When the waiter came with a heavy tray loaded with salmon sandwiches and two big decanters of vodka, I told him to take it up to our room. "Well, well, it sure is nice to see you again, Mr. Farson. Nice to see you. . . ." "And you too," I said, shaking his hand warmly; for never did I meet a friend when more in need. I walked out with the vodka bottle that he had pressed upon me—and there stood the senior submarine officer.

The language was international—I just held the vodka bottle up, gave him the number of our room, nodded upwards—and he grinned. Mac and I were just starting on the salmon sandwiches when he stood in the door. He closed it quickly behind him. I poured a drinking-glass half full of vodka and handed it to him. Took the other, and raised it to him—"Health!" He put his head back, poured the whole half-tumbler down the hatch at one gulp; shook his head, seized mine, and kissed me on both cheeks. Then, before I could get my breath, the door of our room slammed behind him. "Well, of all the things I've ever seen," said Mac, "he *kissed* you!"

Among the American sailors was one boy with a foot the size of an elephant's. He came from Iowa. And he had some beautifully pungent feelings about the Russians. We could only manage one, so we took him up to our room, where he slept on the floor with the blankets we had each given him. "Comfortable?" we asked, when he was full of vodka and salmon (he absolutely would not take either of our two hard beds). "Y-e-es. . . . Boy! *am* I comfortable. . . . Do you know my mother almost made $5,000?" "How come?" "Well, that's what she would have got if I'd been drownded. $5,000!" That was the one regret of *his* experience: eight days in the ice floes in an open boat. . . .

There was only one last hitch. While we were eating dinner with the British, the Major, who was head of Mission, said to me under his breath: "There's a convoy leaving tomorrow." I gasped. "My God," I said, also in undertone, "how I wish we could be put on it." He looked at me curiously: "What makes you think you couldn't?" I told him. "I know," he said. "Even if everything was normal, there would probably not be time to pass you through the usual formalities. The Russians make such a fuss. God knows why; you might think we were fighting them instead of the Germans." He sighed: "Impossible to make them see that all this fuss and bother only makes it harder to help them." And then: "I think we will put you aboard anyway."

When we sat in a corner, he said: "Look here. You and Macloughlin just have your things ready. Don't say anything to anybody. You be ready to be picked up—say, any time after six a.m. tomorrow." I told him we had not unpacked even a toothbrush. "Don't pay your bill!" he said suddenly. "We'll look after that." We sat there smoking: "Frankly," he said, "we were beginning to wonder what had happened to you and Macloughlin. We got the signal from Moscow that you had left, then . . . nothing. . . ." "That's the way I felt," I told him. He began to smile: "You refused to go back to Kuibyshev, didn't you? Hmmmm. . . . Well, you chaps be ready. There's a Captains' Conference. I'll be at it. . . ."

At seven a couple of Tommies showed up and Mac and I were in a jeep before we knew it, hot-foot for the harbour. Murmansk harbour is (or was at that time) only one square mile. It had just been heavily bombed. Two big British ships lay beached, with people still searching for fragments of human remains in one of them, as a bomb had dropped right down her stack as she lay at anchor. The head of the harbour has a small pool, with a slanting stone wall like Dover's: we slid down that on a slatted board ladder to the launch that lay at its foot. The convoy was already lined up. We were taken to the Commodore's ship, the little *Temple Arch*. "Well, goodbye," said the Major, "I think that's done it. And good luck."

I was rather glad as I watched their launch going back that I had once lost my job, the finest job in the newspaper world, for being pro-British. But I was congratulating myself a bit too soon. A *Russian* launch was now coming out to us. And she was coming at full speed. Mac was in with the steward, sharing in the all-around ship's handout of grog. I had told him that I was not drinking: I know myself; I wanted a clear head if I was going to be in trouble. And so I had no illusions now: the Major's kindly offices had not worked. Two surly-looking Russians, of the very worst trouble-making type, came aboard: they began to argue with Captain Lamont. "I'm sorry," he said, coming along to us, for I had called Mac out now. "They want your passports."

Lamont and I stood there talking after the officials had left. "It's a pity," he said. "I wish you had come aboard in the regular way. We're going out pretty soon"—we could feel the tremor as the ship's propeller was turning over—"and if they don't bring your passports back, well . . . I'm afraid I shall have to put you ashore. We can't break the rules of this port." I was with Captain Lamont for twenty-two days—and the ineffable George Currie, a four-striper engineer: *and* a second officer who afterwards got his Master's ticket at the age of twenty-six, and who potted a Junkers 88 on this trip: and all I can say to the men of the *Temple Arch,* from captain to cabin boy, is in pure American: "I'm glad to have met you."

One of the Everests of my emotional life was when, after I had fearfully watched that Russian launch racing back to us, a little Russian midshipman scrambled aboard, gave us a smart salute, and handed us our passports. I was "out".

There have been many stories of convoys, some of them far worse than ours. I have no wish to compete in disasters. But some things on this trip were unforgettable. First picture: as we came near the edge of the ice-pack, trying to get past Petsamo, there was the little *Sabre* ahead of us, almost invisible in the fountains of bomb-sprays all around her: just her guns flashing, all of them, as she answered back. She was so loaded with depth-charges that she looked like a Christmas tree. "Touch *her* off," said George Currie, "and you'd think the whole bloody convoy goes up!" Second picture: Currie himself, as we stood amidships, watching open-mouthed as three bombs came down on us. Two of them failed to explode, though one knocked the ice-doughnuts off the lines of our boats, which we had already swung out: the third went off underneath our keel. Ship jumping like a horse, and the filament of every light broken. Total darkness inside. The Arabs from the fireroom piling up. "Down lads," said Currie, making a sign to them they understood. And, about forty minutes later—the sky splattered with sepia puffs where the convoy's shots were exploding—George Currie coming on deck, stuffing his hands in his pockets, and looking pure W. W. Jacobs. "Tell me, Mr. Currie," I said. "How did you feel down there—with all the lights out?" "Well, lad, I thought I would just close the —— doors and keep out the —— fish."

I used that on the B.B.C., having one hell of a time finding an acceptable substitute for Currie's one adjective. And he heard it! He wrote me from South Shields: "Someone gave me the tic-tac that you would be on the air—and lo and behold! you were talking about *me!*" He got the O.B.E. for this trip, for "the commendable way he brought his ship into port". Captain Lamont wrote me: "I suppose you know Currie and I have joined the ranks of the O.B.E.s." The Commodore got the D.S.O. And on Currie's next ordeal in the Arctic he got the D.S.C. "My husband," Mrs. Currie wrote me, "has gone to the Palace to see the King."

At 2.30 one night (I had just looked at my watch) when I was leaning over the rail with George Currie, saying what a weird thing it was, up here in the Arctic spring, to be in a place where the sun never sets, Currie, who had just come from Lamont, said: "There's a sub somewhere in these lanes, and"—BANG! The stern was blown off the ship directly opposite us. She went down in 2½ minutes. Said chief-engineer George Currie: "What a —— waste! To think of all the trouble that went into the building of that ship!" It was the *Kiev*, on her maiden return from her first voyage. How many of her men the trawlers picked up we could not know. It was the waste, though, that depressed Currie.

At Loch Ewe I was invited to spend the night, and spent two, in the *Sabre*, the little destroyer dripping with depth-charges that we were always afraid would be blown up beside us; and then we should be "hanging on to the horns of the moon", as Currie put it. "That's impossible!" laughed her Commander and his officers in her wardroom, explaining that those things never went off until you set them. He had won the D.S.C. at St. Nazaire. Wearing a pair of immaculate chamois gloves, he steered the whaleboat as we went to shore. And in the Mess I watched a bearded old Commander, who had been called back from retirement, simply bursting at the seams with the love and happiness of being back with his service, the witty old savage. He said: "I'm the Mother Superior of these infants." The Navy was there! There was hardly an officer in that building who had not just come off a tough show or who was not just about to go out on one. Laughter, laughter, laughter. . . . And that was that.

A HOUSE
BY THE SEA

When I got back from Russia and took on the *Daily Mail* job (my articles could be written in the country and dictated over the phone), I decided to do two things I had been wanting to do for some time —to give the sun and salt water a chance to heal my leg (I thought they might do the trick) and sit down and catch up with some of my past years. I wanted to study for a time. Eve and I went down to North Devon and rented a house right by the sea, on one of the most beautiful stretches of coast I have ever seen. A year rolled by, then a house that we had often wished we owned as we saw it when walking along the sands—a little grey house, built of the local stone, standing on its own isolated little plateau overlooking the sea—came into the market. Its owner, appropriately enough, had died in Kenya. This house was the only land on his estate that was not entailed. His son wanted some ready money to pay the death duties, so we made him a price, and he took it. We thought it was the most sensible thing we had ever done in our life. And just about time.

I bought it out of the proceeds of *Going Fishing*. In fact, I bought it because of the fishing. For if ever I saw a stretch of sand and sea that is a surf-caster's dream, we have it. Hardy's made me a beautiful greenheart rod, American pattern; a friend in the Embassy got me over a superb Vom Hofe reel. My publishers, who were used to putting their authors into hospitals or asylums, sent me over the full list of what I had asked them to buy from Abercrombie & Fitch— cuttyhunk line, bloc-tin squids, three-way swivels, 4-oz. pyramidal sinkers, three-ply casts (I am using the American nomenclature), etc., etc.: the same line of tackle that I had used when I was twelve years old, and bought from the same company. I could almost retire on the money I have spent during a lifetime at Abercrombie & Fitch: to walk through that store is an emotional debauch. And *Going Fishing,* as it happens, opens with surf-casting on the New Jersey coast.

But the British fish were too conservative; they had never heard of these American gadgets. For two desperate years, night and day, every turn of the tide, I fished the sea right in front of our house. No fish. A few spotted sand-sharks gave themselves up, the type they call 'nurse'; fine for the cats, but my wife, who does not like their sweet taste, declared that one of them turned in the frying-pan and stared at her as she was cooking some sections of him for us. I also got one suicide bass. By that time, I was in a suicide mood myself. I can't describe my dismay. And I am absolutely certain that if I had been able to do my bit of surf-casting every day, wading out into the sea to plunk a 4-oz. sinker beyond the waves; or better still, if I could have worked a squid through the sea the way I used to do for bluefish—and I love doing that every bit as much as fly-casting— I should never have begun to wade in those oceans of alcohol that I then began to take aboard. To stick it out, and not just pull up anchor and try to live somewhere else, was one of the hardest bits of moral discipline I have made myself face.

Actually, I worked far harder, and with more sense, than I should have done in Fleet Street. We live three miles from the nearest pub. For the first year or two, when I wasn't writing, or sitting beside the radio listening to the news bulletins and the monitoring—and on some days, when the Russians crossed the Dnieper for example, this kept me turning the dials all day—I made a study of the twenty wasted years between the two wars. I had attended many of the international conferences. I bore a grudge against those years, when we were so ready to accept paper formulas instead of facts. In addition to the *Daily Mail* articles I was doing a political feature every week for the Central Press. These articles went to the provincial newspapers of Britain—which, odd as it may seem to anyone who does not know the English Press, presented far more serious and lengthy political articles than did the popular London dailies. The Central Press also syndicated overseas, so I had the pleasure of being able to talk, if only through the printed word, to my friends of the first-war days, Down Under. With the habits graven into me by four-teen years of newspaper routine when I had worked only in the morning, I worked only in the morning. After that, the day was mine.

At first, the problem of what to do with it did not bother me. I tramped the downs behind us with a gun, shot rabbits, and got an occasional partridge. One day I got two partridges, and would have had three had not the face of my wife appeared as I threw up the gun. I did not think it worth the risk of adding her to my very mixed bag. I rented the shooting rights on some farms over by the Taw River, and got a few golden plover when the weather was so cold I could hardly bend my finger to pull the trigger. There were a few days of fair snipe shooting. And here for companion I had a Welsh-man, born poacher, ex-sergeant in the Royal Horse Artillery, the only man I have ever met who could shoot ducks by sound. When the rains came—it rains here, so the locals say, for three hundred days out of every year, and blows a full gale for the remaining sixty-five —this Welshman and I used to lie behind the dykes on the coastal farms and shoot ducks as they came in at night. That is, *he* did. "Duck coming! Duck coming!" he would whisper hoarsely, as we sat there with our heads down and hands covered so that their white would not show. " 'Bout twelve feet up. . . . *Wham! Wham!*" Then he would wade out into the pool, breaking the reflections from the red light up on the pylon over by Bideford, and come back with two ducks.

My hearing had gone long ago. I could not hear the whisper of their wings, to shoot at *sound*. I treasured the romantic excuse that my deafness was the result of Africa: malaria—and gin. I should have been willing to settle for the gin; it meant I should have had some fun for my affliction. But at long last, in Boston, and as late as 1954, when the wife of the Chairman of Little, Brown & Co. had second-row seats for the try-out of Grahame Greene's *Living Room,* and I had to confess to her that I had missed every other word of Barbara Bel Geddes, I went to the ear-specialist she demanded I should see the next day; and he, after giving me the works, eventually landed on the real reason: the awful over-doses I had had of sulfa drugs. He advised me not to go in for any hearing devices, but to take up lip-reading. "But do you know where I *live?*" I asked him; and when I tried to imitate the Devon burr: "Aye she be a proper toad!"—or the Welshman!—he collapsed. "Well then, stay as you are," he ended. "Just as you are; you will hear all that is good for you for the rest of your life." Alas, I see the curlew coming back over our house from the sands every morning, but I no longer hear them. Another one of my senses has petered out.

Then, as writing about Russia put me in the mood of Russia, I spent the evenings of nearly all that first year or so going back and re-reading all the old Russians. Stretched out by the log fire, I lived the story again of Peter and Natasha and of Vronsky and Anna, and tramped through Russia with Gorky, while my cat Roly sat on the arm of my deep chair or on my chest. These were two great compensations: my love of reading, and these animals that came back into our lives, now that we had a place to keep them. For six years of my journalistic life I had never lived in any one country for more than six months—except for that one year in Soviet Russia. I had lived in steamers, Wagon-Lits, foreign hotels, quarrelling with concierges, customs and censors around this bloody world; the only things that ever seemed able to catch up with me were my bills. But here was home again: 2½ acres that we could really call our own— and a place that would be monstrous without a cat and dog. And here I want to say something about the British.

Not long after I returned from my second trip to Africa, when the Colonial Exhibition they were holding in London was such a pathetic flop, I got a letter from the B.B.C.: a controller in the talks division wrote: "I want to ask whether you have material for three rattling good talks about your experiences in East Africa, with reflections thereon. If so, the Home Service would like to place them early in October. . . . I say 'rattling good talks' because the resistance of people here to attempts to interest them in the Colonies can only be overcome by art, and this invitation to you is an invitation to an artist, not just a chap who's recently been there."

Well, I spread myself. The talks sounded pretty good to me as I listened to myself (at the excellent listening-hour of 7.45 p.m.); they read even better in *The Listener*: but not one word from the great British public. As I recall, the only letter I got was from a German baroness, asking me to introduce her to a White Hunter. But the next talk that the B.B.C. asked me to do—ah, that was about cats! And for the following days our postman's legs were bent as he tot-

tered into our house. Among this deluge was a letter from a little
Major in Somerset (I don't know why I should speak of him affectionately as *little*, except that he wrote so endearingly): he said:
"We have just had a white kitten born in our house. We were going
to call him Nero. But after listening to your talk last night we should
like to call him Negley. Do you mind?" I wrote back: "I don't mind,
if Nero doesn't. . . ." So somewhere in Somerset is my namesake,
and I only hope he is as good a Familiar to his master as was my
Uncle Roly. Roly was the finest cat I ever knew. He was a gentleman.

But for the first year or two Uncle Roly and I were very worried
about his sex. He varied. As a result, he ran into every calamity that
a cat can come up against. Both sides attacked him. And a white
cat is very vulnerable at nights. Yet for the first year or so, when
poor old hermaphrodite Roly was on the losing end of every battle,
he would stride in of a morning wearing a bloody bitten ear as
proudly as if it were a carnation.

He was a rough, short-haired cat, not one of your fluffy pussies;
and as with his cousins of the lion family all Uncle Roly's power
was up in front—in those terrifically powerful front legs. When he
was in his accustomed position, on the arm of my deep chair by the
fireplace, staring into the green flames of salty driftwood and thinking thoughts that only a philosophical cat can think, he always sat
bolt upright, his powerful forelegs straight, with his tail curled
around them. But his favourite position for meditation was on my
chest. If he caught me lying back at full length, as I often do when
in a book, he would tentatively stretch out a paw, to make sure it
was all right; then would walk up my stomach, fold his paws under
him as only a cat can, and close his eyes in peaceful thought. We
have sat that way for hours. His gentleness was charming. So was his
trustfulness. He had only one testicle, and his pumping-ship appa-
ratus was unique. Like the female camel, it was straight back. Roly
would back up against the wall, close his eyes, and let go. I don't
know how many times we repainted all the wainscoting of this house.
We kept pots of paint of the right colours handy. And as one of his
friends, Warren Chetham Strode, wrote him in a bread-and-butter
letter "The Grey House fairly reeks of your personality".

His mother, Hepzie, was a member of my London club. She was

born in the warrens of its Stygian basement, where a terrific un-
counted and uncountable community of cats lived and loved with
an abandon that would have petrified its members upstairs. And we
were supposed to be a very Bohemian lot.

I saved her from the streets. One night, after a particularly late
session at the bar (which, so the legend runs, has sunk more good
men than the Goodwin Sands), I found her sleeping on the hall
porter's blotter. Just a little ball of striped fluff: colour between a
March Brown and an Olive Dun. I was out of a cat at that moment.
So I put her in my pocket. We live on a very lonely stretch of this
North Devon coast, on the edge of those three miles of deer-coloured
sands which lie between Morte and Baggy Points. There are only
six homes in all those three miles; and not another house may be
built, thank God—and the National Trust. Just the sea and the sands.

Behind us rise the downs, sweeping up to the sky with great
splashes of golden gorse in the spring; rusty with dead bracken in
winter, an occasional clump of cattle grazing along the skyline, gulls
swirling in a white nimbus after the plough, a hawk hovering at a
fixed point in the sky, a few circling buzzards, millions of rabbit drop-
pings, and the curlews calling. It is a grand place for a cat.

In the spring of 1947, while I was replacing some sea-steps that
the March gale had torn away during the time I was in an asylum
in Switzerland (we have 39 steps, shades of John Buchan), Hepzie
sat on the top step and watched me. I think that cat loved beauty
—loved the sight of daffodils waving against the blue sea; but she
was never a friendly cat, not even with me. Yet like many a beautiful
little cockney, born in London's lower depths, who becomes the toast
of the West End and the Belle of New York—Hepzie was a sort of
Gertrude Lawrence among cats—she was a wow with the toms. Roly
and Becky, his one true love, the one cat that Roly always returned
to (when she let him), were the sole survivors of Hepzie's machine-
gun bursts of kittens. Hepzie met a bitter end, as cats do; but that
is another story. Little Becky is a dead ringer of her, and with a
charming disposition.

The one thing that Becky would not tolerate was unfaithfulness.
After Roly discovered that he was a tomcat he often had to spend
three or four days away from home, covering his constituency. If
he knew that he had been committing adultery on the hill, he would

always "throw his hat in through the door first", so to speak: put his old polar bear head around the door and peer hopefully. But it did not save him.

With a shriek like a calliope, Becky launched herself upon him, tore clawfuls out of him. He was twice her size, but he never hit back. Sometimes he would put up a paw protestingly, as if to say: "Oh, why bring all that up?"

If he had been good, then he was smugness personified. He would hold out his brow to be smelt. Then, after a few sniffs, she would put out her little pink tongue and lick him. And if that wasn't cats kissing I don't know what is. Next they would give themselves a hurried wash all over, sure sign that cats are contented, and get to work on the furniture: One—two—three—four! Sinking their claws in, putting their backs into it. . . .

His turning into a tomcat was terrific. A concussion of catas-trophes. When he was no bigger than a white mouse, our jealous little dachshund bit a hole in Roly's stomach. I caught her red-fanged, with Roly wet and half-dead on the rug. Which explained the mysterious death of many of Hepzie's former kittens. Then, as he grew up, every time he put his nose outside the house some cat took a swipe at him.

I have seen him lying there in the mornings, half his neck-fur torn away, when I thought all he needed was a broken spear in his side to look like the Lion of Lucerne. On such occasions I gave him his breakfast in bed: porridge, with most of the cream off the bottle, and a nice plate of boiled fish. "Confidence," I said to my wife, "we've got to give that cat confidence. Make him know that we are behind him. That, in this house, nobody can touch him. Build up that cat's morale, and I am sure that Roly will come through."

I should like to know the number of miles I have driven when petrol was short—we live eight miles from the nearest small town—to get fish and horse-meat for those cats and our dachshund. Lucy could eat a horse at one meal. Nearly every sunset I took her for a walk along the sand-dunes to get a rabbit: paunching it on the spot and giving her the liver and kidneys right there, while they were still warm. I conditioned that poor faithful dog to think: "*Bang!*—that means something lovely to eat!" And then, for six nights, I would miss every rabbit.

Roly, as he got bigger, went hunting on his own. I would hear that thud down in the kitchen: it was Roly, popping in through the window with a full-size rabbit in his mouth. His favourite place for eating them was on a Persian prayer rug in our dining-room that Eve and I had picked up in Turkey. Blood all over it. And one morning, when I was going up to do a B.B.C. recording in London, Roly had laid two harvest-size rabbits outside my bedroom door—unquestionably for provender. I slipped on them and almost broke my leg as I tumbled downstairs. I was doing a talk every month then to East Africa. I got £15 per talk, recording two at a time, then I went to my club and drank up £30 in the next four or five days. I lost many near-friends, though the good ones stuck it out. But I got so fed-up with myself for turning up here in Devon wishing I have never been born, that I finally abandoned the talks and stuck to straight writing. This was the beginning of the worst time of my life. And in the mornings, when I lay there in agony, old Roly would hop up on the bed, walk up my chest and butt me with his old polar bear nose, as if to say: "I know, old boy. It's hell, isn't it?" And, rousing myself to talk to him, especially if he had been badly torn up himself, I could take an interest in some other life than my own foolish one. No wonder I loved him.

His most formidable enemy was the Black Knight. This was a ferocious, fluffy cat, about the size of a badger. The Black Knight used to ambush Roly right outside our kitchen window. Our terrace would be covered with white fur in the mornings. Like a snowstorm. I always searched for some black fur. And then—I found it! There had been a terrible joust down on our sea-plateau during the night: screams such as could only have come from Hades. And in the morning I found almost fifty-fifty black and white. "Hooray!" I called up to my wife. "Roly is gaining."

It was about this time, I think, that the farmer up behind us on the hill said, "Do you know, Mr. Farson, that your white cat is the father of five white kittens up at our place?" "Wait a minute!" I said. "I'll tell him. Roly will be delighted." Anyway, he *had* changed: and that is just where the Black Knight made his fatal mistake—he came into our house in broad daylight.

We were eating our lunch when we heard that horrible humming. I went into the sitting-room, and there was the Black Knight behind the sofa. Roly was before the sofa. Waiting. Now, I thought, I can finish that black cat for ever, and I picked up the poker. But then I was horrified at what I had intended to do. Do unto other cats as you would have people do unto your cat: that's what I thought. And I put the poker down. This was to be a free fight. No holds barred. No Marquess of Queensberry. Which was exactly what Roly had been waiting for. I pulled out the sofa. . . .

With one pounce Roly had the Black Knight by the neck. With one heavy paw he pressed the Black Knight to the floor. And with his hind paws he went up and down, ploughing the stomach of the Black Knight. It was too horrible to watch. I opened the door. The black cat broke off the engagement. Fled. Roly hot after it. We didn't see Roly for two days. And we have never seen the Black Knight since.

Now as Roly grew older he became more sedate. And it was his sons who now began to attack him. Stalwart cats, absolute replicas; chips off the old block. There was a fight between two white cats below my bedroom window one night that sounded as if all hell had broken loose. And Roly just barely got away with it. But he was still the old champion. Worn out with nights of love, ears chewed from battles, he still smiled when we drove him up to the farm where he used to stay when we went abroad. For as we passed through the countryside, white cats were sitting in lanes, on fences, drowsing before cottage doorsteps, like a set of little figurines. All over the landscape. And I am sure that Uncle Roly thought they were all his own work. As they probably were.

He loved to sit beside me when I was typing, and was present through much of the beginning of this book. In those ice-green polar eyes of his I sometimes saw an expression that showed that he was trying to get through to me. I have often wondered what he wanted to say. At any rate, I was used to him, and wanted to have him with me. I always rejoiced when I heard him coming home at night (for I had hunted all over the hills for him, and four times had to release him from rabbit traps). As he came down the drive, walking with that heavy-shouldered polar-bear gait he had, he would always stop and give a little yowl as he came opposite my bedroom window. "All right," he as much as said. "I'm home." And writing down in the kitchen, in the small hours, with Roly curled up by the warm stove

. . . as I looked out at the two lights winking on Lundy Island, fifteen miles out to sea, with the comfortable thought that there was nothing beyond them for three thousand miles of the open Atlantic until you hit the coast of Labrador, I sometimes felt I was closer to some of the fundamental truths of life in trying to understand Roly than I have ever been before. And then . . . we think he must have been bitten by a badger. Or a fox? For he limped home one noon, when we were beginning to wonder where to start looking for him, with a horrible gash laying open his right hind leg. He got thinner and thinner, that tough old Roly; so weak he could hardly walk. The vet gave him all sorts of injections. Then (perhaps we did have an affinity) I cracked up. I went to Denmark for an operation. Eve kept Roly shut up at nights, waiting for him to get stronger; but the sight of him, with his nose pressed against the window, trying to get out, was too much for her. She opened the door. Out he leapt and up the garden path, and we never saw him again. He vanished. . . .

Sitting on the side-lines of life down here in North Devon, I often felt that I was just letting the years slip away. I had made much too big a break, too quickly; and into the wrong setting. For me, if I could have a free choice, there would be only two alternatives: New York, with all its roars, dirt, discomfort, and the most exciting mental and emotional life that any of today's cities can give you— or a life in some part of the world where men are few and far between. But to live in the woods entirely on your own, as we had lived during those two wonderful years on Vancouver Island, requires an amount of physical strength that is now quite beyond me—and the places just aren't there any more. A Canadian author wrote to me from our lake in British Columbia, asking permission to quote from what I had said about it in the *Transgressor,* and added: "Don't come back. It would break your heart." He enclosed a real-estate development map which showed that the shores of the lonely bay where we had lived in our unpainted shack—where occasionally we saw a deer come gently down to drink, and I could catch all the trout I wanted for our dinner by casting a fly along the reeds at sunset—were now a suburb of bungalow plots. Most of the good places are gone. It took me some years, and I can't say that I have altogether succeeded yet, to realise that the one place where I shall have to live from now on is within myself. Not so easy as it sounds.

. . . if morning skies
Books, and my food, and summer rain
Knocked on my sullen heart in vain:—
Lord, thy most pointed pleasure take
And stab my spirit broad awake.

A very hackneyed little poem? Well, let it be: it is the way I felt. Sometimes, sitting up on the downs and watching the ships headed in for the Bristol Channel; or worse, watching some ship going *out*—the smoke from her freshly-stoked fires trailing behind her like a black rope—I have felt a madness of frustration. The world could still be so beautiful, the world beyond. Yet, would it be? Somerset Maugham could never write another *Gentleman in the Parlour*, about his walk through the Shan States: that world has been poisoned. The East is awakening. Well, let it awaken. And in every country you will find men completely indifferent to the happiness or misery of their fellow men, as throughout Eastern Europe, and others who are making the glamorous East, even as I write, foul and ugly. Let younger, more credulous, more hopeful Westerners write about it. And in the Africa I had seen, and had no wish to go back to (though I did), which the white man is making ugly because of his failure to be decent, I had jettisoned the entire shipload of romantic ideas. I think the white man has served his time under the tropic sun. Therefore, when I thought things over carefully, I knew that I was lucky in my coastal paradise here in North Devon. I think, and I have seen the coast of many countries, that it is one of the most noble stretches of sea and sand anywhere in the world.

I have always felt that a man is a fool to let himself be owned by his possessions, perhaps because I never had much to lose. Or perhaps, belonging to three different families whose outrageous swings of fortune were spectacular even for the United States, I was accustomed to losing things, so that I had learned long ago not to cry over spilt milk. However that may be, when we bought our 2½ acres down here on the Devon coast and began to work on it, it wasn't long before we both realised that the place owned us. I am no gardener. If I put something into the ground I am always sur-

prised if anything comes up. It is my wife who has the green fingers:
the English girl I took out to the woods of British Columbia—who,
as soon as she saw the bay where we moored our house-boat, began
to wonder what she could make grow on it; who carted soil from
the forest, rich with the loam of centuries, placed it between the
curves of the cedar-raft on which our shack floated, and—God knows
they were hot!—had radishes that went down three feet, with all
that water below them, and lettuce that shot up like poplars. I am
only the hired man on this place. I dig where I'm told, when I can't
get out of it.

Our garden, when we first got it, was just a few rows of potatoes
and peas, in an angle of stone wall on a slope facing the sea. Its
previous owners had let it go to seed. Today, to break the salt winds,
it is enclosed by a stone wall six feet high, built by two local crafts-
men—a dry-wall, as it is called, which comes down, in sections, with
every winter's rain. They are great stone-workers, these men of
Devon, the men who sailed under Grenville to smash the Spanish
Armada; but this dry-wall, as I have said, has not stood up to gales
as well as did the good ship *Revenge.* However, no matter: it keeps
me in good shape hefting stones back in place. Over two-thirds of
the garden we made from virgin soil; from grassland that had never
known a spade. I had calluses on my hands like a glass-blower's by
the time those tussocks had been cleared. Espaliered against the
west, inside, section of wall we now have eighteen fruit trees, arms
spread where they will catch most of the day's sun. I double-
trenched, and placed a large stone at the foot of the roots of each
tree, as we put them in. It was a man in a local nursery who told
me that trick of putting a slab of stone at the roots. We have more
pears than we know what to do with every other year, as these seem
to go by alternate seasons. Doyenne de Comice, Buerre Hardy, Jar-
gonelle (which Eve bought because she liked its name: it has not
been successful with us), Conference, William, Laxton Superb. Ap-
ples: Bramley Seedlings, Cox's Orange Pippen, Marie Elizabeth.
Peaches: three trees that have never grown anything softer or bigger
than a green almond.

And every year we have put in at least two dozen pine and birch
trees outside the wall. So that, anticipating the percentage we knew
we should lose by sea winds, we now have our own copse, and this

year we had the cheerful sight of birds nesting in our pine woods. Or perhaps I'd better call it clump. Unfortunately, the bird whose song I like best, the merry blackbird, is also our greatest enemy. To protect our strawberries, currants and raspberries, I worked all one summer building a wire cage sixty-five feet long by thirty-one wide, and it has stood up against gales that have ripped the iron drainage-gutter off our house. I took a trick from old sailing days and made a 'needle' by curving a length of rod and punching a hole in one end; so that I *sewed* the strips of cage-wire together as one would sew a sail or football. I was proudly showing my cage to a friend, when I found that I had caught four blue-tits. He congratulated me on my aviary.

For the first two or three years both the spirit and the flesh were willing—I liked the feel of the good earth between my toes—and there were so many interesting things to do; but now I have to be caught, and will not work until a spade is thrust into my hands. Fortunately, my heart has gone dicky these last few years: I have been advised not to strain myself. When I asked the local doctor, after he had finished sounding me, "You don't think I should do any work in the garden, do you—such as digging double trenches?", he answered innocently, right before my wife: "Oh, of course not! You take it easy." I have.

When we bought the house, it was grim: painted chocolate brown inside. And there was no evidence whatever that any of its previous occupants had ever read a book. That meant years of painting: Eve painted our dining-room walls five times to get the right shade of green. I made bookshelves. I set up a workbench in the garage, collected really an excellent set of pre-war tools, and spent some of the happiest days I have known there. I like the feel of using good tools, of doing precision work. I like the very sounds of carpentry: that smooth purr as a well-set plane peels off a clean curl of fresh wood. I like the *smell* of it. As no two opposite surfaces in this very-much-hand-built house are parallel—no floor with its ceiling; and as no wall makes an exact right angle with any other, most of my jobs have been finished off with a wood-rasp. But the long shelves are slotted and slid into each other; battens support them; and if I do say it myself, they look as if they had been built there when the house was first made. I used a spirit level to parallel the shelves in the Picasso abandon of our dining-room. A ship torpedoed off the coast sent ashore some beautiful planks of fresh Oregon pine; and some of these now form the stand by my desk which holds my 13th Edition of the *Encyclopædia Britannica*. Now every room in this house is walled with books, and, alas, they are beginning to pile up on the broad window-sills. Books, books, books. . . . The bulk were old favourites I had had for ages. And when they were brought down from London, where they had been stored for nine years, and case after case that I opened as they came out of the vans turned out to hold nothing but books, I heard one of the men say to the driver: "*Books!* That's wot's in *them*—nothink but —— books!"

Only the roof of our house shows from the little private road that leads past these six homes. We are the only people who live here all the year round, except another writer and his wife who are just as farouche as we are: we sometimes don't speak to one another for a month. This lonely part of the coast has, thank God, no drop-inners: we can be as isolated as if marooned on a desert island. We have left the slope and plateau before our house, over-looking the sea, just as nature made it. The fine turf that grows on these wind-swept downs has an amazing number of gay wild flowers that come in their seasons; there are masses of sea campion, and primroses in spring on all the grassy banks. We have even left the ferns in their natural state along the edge of our plateau. I think their delicate tracery is one of the most beautiful designs in all nature, but they can be a damned nuisance when they start to march across your place. From the end of September to nearly the end of May no foot-marks mar these three miles of sand, except those of the coast guard on his dawn patrol, or of a few gatherers of driftwood. Sitting in my bed at dawn, or on sleepless moonlit nights, I look straight out on the Atlantic Ocean. I might as well be in a ship at sea. This makes one broody. Self-searching is part of the mood of this place; the sound of the sea is all about you, though after a time you cease to be conscious of it.

The danger, of course, was that I went in over my head every time I stepped out of this mood. The train to London meant the luxury of sitting in the dining-car, of watching the clouds pass by over the rolling West Country, and of gin after gin after gin. . . . I won't say that I regret those gin-inspired reveries, but by the time the train reached Waterloo I had already lost the game. No theatre, no movies, not even friends. . . . Dressing eagerly in my room on these mornings, to be driven to the station, I exulted as I shaved: "Now for some real life!" What a joke.

I was 'conditioned', just like Pavlov's dogs. I had had the privilege, the ordeal, of seeing them in Petrograd: standing in their suspended cement blocks, insulated and isolated from the outer world—and then, at the tick of the metronome, the saliva came. The "Devon Belle" up to London was my 'tick': and the only way I differed from the dogs was that I began to know it. That is why I can now write of it in the past tense.

To break the thraldom I decided to change habitat. I went twice to Norway, ostensibly to fish. But I love Norway too much. I was so happy to get back there that I went on a binge in Oslo that left me quite unable to wade a river. During my alcoholic urgings to go one better than ordinary mortals, and to tell them about it, I came on two good-looking young Norwegians who, when I sat at their table and began to talk about life, told me angrily that they were leaving Norway. "We are bored, bored, bored!" "You mean the Welfare State? Everything's been made so easy for you? No risks?" "Exactly! A man can't live by rules—by this and by that—all his life. With some silly clerk telling you what to do. That is no life for a man!" "Where are you going?" "Kenya!" "What are you going to do there?" "Start an import-and-export business. We hear the fishing is splendid. And there's a lot of money in sharks' livers." By this time I did not know which of us most needed a doctor. When they had gone the head waiter himself came back with the drink I had ordered: "Well, Mr. Farson—how are we?" "We," I said, "are still suffering from shock." And I told him about the two young Norwegians.

"That's true," he said. "A lot of the young people do feel that way. There is something *missing*. . . . I don't know what it is. And you will notice one thing, Mr. Farson: when you talk with some of our intelligentsia they will seem highly anti-American. They will tell you they are afraid of the 'American way of life'. But that's not what they are afraid of: they are angry with the Americans because they don't like the way you are trying to save us from ourselves—to make us build aerodromes in the North to defend ourselves against Russia. This Welfare State has lulled us into a false sense of security and we don't want to wake up—Scandinavia today is living in a dream-world."

I asked him whether he would lunch with me the next day. "With pleasure," he said. "And may I suggest, Mr. Farson, if you don't know what has happened here in Oslo recently, that we go to the ——?" And he named a restaurant I had never heard of. "What would you like to have, Mr. Farson?" I told him. He said: "I will meet you there tomorrow. The lunch will be ordered, the chef is an old friend of mine." He smiled: "You buy the drinks, Mr. Farson, and I'll buy the lunch."

It was a battle that lasted all afternoon. We telephoned his wife to join us. I got Nils Lie, who has translated all my books into Norwegian, to come over. There were two editors of Oslo newspapers there. And all afternoon I upheld the American way of life—until I was tenderly decanted into the night train for northern Norway. I was going to stay with one of the finest Norwegians of them all.

I was going to stay with Axel Mathiesen at the thrumming port of Aalesund, forty miles from any railway. His home was packed with books and salmon rods: the only two things he cared for, except Nina. Here where the *leitmotif* of the port was the *tump-tump-tump* of the heavy-duty engines in the coastal fishing-boats, the scream of gulls, and the silence with which the big ice-scarred sealers slid in from Greenland, Axel was making the most advanced study of that mysterious disease "Seal Finger", trying to identify the virus that gets into the hands of the sealers if they cut themselves skinning, and rots their bones. It is a virus connected only with the seal. The Russians and the Japs were also studying "Seal Finger", and had the same name for it. Axel's Russian wife Nina was a doctor too —they had met while students in Vienna—and their practice covered cases from all over the world: the one disease that sailors always seem to pick up in foreign ports, clap, being first on the list. When Axel tired of his microscope, or of injecting penicillin into sailors' bare behinds, he turned to his fishing rods.

I think the Rauma, pouring down from its snows and glaciers, and racing and jumping through its valley of waterfalls, must be one of the most beautiful rivers in all the world. And to sit on the bank of a river with Axel, eating a lazy lunch, was about as enjoyable a bit of sheer living as I could have wanted. He was a poet at heart, and his own book, *Norsemen Under the Southern Cross*—tales of his two years with the whalers down in the Antarctic—is full of beauty. And now, as I write this, comes a letter: Axel is dead.

I went to Spain. Spain, I fondly hoped, would be the last country to become "modern". But no, in Madrid I found that an over-efficient and commercially-minded tourist bureau, set up by Franco's Government, had put Spain up for sale. All its dignities had been placed on the counter. In Pamplona I found that the Francoites had shot one of my old friends. When I came on another of them, Jesu Christi Basiano, painting in the Cathedral (where the priests had let him have his studio for over twenty years) and asked him about Augusto, he cocked his thumb and forefinger against his head and pulled the trigger: "Augusto," he said, "was too political. Boom-boom." The Falange had shot him. Jesu Christi Basiano and I had taken horses down the high Pyrenees in 1928. At that time he had won the *Prix de Rome*, but his promise had petered out. Now, he showed me a newspaper with his name in big letters all across one page, over an article extolling his one-man show then being held in San Sebastian. But Jesu hung his head. "Life has no gusto!" he said wearily. "Life is dead."

And for the first time in thirteen years I returned to the United States. I made three trips back to my own country, really trying to find my way back to myself. The last of them ends this book. I stood on Brooklyn Bridge at sunrise, looking down on the East River, and thought of the New York I had sailed from forty years before, in August 1914, with the secret vow that I would never again return to the United States, at any rate not to make a living there. Well, a lot of water had run under the Brooklyn Bridge since then.

During these struggles to escape from myself, when I was like a striped-bass on a hook, I wrote to a friend in Switzerland and got him to arrange for me to enter the asylum outside Berne. This is a State institution, the biggest in Switzerland, and the last court of appeal for the demented. Its head was one of the most noted psychologists in Europe. They had 900 cases there, mostly schizophrenics: and when I saw the way these human problems were being studied, the kindness and the good conditions these poor people were being given, I found the place so fascinating that I forgot I was a 'case' myself. I had to be reminded of it. And I am not being irrelevant when I say that seeing all that real human misery made me, by comparison, ashamed of myself. It was very likely the one thing that decided me to pull up, even if I damned near died in the attempt. Nothing that I have ever seen in Switzerland, a country in which I have found a lot to admire, has made me like the Swiss as much as that asylum.

We had among the eight cases in our private wing a man who had been there thirty years. He was strong as a gorilla, the picture of health, and terribly happy. Terribly is the word. He was still a child. He was charming. But when dinner was served he tried to take the whole bowl of macaroni; and it required some restraint, from myself and the others at that table, not to appear to notice it when he got up from his chair and tried to catch the raindrops that were sliding down on the outside of the window-panes. Otherwise the talk at dinner was almost uncannily normal. There was an Austrian doctor there, for a time, who was one of his country's champion skiers. His schizophrenia had first come upon him while he was actually operating on a patient. He was in Switzerland to have a lobotomy performed. The psychologist at the head of the institute did not believe in this operation, and tried to talk him out of it; and when I asked him why he had finally agreed to it, he said (for we had reached that stage of friendship where we could talk like this): "Because, if I had not, he would have committed suicide. He told Doctor —— (one of the Swiss skiers and son of a former President of Switzerland) that he would kill himself. I know that type. He would have done it." I was playing about with my camera there, taking photos indoors, etc., to amuse myself. The Austrian asked me to take one of him: "Before I have the operation," he said with a melancholy smile. I took several. They show a dark, worried, but very intelligent face. I left the place to go trout fishing in Italian Switzerland, but paid it a visit when I came back through Berne. The Austrian doctor was still there, and the pads of bandage had not yet been removed from the sides of his head. He greeted me with the smile of . . . a peasant, perhaps?

I began *The Sons of Noah* in that place. On one side of me was a wealthy Swiss whom I never saw, though I heard him. This was when he was hurling himself about in his bed. He was a D.T. case, last stages: he always insisted that they had put a woman or a horse in his bed, I forget which. On the other side was an American, a peculiar case, who had coffee with me in the mornings and seemed absolutely normal. But—mysterious. In this case a horse actually did come into the case: someone sent him a horse from Morocco. He asked leave to go into Berne, to ride it: went to St. Moritz, and never came back. He was quite wealthy, and had been a member of our diplomatic corps; and several years later he wrote me a letter from the States. "I've got a lot to tell you," he said, still mysterious, "when I see you." I've lost the letter and forgotten his name, so he will always be a mystery to me.

The asylum was the centre of a big farm, worked for the most part by patients. I used to sit and read in the sun, and watch them tending the flower beds. They loved to do that, and it was moving to see with what skill and tenderness they looked after the plants. They sent baskets of table-flowers into Berne. In the late sunsets I would go into the dairy and stand behind the huge biscuit-coloured Swiss cattle, and get that warm smell of animals and fresh hay. They had a special farm some distance from the asylum where they were reclaiming some of the more hopeful cases; passing them out eventually to mountain farming-families in Switzerland, where they could enjoy a normal life. The Professor took me there to eat Christmas dinner with them. Their toastmaster made an almost frighteningly witty speech . . . and I danced with the inmates of the asylum at their big ball that Christmas Eve. I saw exactly the same scene years later in New York—watching Olivia De Havilland in the *Snake Pit*.

Finally, as I have said, the great Herr Doktor Professor gave it up: "Keep your conflicts," he told me one day. "It is better for you not to be a normal man."

I had one more go at a "cure". And this was in England, a little too near home to make me want to write about it. Anyway, I'm bored with showing my sores in the market-place. The most interesting thing about that place was a friend I made there. I came out of—whatever it was—one morning to find myself lying on a bed only a foot from the floor, with two doctors and the head nurse standing by me, and a man in a worn camel's-hair dressing-gown sitting in a chair in the corner. I did not know how long I had been in that bed. "I want to introduce you to a fan of yours," said the head doctor. "This is Colonel ——" And the man in the corner stood up and came over to shake hands with me. A little later (I must have fallen back again under the influence of whatever drug they had given me) the Matron came back and asked me whether I would mind sharing a room with Colonel X. "He is very lonely," she said. They helped me downstairs and I sat on the bed of the room I was to share with this other case.

It was my collapse at the tail end of a terrific fall from grace in London that had made me accept a friend's advice to enter this home. I had my one good suit on, and had just tremblingly got into it upstairs. Now as I took it off the colonel came across and hung my coat on a hanger. When I leaned forward to unlace my shoes, and nearly slid on to the floor, he got down on his knees and did the job for me. "Don't do that!" I snapped in my humiliation. "It will be all right," he said stubbornly. "I know where to put things in this room."

I lay there. The nurse had told me that he was an Australian who had been in France in the first war. He had had a breakdown, his present illness, in New Guinea, in the second one. This was the third place he had tried in England, and he had been here some time. I saw him sitting there, rigid, eyes fixed on me. "Tell me," I asked, "is there any real *green* country in Australia? What's the Murray River like?" For a moment I thought he had not heard me. Then he began to talk. A little later we were both lying back in bed, and he was going on, thirteen to the dozen. "Let me show you my daughter's picture," he said. "And that's my son. He is in the Navy. . . ." He put them back on the table at the foot of his bed. "You know, sometimes . . . when I lie here at night . . . it's as if I could hear them speak to me."

They were giving me insulin shocks then. And you are not supposed to take any liquids until they give you that warm glass of sugared water. "There's my tea," he said. "If you'd like to have it?" "No, thanks. I'll just go through with it." "I'm glad to have met you," he said. "You're just like your books."

One night I woke up to find him feeling my face. I lay perfectly still. Then his fingers ran down over the length of my body. Then I heard him breathing somewhere else, but I couldn't make out where. I had been instructed to take his cigarette away from him after he had been given his last heavy shot in the arm to make him sleep. I fell asleep once myself, and woke up to see his pyjamas burning from the cigarette that had dropped on them; so I had made it a point to know where the switch was at the foot of my bed. I leapt out now and turned on the light. And there was my colonel *under* my bed—but not only that: he had made himself into a U so that his feet were sticking out and he was bent forward over the cross rod which ran between the bed-legs. "Now you lie back," I said, pushing gently to straighten him out, "and *stay* there—and I'll pull you out." I did. I took him by his legs and hauled him out from under. Then we both sat there on the floor, at two o'clock in the morning, and laughed our fool heads off.

"What on earth's the matter with you?" said the night nurse, rushing in, because laughter in that place was really alarming. "Nothing," we said in chorus. "Nothing, nothing, nothing. . . ." And when she left we still sat there. "Of all the damned things!" said the colonel, "this is the damnedest!"

"But what on earth were you doing?" I asked, "under my bed?" "God knows . . . I was looking for something. Can't think what it was."

One night when neither of us could sleep, and we had finished our cigarettes, I said I would go along to the night nurse and get us some. She refused to give me any, though there were some right before her. I dithered with rage. Then I fought it down and went back to the colonel. The instant I told him what had happened he blew up. He leapt from his bed and got his pad and fountain-pen. "I'm going to write to Menzies!" he said. I saw the harm I had inadvertently done. "Don't you be such a fool," I said. "If you write to Menzies, or even to Australia House, you will be doing the one thing that will keep you here—that will show you are uncontrollable. You keep your shirt on. We've got to be level-headed about this—both you and I—I'm going to read a book now. Which one of these do you want?" I got up and took his pad and pen away from him. The next day he went 'over the edge'. I saw him trying to put his arm through the blanket, searching it for armholes as if it were the top piece of his pyjamas. Then he got to his feet and took my typewriter off the bed-table and walked around the room, holding it before him like a priest with an offering for some heathen god. I went out into the corridor and found the Matron. "Colonel X," I said, "is going mad. He needs attention." She nodded. "I know it." And they put him in the room upstairs, with its bed on the floor, where I had found myself on the day I had met him.

They gave him the electric shocks. Then the Matron came in one morning, smiling: "Colonel X says he would like to come back with you. Do you mind?" I asked her to tell him he was welcome. He came in, a little weak, and very pessimistic. But otherwise he seemed all right. I followed him up after I left and learned at last that he was finally back in Australia. And if he reads this, which he very likely will, he will know that I hope he is going strong. Also, he will probably be pleased to know, I have had my last go at that kind of 'cure'. The English psychologist who was looking after me—the only man apart from Bumke that I have had absolute faith in—was in complete agreement. "The one thing that will ever make you stop drinking," he said, "is your own common sense." He tapped his head: "If *this* doesn't make you stop, nothing will."

BROOKLYN
BRIDGE

Thomas Wolfe wrote that only the dead know Brooklyn. I believe that only a hyperinsomniac can get to know New York—so automatically cruel yet so eager to be friendly, with its shy, defensive, trigger-sensitive heart. Everywhere under its hard shell is the desire to find a friend. David Reisman could not have thought of a better title than *The Lonely Crowd*. Everyone wants to belong. By day there are too many people, there is too little space and time: no New Yorker can be himself: there is no room for individualism on its assembly belt. And as the skyscrapers shoot higher and higher, breathtakingly beautiful as they put their heads in the clouds (which, odd as it may seem, can be said of the ideals of American civilisation, even though they have not been fulfilled), man becomes smaller and smaller, until he feels that he just no longer counts. His technical efficiency has made him the plaything of forces beyond his control. That is the desperate belief at the back of the average New Yorker's mind: it explains his feeling of uselessness, his *empty* feeling. New Yorkers talk, even the rich, as if all the life had been squeezed out of them; and as for hard-working people—well, they get a wage that should give them a life that has never before seemed possible, and yet still have a sense that the city is cheating them. New York realities *hurt*, and no one can make you know this more tersely than its taxi-drivers: "Yeah! Christ, but this town is gettin' hard to live in! Either this old burg is gonna blow up, or——" I know no other great city which lives in such a constant state of expectancy, of *conscious* transition—towards what?

The best time to see New York is when most of its inhabitants are asleep. Then it's tolerable, even beautiful. The 400,000 commuters who pile in every morning and fight their way out at night are away from the city; they are asleep in their dormitory towns. Any New Yorker you find up will be a *real* New Yorker. Tired, taut, often used-up, he is commonly in the mood to tell you exactly what he thinks about life. It can take your hair off. And if he happens to be one of those alcoholic melancholics, which it's a 1-to-4 chance that he will be, you might get into a conversation, even be given an admission, that will leave you thinking that this was how O. Henry got the material for *The Furnished Room*. . . . These are the confidential hours: the hours, say, between three a.m. and when the iceman cometh. For he still comes—around six, delivering pails of cracked ice to pack the red Coca-Cola machines in the drug stores, about the time when the white-clad chefs behind the eating-counters turn on their hot-plates to serve the city's best breakfasts. It is in those three hours just before dawn that New York has its guard down.

I reached these conclusions in a Hamburger Heaven, the one just west of Madison on 58th Street. Walter Winchell was perched on a stool four down from mine, though I did not know it until after he had gone out: I was listening to the man at the cash-register tell me how he had walked out of Burma with Vinegar Joe Stilwell. Winchell and his crowd, three men and a girl, slid off their stools; he paid their check, and they climbed into two *Journal-American* cars that had been waiting in the darkness outside. "Did'ya notice the three men? They're coppers," said the man at the cash-register as he filed their bill. "Plain-clothes men. Girl's a hen-reporter. Winchell must be on to something pretty hot." I told the cashier that if I had stood up Winchell would have had another item for his column: the tail of my bath-robe was out. But he only shook his head: "That's nothing. Had a woman in here the other night, mink coat—and not one damn' stitch under it. What you might call the tail-end of some booze-fighting party in this neighbourhood. Mister, nothing surprises New York at this hour of the morning." I paid my check, and walked back to my hotel to dress.

When I came back to the Hamburger Heaven at eight, I found the man from Burma in as tight a spot as he had ever been with Vinegar Joe—he had lost the key to the cash-desk. White-faced, he was scrabbling around under it. The proprietor had come on duty, was leaning down to curse him, then rising to hold at bay an angry line of customers who were demanding to have their bills taken and given the change. "That man mos' scared to death!" said the big Negro who gave me my coffee. "Mister, they tells me you writes books. Wish you would tell *me* how to write a book. I got a lot of things *I'd* like to say." I told him that all he had to do, then, was write what was going on at the cash-desk: "And let me know the end of it." He solemnly shook his head: "I can tell you that, right now. That man done seen his las' night in *this* place."

It has been my custom, when I return to New York—I am a hyper-insomniac, as I've hinted—to take buses and ride either up or down the entire length of the city in the early hours. I like to watch it when the people are coming to their day's work, or just going off it. One morning I watched the sunrise on Brooklyn Bridge, looking down into the East River. The ships of all the world lay at their piers at the foot of New York's receding Aztec skyline. White puffs from the tugs in the river: the hoarse moan of a big ocean liner over in the Hudson, signalling her departure: the Statue of Liberty, arm up-raised above the swirling, sun-bright tides of the Bay—there it all was: the city where I had held my first job, over forty years before.

A few years earlier, when I had come back to the United States for the first time in thirteen years, it had been on the little 8,000-ton Danish ship *Jutlandia,* later to be their hospital ship in Korea. We arrived at night. And as we were going to dock at Hoboken, over on the Jersey side, we shaved Bedloe's Island so close that we could look up and see the green verdigris on Liberty's arm, reflected in the floodlights. Her face, looming in the sky above us, had a sort of half-reality, the look of a portent, like the face of the King on the battlements of Elsinore. "You are there!" I said. And as I did, my arm was gripped and shaken roughly. . . . It was Fritz Busch. I saw that he was weeping. Anyone who knows his story—how he threw his conductor's baton straight at his old friends in the Dresden Opera House as he saw them sitting there supinely while the young Nazi thugs in the audience stamped their feet and shouted: *"Raus Busch! Raus Busch!*—will not need to be told what that face in the sky meant to him. "There she is! There she is!" he cried, digging his fingers into me. "That old lady still means something!" I told him she did to me. But what?

It had been a twelve-day trip, and all the way over from Copenhagen Busch had been lyric about the life of the artist. He would even tap me on the shoulder as he came past my table in the dining saloon: "You must live the life of the artist! It is the only life." For him, to get back to New York was to return to the world he had lost in Europe. "It has come over here," he said. "Europe has killed us, driven us out. . . . Over here we can breathe again. To conduct in New York, ah! . . . I can rise to heights!" New York, he said, brought out all the best in him. "It is so *vital!* Europe is dead."

I knew it. All the races were coming to flower in America. It was still the last frontier. There was a feeling of transition in New York, and all New Yorkers were conscious of it: something really was happening. It wasn't merely a question of a skyscraper being here today that hadn't been here yesterday; it was a new feeling of exhilaration men felt, a new sense of something buried under these stones of beauty. We had seen the city changing from hope to hopelessness, and beginning to hope again. I can give the moods and dates of my own periods of transition in New York City. There was the period when I, like all Americans, was awed by the size of its buildings—just the height, not the beauty of them. Those were the days of Progress. That had turned out to be a myth. We knew that the ruins of a better city lay under the lava-layer of skyscrapers and canary-bird flats that were being built. This was the period, that of triumphant materialism, when New York began to affront one. And when I stared up at the sight of a riveter, poised on his steel girder hundreds of feet in the sky and leaning slightly against the wind as such aerial steelworkers have to, and when I watched him nonchalantly catch a red-hot rivet in a tin-can as it was hurled to him from the forge and then lean against his thudding pneumatic drill as he drove it home, this—the sight that once thrilled me to the marrow—now made me desperate. It was the end of the New York I had loved.

Today, in business hours, New York seems a civilisation where people are being driven mad by the things they make—"You have made me, you must sell me"—with every human being geared to that imperative. Our advertisements have become a nightmare in an insane asylum. Idiot's delight. The U.S.A. does not have to lie on the couch for the psychiatrist: all the case-history *he* needs is in the magazines in his waiting-room. But that is not the New York of Sunday morning, with the leaves changing to their glory of autumn colours, people feeding the squirrels, and some of the older inhabitants, German-Jews mostly, playing chess on the top of a rock, at open-air tables with chequer-boards made in the cement; with men in windjackets—city janitor types—intent on their games in the warm sun, and looking up occasionally at that lovely sight of the low islands of blue clouds floating along the upper levels of the skyscrapers; with a green truck of the Park Commissioner's come to attach a gold wreath to the new bust of Schiller. . . . And what love those solitary loungers lavish on the squirrels who climb confidently up their knees to be given the expected peanut: these little grey furry ones who still place such trust in man! That is very comforting, such faith, even if it's only from a dumb squirrel. For the man knows that if he sat on the same bench after the sun went down he would have his throat cut.

De Tocqueville wrote many years ago of the low tastes of the democracies compared with, say, that of aristocratic England. Well, here lies the clue—in the changing tastes of New York. The stream of immigrants from Europe has dried up: manufacturers no longer have the markets that derived from that peasant background. Now, New York is demanding perfection, nothing less; and it is getting it. This is the new city, the one that will be always in transition. I was troubled about how I should be able to express my present mood about life in the United States. But, looking back and thinking of Fritz Busch—of the artistic world, and the fact that he seemed to be returning to his own people when he came back to New York—I know I can give no better picture of the city I see coming than the one I used to look at every night, after six, from my rear window. It was of the ballet school across the street, in Carnegie Hall. Here every night, as my wife and I were getting ready to go out to dinner, we saw girls being trained in graceful movements; and one room was for minute tots. And the night we saw the New York Ballet dance the *Nutcracker* the most delightful of the child dancers had been a Chinese. On some evenings I sat there for an hour or so, watching those little dancers across the road: thinking of New York, its museums and art galleries, its theatres and its shops; of Sunday morning in Central Park, and of how the rich loam of all Europe, Africa, and Asia was now blending to grow the new city. Here, in the dirtiest, the most corrupt, the most dangerous city on earth, was the new frontier of the United States.

INDEX